From Frontier Town
to Metropolis

Portrait of Antonio de Villavicencio y Verástegui by an anonymous painter. Casa Museo 10 de Julio, Bogotá.
Source: Javier Ocampo López, "Antonio de Villavicencio y Verástegui" in *Gran Enciclopedia de Colombia*, accessed August 16, 2005, on www.lablass.org/blassvirtual/letra-b/biogcircu/villanto.htm.

It is fitting that the city of Villavicencio takes its name from Antonio de Villavicencio y Verástegui for he played a significant role in the early struggle against Spain. Although he was born in Quito, his family moved to Bogotá while he was still a child. His parents sent him to Spain to complete his education, where he prepared himself to serve in the Spanish Navy. Villavicencio fought in the disastrous Battle of Trafalgar (October 25, 1805) that ended by virtually destroying the Spanish Navy. After the Napoleonic invasion of Spain he returned to Venezuela in 1810 as an agent of the junta that was ruling on behalf of the deposed king, Ferdinand VII. On learning that the patriots in Bogotá had declared complete independence from Spain on July 20, 1810, Villavicencio decided to join their movement. He fought in several battles against the Spanish, and he was serving as governor of the Province of Tunja when the Spanish Army led by General Pablo Morillo took control once again of Nueva Granada. Villavicencio was captured and tried as a traitor. He was executed on June 6, 1816.

From Frontier Town to Metropolis

A History of Villavicencio, Colombia, since 1842

Jane M. Rausch

ROWMAN & LITTLEFIELD PUBLISHERS, INC.
Lanham • Boulder • New York • Toronto • Plymouth, UK

ROWMAN & LITTLEFIELD PUBLISHERS, INC.

Published in the United States of America
by Rowman & Littlefield Publishers, Inc.
A wholly owned subsidiary of The Rowman & Littlefield Publishing Group, Inc.
4501 Forbes Boulevard, Suite 200, Lanham, Maryland 20706
www.rowmanlittlefield.com

Estover Road, Plymouth PL6 7PY, United Kingdom

Portions of chapters 1–5 first appeared, in an earlier form, in Jane M. Rausch,
The Llanos Frontier in Colombian History, 1830–1930 (Albuquerque:
University of New Mexico Press, 1993).

Excerpts from chapter 6 first appeared in Jane M. Rausch, *Colombia: Territorial Rule and the
Llanos Frontier* (Gainesville: University Press of Florida, 1999). Reprinted here with
permission of the University Press of Florida.

Illustrations 1.1, 1.2, 2.1–2.3, and 3.1 are by Edouard Riou and were published in 1878
from sketches by the French botanist Edouard André during his travels through the Territory
of San Martín in 1875–1876. André's accounts, with Riou's illustrations, were first published
in *Tour du Monde* (Paris) 35: 1st sem (1878), 129–224. They were later reproduced in
Eduardo Acevedo Latorre's *Geografía pintoresca de Colombia* (Bogotá: Litografía Arco, 1968),
115–22.

British Library Cataloguing in Publication Information Available

Library of Congress Cataloging-in-Publication Data
Rausch, Jane M., 1940–
    From frontier town to metropolis : a history of Villavicencio, Colombia, since 1842 /
Jane M. Rausch.
        p.   cm.
    Includes bibliographical references and index.
    ISBN-13: 978-0-7425-5473-3 (cloth : alk. paper)
    ISBN-10: 0-7425-5473-2 (cloth : alk. paper)
    ISBN-13: 978-0-7425-5474-0 (pbk. : alk. paper)
    ISBN-10: 0-7425-5474-0 (pbk. : alk. paper)
    1. Villavicencio (Meta, Colombia)—History. 2. Frontier and pioneer life—Llanos
(Colombia and Venezuela). I. Title.
    F2291.V48R38 2007
    986.1'94—dc22
                                                                    2006034685

Printed in the United States of America

∞™ The paper used in this publication meets the minimum requirements of
American National Standard for Information Sciences—Permanence of Paper
for Printed Library Materials, ANSI/NISO Z39.48-1992.

Contents

List of Illustrations, Maps, and Photographs   vii

Preface   ix

1   The Llanos Frontier and the Founding of Villavicencio   1

2   Villavicencio during the Federation Era, 1863–1888   23

3   Villavicencio during the Era of Regeneration, 1886–1899   47

4   War and Dictatorship, 1899–1909   65

5   Capital of the National Intendancy of Meta, 1909–1930   77

6   Villavicencio during the Liberal Republic, 1930–1946   101

7   La Violencia and Its Impact on Villavicencio, 1947–1953   117

8   The Rojas Pinilla Dictatorship and the Pacification of the Llanos, 1953–1958   135

9   Villavicencio during the National Front, 1957–1974   149

10   Villavicencio, 1974–Present: The Search for Civic Identity   173

11   Villavicencio and the Llanos Frontier   197

Bibliography   211

Index   221

About the Author   231

Illustrations, Maps, and Photographs

ILLUSTRATIONS

Frontispiece	Portrait of Antonio de Villavicencio y Verástegui	ii
1.1	Lost in the Llanos	11
1.2	A Rodeo in the Llanos	12
2.1	Villavicencio and the Llanos	25
2.2	Arrival in Villavicencio	26
2.3	A Church in Villavicencio	34
3.1	Growing Coffee in the Llanos	58
6.1	Llanero Musical Group: Harp, Maracas, and Four-String Guitar	111

MAPS

1.1	The Llanos of Colombia	3
5.1	Plan of Villavicencio, July 19, 1916	80
6.1	The Llanos in 1930	102
9.1	Plan of Villavicencio, 1965	157
9.2	Cattle Movement in the Llanos Orientales of Colombia, 1972	166
10.1	Department of Meta	175
10.2	Municipio of Villavicencio, 2005	179

PHOTOGRAPHS

2.1	José de Calasanz Vela, 1840–1895	36
5.1	Mauricio Dieres Monplaisir, 1887–1947	82
10.1	Villavicencio 2006	177
10.2	Villavicencio Cathedral, 1998	184
10.3	Breaking a Wild Horse	193

Preface

In 1940, the town of Villavicencio, the capital of the Colombian intendancy of Meta, was located just 120 miles from Bogotá, but the towering Eastern Andean Cordillera that reaches heights of 19,000 feet blocked easy access between the two cities. As a result, although it had been founded one hundred years before, Villavicencio remained an isolated frontier outpost. Nestled in the piedmont region on the eastern side of the cordillera, the town was, and still is, called *"El Portal de la Llanura"* (Gateway to the Plains), because beyond it stretched out in all their glory the Llanos Orientales or eastern tropical plains. Covered by tall grass, these plains are bisected by tree-lined, fast-flowing tributaries that join the Orinoco River. Together they form the geographic region known as Orinoquia, which encompasses 220,000 square miles of territory and extends eastward through Colombia and Venezuela.

With a population of some twenty-eight thousand people in 1940, Villavicencio was the largest city in the Colombian portion of the Llanos, yet despite efforts of nineteenth- and early twentieth-century governments to encourage the development of the Meta territory, most would-be colonists were deterred by the harsh climate (nine months of heavy rain and three months of drought); the prevalence of diseases (malaria, yellow fever, cholera, hookworm, and tropical anemia); and the fact that only one unreliable road linked Villavicencio to Bogotá. Given these formidable obstacles, it is not surprising that in 1940 the territory had, besides the twenty-eight thousand *villavicences*, just 23,674 inhabitants, scattered throughout its 85,220 square kilometers.

Fast forward to the year 2005. Despite, or perhaps because of, civil war and unrelenting violence between guerrilla groups, narco-traffickers, paramilitaries, and the Colombian army, Villavicencio has become a medium-sized metropolis of 273,511 inhabitants, complete with high-rise buildings and urban slums, which is anticipating the construction of its first modern shopping mall. It is still the capital and largest urban center in what is now the Department of Meta that currently has 583,418 inhabitants of which nearly half live in Villavicencio. Likewise, it remains the gateway to the plains lying farther to the east and south, because in the last thirty years the cutting edge of the frontier has moved beyond Villavicencio to newly founded towns and ranches in the piedmont and the savanna *más allá* (farther away).

The purpose of this study is twofold: first, to trace the history of Villavicencio from its founding in 1842 to the present to explain how over the passage of one hundred and fifty years, a remote outpost became, by the twenty-first century, a thriving metropolis; and second, to show how its development has modified ideas about the fundamental nature of Colombia's eastern frontier. To accomplish these objectives, this monograph draws on data collected for previous books about the Llanos, but by focusing on the major city of the region, it goes beyond them.[1] Although the last ten years have seen a spurt of books published in Colombia about Villavicencio,[2] there is still no satisfactory history of the city available in English. *From Frontier Town to Metropolis* seeks to fill this gap, to take its place among the growing literature on Latin American cities, and to change ideas about the role of frontier regions in South America.

My fascination with Villavicencio began in 1964 when I first visited the city as a graduate student and was struck by its similarity to portrayals of nineteenth-century frontier towns in the western United States. *East of the Andes and West of Nowhere*, the evocative title of a book about Villavicencio written by Nancy Bell Bates in 1949, seemed an apt description of the city's location. The immensity of the Llanos that lay beyond it with their promise of limitless opportunity captured my imagination and determined the direction of my subsequent scholarly career.

During the next forty years, while I was conducting research on the Llanos in Bogotá at the Biblioteca Nacional, the Biblioteca del Ministerio de Gobierno (now the Ministerio del Interior), the Biblioteca del DAINCO, the Biblioteca Luis Angel Arango, and the W. E. B. DuBois Library at the University of Massachusetts, Amherst, the rapid growth of the town remained pivotal to my understanding of the dynamics of Colombia's eastern frontier. Likewise, the emergence of a group of professionally trained Colombian scholars determined to preserve the history of the city and the Llanos has been an exciting development to behold. Without their outstanding publications this book could not have been written, and I am especially grateful to María Eugenia Romero, Nancy Espinel Riveros, Tomás Ojeda Ojeda, and Miguel García Bustamante for their valuable insights. I also wish to thank Frank Safford for his helpful comments; Jessica Gribble for editorial assistance; Donald Sluter for designing a fine set of maps; Peggy McKinnon for preparing the manuscript; Jack Tager for creating the index; John Loy, who first suggested this project in 1973; and finally Marv Rausch, whose unflagging support made the completion of this work possible. For its errors and shortcomings, I alone am responsible.

NOTES

1. Jane M. Rausch, *A Tropical Plains Frontier: The Llanos of Colombia, 1531–1831* (Albuquerque: University of New Mexico Press, 1993); Jane M. Rausch, *The Llanos Frontier in Colombian History, 1830–1930* (Albuquerque: University of New Mexico Press, 1993): and Jane M. Rausch, *Colombia: Territorial Rule and the Llanos Frontier* (Gainesville: University Press of Florida, 1999).

2. See, for example, Nancy Espinel Riveros, *Villavicencio: dos siglos de historia comunera, 1740–1940,* 2nd ed. (Villavicencio: Editorial Juan XXIII, 1997); Carlos Burgos M., *Crónicas y anécdotas regionales: Villavicencio años 1900* (1999); Tomás Ojeda Ojeda, *Villavicencio entre la documentalidad y la Oralidad, 1880–1980* (Villavicencio: Edición Corocora Orinoquense, 2000); and two books by Miguel García Bustamante, *Un pueblo de frontera: Villavicencio, 1840–1940* (Villavicencio: Universidad de los Llanos, 1997) and *Persistencia y cambio en la frontera oriental de Colombia: El piedemonte del Meta, 1840–1950* (Medellín: Fondo Editorial Universidad EAFIT, 2003).

1

The Llanos Frontier and the Founding of Villavicencio

In 1842 when Esteban Aguirre built his house in the piedmont zone of the Eastern Andean Cordillera at a site known as Gramalote (later renamed Villavicencio) between the Guatiquía and Río Negro rivers, the Llanos formed part of the peripheral lowland territories of the independent state of New Granada. These regions, which included the Amazon Basin lands and the Pacific Coast, as well as the Llanos, accounted for two thirds of New Granadan territory, but because of their geographic isolation and unhealthy tropical climates, all three areas remained lightly populated and largely outside the sphere of national political influence. Nevertheless, from the arrival of the first conquistadors in the sixteenth century, the Llanos emerged as a unique frontier. The purpose of this chapter is, first, to explore the nature of this frontier as it developed during the colonial and independence eras and, second, to suggest that the official founding of Villavicencio on October 21, 1850, was the result of spontaneous colonization rather than policies adopted by the national government.[1]

THE GEOGRAPHIC SETTING

While three magnificent branches of the Andes mountains run north to south through the Colombian heartland, no less imposing are the vast grasslands that lie to the east of them. Bounded on the north by the Coastal Range and by the Orinoco and Guaviare rivers on the south, they account for 250,000 square kilometers of Colombia and 300,000 square kilometers of Venezuela. From an altitude of a few hundred feet at the base of the Andes, the plains slope gently toward the Orinoco, broken here and there by low mesas. They are drained by numerous tributaries of that great river, the largest being the Apure, Arauca, and Meta rivers. Although they are hot throughout the years, the Llanos are alternately flooded and dry in response to changing conditions of weather and terrain. The rainy season, or "winter," begins in May and intensifies between June and October, when much of the land becomes flooded. During the dry season, or "summer," from December to March, the swollen rivers recede; the land becomes parched, and the grass turns brown and brittle because of lack of moisture. Dense forests line the streambeds and cover the base of the mountains, but the typical vegetation is tall, coarse grass with some dry, scrubby forest and scattered palms. In this difficult environment characterized by clouds of noxious insects, a brutally hot climate, and unappetizing pasturage, cattle and horses introduced by the Spanish in the sixteenth century managed to adapt and thrive, grazing freely in large numbers over the open grassland and forming the basis for the distinctive Llanero subculture that had evolved by the eighteenth century.

On the Colombian side of the border, the Meta and Casanare rivers divide the region into three large sections known in colonial times as the Llanos of San Martín (Meta), the Llanos of Casanare, and the Llanos of Arauca. The Llanos of San Martín have a second mountain range, the Serranía de la Macarena, which is detached from the Andes and distinct in its formation. La Macarena is an extensive sandstone plateau, which rises to an altitude of over two thousand meters and is stratigraphically related to the Guiana highland complex. These mountains have been weathered into fantastic forms, leading early explorers to believe that they could see spires and turrets of old cities. Once these explorers assured themselves that La Macarena was not El Dorado (a land inhabited by natives possessing great wealth), they were content to leave it alone. It remained a rugged, virgin wilderness until the twentieth century when the Colombian government declared it a national park.[2] The rest of the Llanos of San Martín is divided into two zones, the Meta Cercano and the Meta Lejano. The Meta Cercano includes the plains lying between the Eastern Cordillera, La Macarena, and the Metica River, which stretch from west to east for fifty to eighty kilometers. The Meta Lejano is a zone of plains sloping gently toward the Orinoco and Guaviare lying east and south of Meta Cercano. In colonial times this region was called the Gran Airico. Today, it takes its name from the major river that flows through it, the Vichada.[3]

Before the arrival of the Spanish, the portions of the Llanos of San Martín and Casanare near the mountains were occupied by Arawak-speaking Achagua, Sáliva, and Tunebos who used slash-and-burn agriculture to raise food crops and supplemented their diet by hunting and fishing. Scattered farther east throughout the open plains were the nomadic Guahibos (also called Chiricoas), who depended on hunting and gathering. The mobility

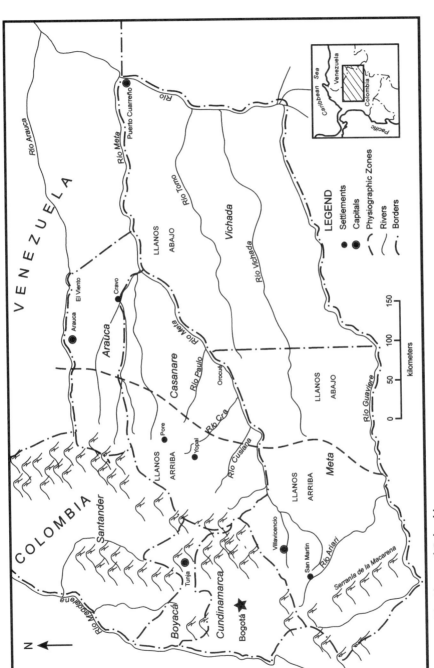

Map 1.1. The Llanos of Colombia

of these people made them excellent fighters, and they were more successful in resisting conquest by the Europeans than the sedentary groups to the
west.[4]

COLONIAL ANTECEDENTS

Between 1531 and 1650 five Spanish-led expeditions starting from Bogotá
and three German expeditions setting out from the Welser colony in
Venezuela explored the Colombian Llanos, each motivated by the conviction that somewhere in these plains lay the mythical kingdom of El Dorado. All these expeditions failed in their ultimate objective, but their leaders did establish the first Spanish cities in the Colombia Llanos. In Meta,
Juan de Avellaneda founded San Juan de los Llanos in 1555 on the banks
of the Ariari River where he had discovered a significant amount of alluvial
gold (at the site now occupied by San Juan de Arama). On a second trip
from Bogotá, Avellaneda brought cattle and settlers. For a while, the inhabitants of the little outpost thrived by extracting a modest amount of gold
and supplying expeditions that stopped on their way to search for El Dorado, but by the end of the century both the mines and the Indians enslaved
to work them were depleted.[5] After San Juan declined, Captain Juan de
Zarate began the town of San Martín in 1641, but this settlement showed
little prospect of expansion.

The main focus of Spanish colonization was to the north in the Llanos of
Casanare and Arauca. Here in the piedmont region resided larger concentra-
tions of sedentary natives. After the Spanish conquered the Chibcha in the
Andes highlands in 1538, they divided up the Indian villages around Tunja
and assigned them to Spanish *encomenderos* (holders of *encomiendas*—an institution whereby groups of natives were assigned to a Spaniard with the
duty of paying him labor or tribute. In return, the encomendero was to provide instruction in the Christian religion.) By 1544 these grants included Indians in the piedmont of Casanare who had formerly paid allegiance to the
Chibchas. Pauto and Támara, the two oldest towns in Casanare, were established as *doctrinas* (curacies) in those years, and in 1551 Chita and La Sal
were added. Augustinian missionaries administered these towns whose residents were mostly encomienda Indians who raised cotton and wove cloth
for the markets in Tunja and Bogotá.[6]

In 1588 Captain Pedro Daza founded the first Spanish city in Casanare,
Santiago de las Atalayas, located near the Cusiana River at the foot of the
cordillera southeast of Tunja; and he divided up the surrounding Achagua
villages into encomiendas. By 1620 the crown had designated the city as the
capital of the Provincia de los Llanos, an immense, largely unknown area
that included the Llanos of San Martín and extended to the Orinoco. By the

mid-seventeenth century, Santiago was sending twelve thousand *varas* (measure of length equivalent to about thirty-three inches) of cotton cloth back to Tunja as well as six thousand pigs and five thousand head of cattle.[7]

In 1662 a Junta de Propaganda Fide, which met in Bogotá, began a campaign to convert the Indians in the Llanos by dividing up the territory into five zones and assigning responsibility for each one to a different religious order. Casanare natives were distributed between the Augustinians, Recoletos, and Jesuits, while the Dominicans and Franciscans received the tribes living in the Llanos of San Juan and San Martín.[8] By 1760 the Augustinians controlled nine mission towns with 6,458 inhabitants while the Jesuits administered eleven towns with a total of 7,620 Indians. In Arauca to the northeast, the Recoletos had three towns with 300 inhabitants.[9]

In the Llanos of San Martín, the Dominicans continued to administer the town of Medina, which they had founded in 1620 before the Junta de Propaganda Fide edict, but they made little effort to expand their operations.[10] The Franciscans, who arrived in San Juan and San Martín in 1662, were more energetic. By the early eighteenth century, they ruled six small missions, whose populations of Sálivas and Achaguas fluctuated daily from a handful of individuals to as many as sixty in each village. The leading missionary enterprise in the territory was the Jesuit-run Hacienda of Apiay, an estate located at the headwaters of the Guatiquía, consisting of 11,498 hectares and 1,683 cattle divided into three *hatos* (ranches)—Apiay, Cumaral, and Patire.[11]

After the crown expelled the Jesuits in 1767, the Dominicans, Franciscans, and Recoletos took over their missions in Casanare, but the Junta de Temporalidades (a committee composed of the viceroy, the archbishop, a judge, and an attorney) sold the haciendas that had been attached to the missions to private individuals. In 1797 a Nicolás Bernal bought the Hacienda of Apiay in the Llanos of San Martín for four thousand two hundred Colombian pesos, and after he had passed it along to his heirs, the groundwork was laid for a legal battle over the ownership of this important property, which would not be resolved until the twentieth century.[12] In addition, the Franciscans relocated one of the former Jesuit missions, Jiramena, to the Meta River, where in 1806 it had 140 neophytes. At that time, they ruled 1,542 Indians in six other reductions in the Llanos of San Martín—Túa, Mayoral, Cabuyaro, Campo del Arrojo, Concepción de Arama, and Maricuare.[13] After the War of Independence, only Jiramena remained.

In sum, before 1810 the settled population of the Llanos of San Martín consisted of two Spanish towns, San Juan de los Llanos and San Martín, and the seven Franciscan missions which, taken together, did not exceed two thousand people. In contrast, Casanare (including Arauca) had a population of 20,892 including 1,535 whites (7 percent), 15,189 Indians (73 percent), 4,025 mestizos (10 percent), and 119 black slaves (less than 1 percent).[14]

Pore, founded in 1649, had replaced Santiago de las Atalayas as the capital of the Provincia de los Llanos, and there were five other Spanish towns and twenty-three Indian missions. Casanare was economically linked to the highlands, because its creole inhabitants maintained a vigorous trade with Tunja in textiles, pottery, articles of wood and straw, and cattle. In this area of the Llanos, three hundred years of European subjection had ravaged the Indian cultures. Spanish demand for slaves, encomienda workers, and Christian converts devastated the Achaguas, Sálivas, and Tunebos, forcing them to sacrifice much of their original way of life to survive within the new system. More fortunate were the Guahibos, who as foragers proved to have more flexibility in countering the Spanish threat. Learning to ride the wild horses, they attacked missions and haciendas and in general waged a fierce resistance against the white intruders. By the nineteenth century, the once powerful cultivators had dwindled to a scattering of different tribes while the Guahibos roamed the plains with impunity outside the line of Spanish control.[15]

Despite the different settlement patterns, on the Spanish side of the frontier in both the Llanos of San Martín and Casanare, *mestizaje* (race mixture) was producing a regional subculture that blended European and Native American traits. The whites attempted to impose their political organization, language, forms of labor, and religion on the Indians, but to survive in the Llanos they had to adopt some native practices. The Indians showed them how to build houses out of palm leaves, fashion tree trunks into boats, and fish in the rivers. They taught them how to grow yuca (cassava or manioc), *plátanos*, and corn. Both the Indians and Spanish hunted deer, tigers, and tapirs with pointed sticks, lances, and bows and arrows. Achagua and Guahibo words became part of the regional dialect, and Indian religious beliefs made their way into Catholicism. The blend of the two traditions was especially evident in the lifestyle of the mestizo vaqueros (known as Llaneros) who worked on the hatos and gained fame as patriot soldiers during the wars of independence.[16]

THE WARS OF INDEPENDENCE

New Granada's struggle for independence from Spain, which began in 1809 and did not end until the patriot victory at the Battle of Boyacá on August 7, 1819, was far more traumatic for the Llanos of Casanare than for the regions south of the Meta River. Learning of Napoleon's invasion of Spain in 1808, José María Rosillo, Carlos Salgar, and Vicente Cadena raised the cry of rebellion in Socorro, Santander, on January 11, 1809, accusing Viceroy Antonio Amar y Borbon of planning to hand New Granada over to the French. They made their way to Casanare hoping to win the sympathy of the authorities and the people. Their attack on Pore backfired, and the Spanish quickly sent a militia to quash the uprising.[17] Despite this setback, once the struggle for independence engulfed the highlands in 1810, rebel sympathizers quickly seized control of the Provincia de los Llanos, and in Arauca, Llaneros fought bravely to repel an invasion by Venezuelan royalists.

After the collapse of the First Republic aIn Bogotá in 1816, highland patriots retreated to the Llanos to make Casanare the base of their resistance movement against the Spanish Reconquest. In August 1818 Simón Bolívar, who had installed his headquarters at Angostura, Venezuela, and formed an alliance with José Antonio Páez in Apure, decided to send Francisco de Paula Santander to Pore to organize the disparate Llanero guerrilla factions into a new army. The following year, Bolívar led this army in a historic march across Casanare and up the Eastern Cordillera to deal the Spanish a stunning defeat at the Battle of Boyacá on August 7, 1819.

The long war was traumatic for Casanare and Arauca. It disrupted the population, decimated the livestock, and depleted the economy. The army recruited some of the mission Indians, while others fled to the wilderness, leaving only three missions intact by the time the fighting ended in 1819. The Llaneros, lacking opportunities for gainful employment when they were dismissed from the army, joined bands of rustlers who plundered the few remaining hatos. The halfhearted efforts by Gran Colombian leaders in Bogotá to redress these conditions were not reassuring. In 1830 General Juan Nepomuceno Moreno, a patriot hero and powerful caudillo, overthrew the provincial government and declared that Casanare would secede from New Granada and join Venezuela. A year later Moreno led a Llanero army over the cordillera to help overthrow a dictatorship imposed by Rafael Urdaneta. Once they were in command, the highland leaders, who had first welcomed Moreno's assistance, firmly insisted that he return with his "barbarous" horde to the Llanos. In December 1831, Casanare, rebuffed by Venezuela, officially rejoined the republic of New Granada.[18]

In contrast, the War of Independence had far less devastating economic consequences for the Llanos of San Martín. During the early years of the struggle, no conflict occurred south of the Meta River. During the Reconquest, a Spanish army on orders from Pablo Morillo did seize Medina and San Martín but did not advance farther out into the plains. In 1818, the patriot chieftain, Ramón Nonato Pérez, retook both positions, expelling the royalists forever.[19] Moreover, the war did not drastically alter the political administration of the region south of the Meta. At some point in the eighteenth century the crown had detached the Llanos of San Martín from the Provincia de los Llanos and placed them under the direct jurisdiction of Santa Fe de Bogotá. This arrangement continued during the Republic of Gran Colombia, with San Martín forming one of eleven cantons in the province of Bogotá which, along with the provinces of Neiva, Mariquita, and Antioquia, made up the Department of Cundinamarca.

THE AFTERMATH OF THE COLLAPSE OF GRAN COLOMBIA

After the collapse of the Republic of Gran Colombia, due to the withdrawal of Venezuela and Ecuador in 1830, the leaders of New Granada, or present-day Colombia, reorganized the political administration of the territory that remained under their control. The Fundamental Law of November 21, 1831, abolished the departments but left the provinces intact. Casanare (including Arauca) with its capital at Pore became one of the thirteen provinces, while the Llanos of San Martín remained a canton in the province of Bogotá. This district, which consisted of two towns, San Martín and Medina, and three parishes, Cabuyaro, Concepción de Arama, and Jiramena, was authorized to send one delegate to the provincial assembly that met each September in Bogotá. Because San Martín was the only canton in the province that failed to hold a presidential election in 1832, it is unlikely that a delegate was ever selected.[20]

The census of 1835 set the population of Casanare at 15,948 (including 3,599 inhabitants of the canton of Arauca)—a dramatic decline of nearly 25 percent from the estimated 1810 population of 22,000, which is attributable to disease, war casualties, and the flight of mission Indians.[21] Neither the 1810 nor the 1835 figures counted Indians living outside white control, but in a separate report dated May 22, 1835, Governor M. Arenas estimated that there were 6,625 Indians living independently in tribes and *capitanías* (units ranging from 100 to 700 members loyal to a single chief). He added that the eight capitanías of Achaguas along the Vichada River interacted peacefully with the colonists, but others such as the ten Guahibo capitanías along the Casanare and Meta rivers were "indomitable, treacherous murderers," who preyed on nearby hatos and river commerce.[22] In 1836, Arenas submitted a detailed statistical summary of provincial economic activity. If Arauca is omitted, there were 15,823 cattle, 466 goats, 811 horses, 402 mules, 79 burros, and 190 sheep in the other five cantons. Casanare produced cacao, coffee, honey, cheese, salt, cotton, corn, rice, straw hats, and pottery, and sent hides and live animals to highland Boyacá and Venezuela.[23]

It is clear that although Casanare had regained political autonomy in 1831, it had yet to recover from the damage caused by the wars. As the second smallest of the thirteen provinces (only Riohacha with a population of 14,514 had fewer people), it had little national influence, being limited to one senator in the twenty-six-member upper house of Congress and one representative in the eighty-four-member lower house. Throughout the nineteenth century, its more populous neighbor, Boyacá, to which it maintained close political, demographic, and economic ties, dominated the region. When modernization, propelled by export booms in tobacco, quinine, and coffee, transformed western Colombia into the economic heartland,

Casanare shared the catastrophic decline of Boyacá, which by 1870 had become the poorest state in the Colombia federation.[24]

In the first decades after 1831 the principal problem in the Llanos of San Martín continued to be a lack of population. Writing in 1832, geographer Feliciano Montenegro Colón asserted that the canton had no more than 421 houses and 1,530 inhabitants. A census conducted in 1835 failed to give a population figure, but it listed 453 houses in the canton. Farmland was valued at COL$19,223 and grazing land at COL$20,500. The census revealed that there were 12,127 head of cattle, 499 horses, 50 mules, 39 pigs, and 21 riverboats. Economic activities included cultivation of cacao and coffee; production of honey, cheese and salt; and manufacture of straw hats and pottery.[25]

Rufino Cuervo, the governor of Cundinamarca, was impressed by the potential wealth of San Martín. In his annual message of 1832, he noted that the canton had rich deposits of salt and was extremely fertile. "It has a navigable river and is so extensive that its limits are lost in countries where civilization had not penetrated, but it is almost completely unpopulated."[26] The following year, Cuervo proposed a law to permit people convicted of vagrancy and other crimes to serve out their sentences in the Llanos. As he explained:

> The vast and meritorious canton of San Martín calls for people; to it can be sent the men who have been lost in the larger society in order that at the side of innocent and hard working citizens, in the midst of fertile and uncultivated fields and without temptation to dissipate themselves, they can dedicate themselves to work, forget their bad habits, make their own fortunes, augment the population and contribute to the prosperity of the state.[27]

The legislature did not approve this measure but the scheme to transport criminals from the highlands to populate the Llanos of San Martín was periodically revived until, in 1907, the government began the first national prison at the town of Acacías near Villavicencio.

Efforts to encourage missionaries to return to the territory were unsuccessful. In 1834, after the *jefe político* (chief political official) of San Martín reported that there were no missions in his jurisdiction, the provincial legislature voted to reestablish missions at Jiramena and San Antonio. Governor Cuervo sent the resolution to the secretary of state for approval, pointing out that evangelization would be easier south of the Meta River than in Casanare because the Indians were more docile and because the jefe político was eager to assist the missionaries.[28] Three years later, however, there were still no Franciscans in San Martín. In February 1837, the jefe político wrote that a measles epidemic was claiming many victims, and because all the parishes lacked priests, there was no one to administer last rites. When he investigated this complaint, Archbishop Manuel José Mosquera discovered that Fr. José María Molano, a Franciscan who was supposed to be serving the parishes of San Martín and San Juan, had deserted his post for unknown reasons.[29] On September 4, 1837, President José Ignacio de Márquez ordered missions reestablished at Jiramena and San Martín, and in March of the following year, Fr. Gregorio Becerra left Bogotá to take charge of them, but whether he arrived is uncertain.[30]

In the meantime, the area between the *caños* (slowly moving streams of water) Gramalote and Parrado at the base of the Eastern Cordillera continued to serve as a resting place for ranchers coming from the Llanos of eastern San Martín who planned to drive their cattle up the mountain to the market in Bogotá. There they met with buyers and muleteers from the capital who found lodging in primitive inns that sprang up to house the transients. It was already obvious that the site was an ideal location for the establishment of a town that would serve as a gateway to the highlands to the west and the Llanos to the east.[31]

AN OLD FRONTIER

By 1830, three hundred years of European contact had transformed the ecology of the Llanos. Cattle and horses grazed on plains that had previously supported no animals larger than the jaguar. On the piedmont edge of the frontier, the Achaguas, Sálivas, and Tunebos, once powerful cultivators, had been decimated or absorbed into Spanish society by missionaries and encomenderos; to the east, Guahibos, no longer peaceful foragers, dominated large portions of Casanare, Arauca, and almost all of San Martín, and they were determined to resist further encroachment. Both whites and Indians cut down the gallery forests in the piedmont and along the rivers to plant crops. They systematically burned the dry savanna grass to produce better pasturage for the cattle, but surprisingly enough, as geographer John Blydenstein has pointed out, man's direct influence on the landscape was slight because of low population density. It was not until the massive influx of *colonos* (settlers who farm or graze cattle on public land without legal title to the territory) into the Department of Meta after World War II that the piedmont forest began to disappear, leaving chronic erosion and scarred mountain slopes.[32]

The tropical climate, which had deterred the Spanish from occupying the Llanos in large numbers, continued to discourage colonization throughout the nineteenth century. Agustín Codazzi, the Italian geographer who surveyed Casanare in 1855, flatly concluded that immigrants from highland New Granada could not survive in the plains. Besides the dangers posed by Indians, tigers, snakes, crocodiles, and mosquitoes, the heat in some sections was so intense that a thermometer registering 30°C (87°F) at 8:00 PM dipped only to 29°C (84°F) by 11:00 PM. The merciless sun caused rivers to evaporate quickly and converted them into stagnant pools filled with rotting fish, and plants emitted fever-causing poisonous fumes. Codazzi believed that the grass itself also gave off fumes that caused epidemics similar to cholera. Temperatures were lower near the cordillera, where cool breezes blew down from the mountains; but these early morning drafts chilled the lightly clothed inhabitants, causing typhoid fever. He concluded that given such perils, the only people who could survive in the Llanos were Africans or Venezuelan Llaneros who were already acclimated to similar conditions.[33] The continued high mortality rate in the plains bore out Codazzi's warning that diseases posed great dangers to Europeans, even though his explanation of their causes had little basis in scientific fact.[34] It was not until the twentieth century that public health officials realized that malaria, yellow fever, cholera, and tropical anemia could be controlled by mosquito eradication, proper sanitation, medication, and diet and that colonists could move into the Llanos without fear of expiring within a few months or years.

The leaders of New Granada inherited from the Spanish an old frontier that was characterized by a unique cowboy subculture and deeply rooted Hispanic institutions—towns, missions, and ranches. Like the viceroys before them, they neglected the Llanos to develop the western heartland of the republic, where economic resources were indisputable albeit dependent on efficient transportation along the Magdalena River. They did not ignore the east completely, but as we shall see in the following chapters, the emergence of Villavicencio as the primary city in the Llanos of San Martín, was more the result of spontaneous settlement by colonos from the slopes of the

Illustration 1.1.   Lost in the Llanos
Source: *Geografía pintoresca de Colombia* (Bogotá: Litografía Arco, 1968), 115–22.

Illustration 1.2.   A Rodeo in the Llanos
Source: *Geografía pintoresca de Colombia* (Bogotá: Litografía Arco, 1968), 115–22.

cordillera in Cundinamarca and Tolima than the aborted attempts by national governments to promote its growth.

SPONTANEOUS COLONIZATION AND THE FOUNDING OF VILLAVICENCIO, 1831–1863

With the establishment of the Republic of New Granada in 1831, Colombia's two enduring political parties began to take shape. Between 1831 and 1849, legislators, deeply influenced by the Catholic Church, guided the fate of the republic under the leadership of presidents Francisco de Paula Santander, José Ignacio de Márquez, Pedro Alcántara Herrán, and Tomás C. de Mosquera. In 1849 the election of Liberal José Hilario López saw the initiation of a plethora of reforms that marked a watershed in Colombian history. Between 1849 and 1853, the Liberals moved quickly to end the state tobacco monopoly, reduce tariffs, abolish slavery, expand civil liberties, rescind the death penalty for political crimes, and give local government more control over the church. All of these reforms were incorporated into the Constitution of 1853, which broadened suffrage by ending property and literacy requirements; instituted direct, secret elections; and provided for the election of many previously appointed officials.

Despite their ideological differences, both the Conservative and Liberal regimes were eager to encourage the development the Llanos of San Martín. Yet, the founding of Villavicencio in 1850 was due more to spontaneous colonization than to any of the flawed policies of the national government.

Spontaneous Colonization

In the 1840s, despite three hundred years of continuous Spanish occupation, the canton of San Martín, with its five small towns, was an isolated New Granadan outpost surrounded by tropical wilderness. In 1844 the towns of San Martín, Medina, and Jiramena had 647, 519, and 270 inhabitants, respectively, and Cabuyaro and Concepción de Arama were mere collections of huts. The prewar Franciscan missions had disappeared, although groups of Indians occasionally notified the jefe político of their willingness to settle down if he would send them a priest. There were five or six thousand cattle in the canton, with three hundred horses, and a few mules and pigs. Trade was mainly with Quetame, Fosca, and Cáqueza—Cundinamarcan towns located along the mule path that led to Bogotá—a road virtually impassable during the nine-month rainy season.[35]

However, the lure of open, fertile land could not be denied, and about this time, some adventurous *vecinos* of Cáqueza and Quetame, weary of living in grinding poverty, decided to seek their fortunes in the Llanos to the east. The first was Esteban Aguirre, who built his house in a place called Gramalote, at the foot of the cordillera between the Guatiquía and Río Negro rivers.[36] Soon his wife, Matea Fernández; his son-in-law, Libardo Hernández; and fellow *caqueceños* (people from Cáqueza) Silvestre Velásquez and Francisco Ardilla joined Aguirre. Gramalote's remoteness also made it attractive to army deserters, escaped prisoners, and individuals fleeing debts. With natural salt mines at Cumaral and Upín nearby, it was also a convenient resting place for Llaneros coming from the east, who were driving cattle raised around San Martín to markets in Bogotá. By 1845 there were more than one hundred colonos living in a small *caserío* (village) of thatched huts.[37]

The lawlessness of the new settlement was notorious. In 1845, the governor of Bogotá, Alfonso Acevedo, ordered the jefe político of Cáqueza to go to Gramalote and arrest Vicente Carillo, Jacinto Chaco, and Atanacio Jura, who were seizing *baldíos* (public lands), forcing newcomers to pay illegal taxes, and forbidding them to grow sugar cane and cacao in certain areas. The jefe político was told to assure the colonos that baldíos were national property and that they could live on them and cultivate sugarcane and cacao without paying rent. He was ordered to choose an official site with an abundance of water for the town of Gramalote and to design a plan for it that included a plaza, at least eight streets, and locations for the chapel, *casa cural* (priest's residence), school, jail, and *casa municipal* (town hall). Finally, he was ordered to improve the road between Gramalote and Quetame so that it might become the principal route of the cordillera, enabling an alternative trail known as La Cabuya to be discontinued.[38]

A year later, Congress declared the canton of San Martín a special territory to be ruled by a prefect appointed by the president. The Law of May 10, 1846, which organized the territory, promised 60 *fanegadas* (land measure; 1 fanegada equals about 1.6 acres) of baldíos to colonos who agreed to cultivate the land and proclaimed that Indians who accepted "civilized life" would be exempted from civil and religious taxes for their lifetimes.[39] The territorial scheme was rescinded in 1850, but Gramalote continued to grow. Dr. Ignacio Osorio, the *cura* (parish priest) of San Martín, consecrated its first church, Nuestra Señora de la Concepción, in 1848, and the town was divided into two *partidos* called Gramalote and Cumaral.[40]

When López abolished all of New Granada's special territories on June 22, 1850, San Martín once again became a canton in the province of Bogotá, but it still enjoyed special privileges. The Law of June 22 authorized the national treasury to spend sixty-one thousand *reales* on its churches and public buildings. It directed the provincial legislature to distribute up to twenty-five thousand fanegadas of baldíos among its parishes and empowered the president to award up to sixty fanegadas to colonos on the condition that they occupy and cultivate the parcels. Finally, the law exempted all the inhabitants of the canton from paying taxes other than those imposed by their parish *cabildos* (town councils).[41]

In September 1850, the provincial legislature elevated the caserío of Gramalote to the status of *distrito parroquial*, and on October 21 it approved its new name, Villavicencio—suggested by the local priest, Manuel Santos Martínez, in honor of independence hero Antonio Villavicencio, who was executed by the Spanish on June 6, 1816 (see frontispiece).[42] The town now had a population of 349—191 men and 158 women. In 1852, it replaced San Martín as the capital of the canton, receiving its first jefe político, Nicolas Díaz, and a unit of the national guard. Mail service with Bogotá via Cáqueza was already functioning, and in August the provincial government sent a doctor to vaccinate the inhabitants against a smallpox epidemic that was sweeping through the canton.[43]

Padre Santos Martínez was not the first priest to say mass in Villavicencio—that distinction belonged to Dr. Osorio—but Santos Martínez performed the first recorded baptism and did much to stabilize the community in its early days. His proposal to populate nearby Jiramena with beggars from Bogotá attracted national attention in 1854, but the experiment failed when the four hundred destitute people that he rounded up from the streets of Bogotá and transported to Jiramena quickly deserted. By March of 1855, when only thirty-six of the new colonos remained, Santos Martínez abandoned the project and devoted his energies to founding a hospital in Villavicencio.[44]

Although Villavicencio was the first newly settled viable town to appear south of the Meta in the nineteenth century, its existence was precariously dependent on trade with Bogotá, 125 kilometers away via a rough trail that ascended three thousand meters over the Eastern Cordillera to the capital. Winding up and down mountain slopes as it followed the Río Negro, the road required travelers to ford streams and cross deep *quebradas* (ravines) using flimsy bridges accessible only by mules. For nine months of the year rains and landslides cut off most communication. Repairs on the road fell to the Cundinamarcan towns that relied on it—Chipaque, Cáqueza, and Quetame.[45] Even when the legislature signed a contract for the construction of a *camino de herradura* (mule path) between Cáqueza and Apiay, as occurred in 1852, the entrepreneur, stymied by heavy rains and insufficient funds, did little more than make the most obvious repairs.[46]

In 1855, the British firm of Stiebel, Rothschild, and Son hired Ramón Guerra Azuola, a Colombian engineer, to survey the Meta River and the road connecting it with Bogotá, to ascertain the feasibility of river transport. Joining a party that included nine Englishmen and a French botanist, none of whom spoke Spanish, Guerra Azuola departed from Bogotá on March 10, 1855, reaching Villavicencio five days later, and Macuco, on the Meta, on July 14. His wry account of his experiences, in his *Apuntamientos de viajes*, includes a pessimistic report about the development possibilities of the main "highway" to the Llanos.[47]

Guerra Azuola began his narrative by recalling that the group had set off at a gallop from Bogotá on a beautiful morning and that his companions were in high spirits until they reached the "sad and miserable village" of Yomasa, two leagues south of Bogotá.[48] At the engineer's request, the party stopped to allow him to unpack his instruments and take scientific observations to determine if the trail could be transformed into a cart road, but the Europeans endured the two-hour delay with ill grace. In a more somber mood, they continued along the trail up the mountain rim southeast of the Sabana of Bogotá. They passed through the gloomy Boquerón de Chipaque, at 3,144 meters altitude and started down the mountain to reach the town of Chipaque at 6:30 PM. This hamlet, at 2,512 meters, was a regular overnight stopping place for wayfarers from Bogotá, yet it offered neither corral nor inn. There was nothing to eat, and because their pack mules had not yet arrived, the weary travelers had neither bedding nor candles to light the darkness. Ravenously hungry, they spent the night lying on the floor of a hut, surrounded by bundles of yuca and cabbages and tormented by insects. The next day, they followed the Cáqueza River down the mountain to the town of Cáqueza, "where we gave a splendid demonstration of the strength of our mouths and the astonishing capacity of our stomachs." Cáqueza, at 1,600 meters, was "a sad town where there is a jefe político and *juez letrado* [judge], but in all the rest is as miserable, solitary and apathetic as any other Indian town." Already, the sharp, twisting descent of the mule trail from the Boquerón had convinced Guerra Azuola that transforming it into a cart road would be "a colossal project" that would require extending the roadbed eight leagues to negotiate the turns.[49]

More encouraging was the next section of the trail from Cáqueza to Quetame, which he described as "one of the best laid out that I have ever seen. Rigid in direction, soft in descent, skillfully taking advantage of the accidents of the terrain—all indicated that the hand which laid it out was expert and knowledgeable." Nevertheless, at Quetame, the path was interrupted by a deep quebrada, a gorge cut by the Río Negro. In the dry season travelers climbed down into the quebrada to ford the river, but during the rainy season and without a bridge, they were forced to cross it by standing in a basket that was suspended from a cable and hauled across the chasm. This makeshift arrangement severely restricted commercial use of the trail and was also a sore point for the inhabitants of Quetame, who lived on both sides of the quebrada. Because of the difficulties in crossing the river, those living on the right side demanded that town offices be located on their bank, "so that they could go to Bogotá without wetting their stirrups," while those on the left bank felt the same way. "Today things have reached such a state," wrote Guerra Azuola, "that one side has only to propose some improvement for the other side to oppose it, and so they live in eternal war, being themselves the victims of such quarrels. Of course in Quetame there is no school because it can only be built on the river, which would be the only neutral site acceptable to both camps. What a pity that a town remains in *barbarie* [rusticity] and tears itself apart for lack of a bridge!"[50]

From Quetame the trail continued in an easterly direction to Villavicencio, but this third section was the worst of all. Careening up and down the mountain, blocked by tree roots and landslides, it passed over dizzy precipices making heavy going even for the mules. Torrents of water poured off the slopes, causing rock- and mudslides, and nearly all of the quebradas were impassable during the rainy season. The bright spot in this difficult journey was the Buenavista outcropping above Villavicencio, where the travelers got their first view of the Llanos, which spread out before them, blending into "the horizon like a vast green sea." As Guerra Azuola observed, "On seeing this *llanura* a man becomes sad to think that he will have to leave it in order to climb once again the high crests of the mountains where cold, fog, and storms reign."[51]

The party made its triumphal entrance into Villavicencio at 4:00 PM on March 15, "without further problem than three bruised Englishmen and the loss of two horses that had died on the road." Although Guerra Azuola's notebook contained pages of calculations, he resolved to report to Stiebel, Rothschild, and Sons that transporting goods between the Llanos and Bogotá was technologically unfeasible, a judgment corroborated a year later by

Agustín Codazzi.[52] In a report submitted to the national government, Codazzi affirmed that for many more years geographic obstacles would limit commerce between Bogotá and Villavicencio to cattle driven on the hoof up the mountain. The government might profitably spend four or five thousand pesos to improve the road for that purpose, but the building of a full-fledged *camino de rueda* (cart road) was a task that might be better undertaken by future generations.[53]

Guerra Azuola was not especially impressed by what he found in Villavicencio, although he did recognize the potential of the town. He wrote:

> Villavicencio is a little town of recent date. Its inhabitants are poor and ignorant and while its location offers them the greatest advantages to advance and become rich, these same advantages hinder their efforts, since they don't know how to make use of them, because of the contrast between the customs of the Cordillera and the Llanos, between the industries of the highlands and the speculations of the hot country.[54]

The 1860s Brings a Second Wave of Immigration

The spontaneous immigration of colonos from Cáqueza and Quetame in the 1840s had laid the foundation for Villavicencio. In the 1860s there was another wave of immigration, set off by the civil war of 1859 to 1862, which returned Tomás C. Mosquera to power and redoubled the efforts of merchant families in Bogotá to cash in on the coffee boom by buying lands in the valleys of Cundinamarca and the hot country. Unlike their peasant predecessors, the people who came to Villavicencio in the 1860s had capital to invest and political influence in Bogotá.[55] Their enthusiasm and commitment to their adopted region opened a new era for Villavicencio and the Llanos of San Martín.

The Liberal revolt of 1859 broke out in Santander and spread rapidly to Boyacá, Bolívar, Cauca, and Cundinamarca. Although Mosquera proclaimed himself provisional president in 1861, it was not until October 25, 1862, that the last Conservatives surrendered at Yomasa, near Bogotá. The conflict reshuffled the Liberal party. Some men, such as Julian Trujillo, Santos Acosta, and Santos Gutiérrez, gained fame and experience for their military exploits, but others lost their lives; the most notable was José María Obando, who was killed during a skirmish near Bogotá on April 19, 1861. After their defeat at El Oratorio on August 16, 1860, virtually the entire Liberal leadership of Santander was captured and imprisoned.[56]

Discouraged by the destruction caused by the fight in Cundinamarca, many young men decided to seek their fortunes in the Llanos. In 1860, Manuel Fernández arrived in Villavicencio without a *real* in his pocket. He worked hard, bought two ranches and one thousand cattle, and was able to educate his large family in the best *colegios* of Bogotá. Ricardo Rojas R.

arrived equally penniless in 1862 and became one of the leading landowners in the Llanos of San Martín by the end of the century.[57] In 1864, at the age of twenty-eight, Sergio Convers left his store on Bogotá's Calle Real to travel to Villavicencio, where he was enchanted by the beauty and fertility of the land. He had planned to cultivate indigo, but his mother-in-law, Araceli Fernández de la Hoz, the wife of Agustín Codazzi, persuaded him to try coffee, a crop she had seen growing in Venezuela. Convers bought land in Apiay in 1865. He cleared away the forest on seventy-five hectares to begin his Hacienda El Buque and planted eighty thousand coffee trees. At about the same time, his neighbors Narciso Reyes and Federico Silva were planting seventy thousand coffee trees on their Hacienda Ocoa. Both El Buque and Ocoa had machines to shell and wash the coffee beans, and Ocoa had a drying stove.

Other Bogotanos who settled down near Villavicencio to grow coffee, cacao, or cattle were Santiago Gutiérrez, Nicolás and Ciriaco Castro, General Helidoro Ruíz, Joaquín Piñeres, Celestino Martínez, J. A. Sucre, and José María de Francisco, but the most tireless champion of the region was a Liberal lawyer and journalist from Antioquia, Emiliano Restrepo E.[58] Born in Medellín on September 14, 1832, Restrepo earned a law degree from the Colegio del Rosario in 1853 and was a judge in Antioquia before moving to Bogotá, where he served as secretary of government of Cundinamarca and defended Mosquera during his trial in 1867.[59] A year later, lured by glowing tales of the fertility and natural wealth of the region, he made his first trip to the Llanos of San Martín. Restrepo's three-week trip took him to Villavicencio, the Salina of Upín, and the Sabana of Apiay, where he visited the estates of Nicolás Castro, Narciso Reyes, and Federico Silva. He returned to Bogotá convinced that the Llanos were destined to be "the location of a rich, civilized and populous nation."[60] Restrepo bought several tracts of land around Villavicencio, began his haciendas La Vanguardia and El Salitre and later founded a cacao plantation. As a congressman representing Cundinamarca from 1870 to 1871, he lobbied successfully for improvements on the Bogotá-Villavicencio road. Restrepo was deeply involved in national politics throughout the Federation Era, but he still found time to promote the interests of the Llanos. Perhaps more than any other event, the publication of his book, *Una excursión a los llanos de San Martín*, in 1870 anchored within the national psyche the conviction that the plains south of the Meta River represented the "future of Colombia."

In her noteworthy monograph, *Frontier Expansion and Peasant Protest in Colombia, 1830–1936* (1986), Catherine LeGrand has suggested that Colombia integrated frontier regions into its economy during the nineteenth century through a two-step process. With the exception of Antioquia, where from the beginning merchants and land speculators played a pivotal role in directing colonization, the hinterlands were first opened by peasant squatters, who migrated to the wilderness seeking economic opportunity and independence. After a decade or two, profit-seeking entrepreneurs appeared on the scene, extending control over the land itself and the peasants' labor by asserting private ownership to vast areas of public domain.[61] The evidence suggests that something of this sort also occurred in the Llanos of San Martín. The entrepreneurs who arrived in the 1860s encroached on the rights and independence of the peasants who had come before, but they also used their influence in Bogotá to stimulate the first concerted national effort to develop the Llanos frontier. The resulting territorial initiative, set in motion during the Federation Era (1863–1888), would bring about the unprecedented expansion of Villavicencio and, along with it, the Llanos south of the Meta River.

NOTES

1. Cámara Provincial de Bogotá, Ordenanza #106 de 21 de octubre de 1850 created within the Cantón de San Martín a "Distrito Parroquial" to be known as Villavicencio, which would encompass the former Corregimiento de Gramalote. The long, involved debate over the precise date of the founding of Villavicencio will be discussed later.

2. F. O. Martin, "Exploration in Colombia," *Geographical Review* 19 (1929): 629–33.

3. Raye Platt, "Opportunities for Agricultural Colonization in the Eastern Border Valleys of the Andes," in *Pioneer Settlement* (New York: American Geographical Society Special Publication 14, 1969), 89.

4. The most complete study of the various native tribes of the Llanos can be found in *Introducción a la Colombia Amerindia* (Bogotá: Instituto Colombiano de Antropología, 1987).

5. Pedro de Aguado, *Recopilación historial*, 4 vols. (Bogotá: Empresa Nacional de Publicaciones, 1956–1957), 1: 569–81.

6. José Pérez Gómez, *Apuntes históricos de las misiones agustinianas en Colombia* (Bogotá: Casa Editorial de la Cruzada, 1924), 123–26.

7. Marcelino Ganuza, *Monografía de las misiones vivas de agustinos recoletos (candelarios) en Colombia*, 3 vols. (Bogotá: Imprenta de San Bernardo, 1921), 1: 176–78.

8. Juan Manuel Pacheco, *Historia eclesiástica: La consolidación de la iglesia—siglo XVII*, 2 vols. (Bogotá: Ediciones Lerner, 1975), 2: 656.

9. Rausch, *A Tropical Plains Frontier*, 62.

10. Alonso de Zamora, O. P., *Historia de la Provincia de San Antonio de Nuevo Reino de Granada* (Caracas: Editorial Sur America,1930), 381–83.

11. Gregorio Arcila Robledo, O. F. M., *Las misiones franciscanas en Colombia* (Bogotá: Imprenta Nacional, 1910), 259–61; Germán Colmenares, *Las haciendas de los jesuítas* (Bogotá: Universidad Nacional de Colombia, 1969), 127.

12. The best discussion of this battle can be found in Espinel Riveros, *Villavicencio*, 75–96. Espinel Riveros also makes the case that the year 1797 marks the

founding of Villavicencio, because the territory occupied by the Hacienda Apiay approximately corresponds to the modern location of Villavicencio (182).

13. Rausch, *Tropical Plains Frontier*, 113–14.

14. Archivo Histórico Nacional, Bogotá (hereafter cited AHN), José Caicedo, Provincia de los Llanos: Padrón formado en el año de 1778. Morcote, October 14, 1778.

15. Rausch, *The Llanos Frontier*, 11.

16. Manuel Zapata Olivella, *El hombre colombiano* (Bogotá: Canal Ramirez-Antares, 1974), 356–60.

17. Enrique Otero d'Costa, "La Revolución de Casanare in 1809," *Boletín de Historia y Antigüedades* (hereafter cited as BHA) 17 (1928): 530–46.

18. Rausch, *The Llanos Frontier*, 12.

19. Oswaldo Díaz Díaz, *La reconquista española*, 2 vols. (Bogotá: Ediciones Lerner, 1964–1967), 2: 117.

20. David Bushnell, "Elecciones presidenciales colombianas, 1825–1856," in *Compendio de estadísticas históricas de Colombia*, ed. Miguel Urrutia and Mario Arrubla (Bogotá: Universidad Nacional de Colombia, 1970), 223.

21. Fernando Gómez, "Los censos en Colombia antes de 1905," in Urrutia and Arrubla, *Compendio*, 21.

22. AHN, Gobernación de Casanare (hereafter cited as GC), volume (hereafter cited as vol.) 16, folder (hereafter cited as fol.). 17.

23. AHN, GC, vol. 16, fol. 225.

24. Helen Delpar, *Red against Blue: The Liberal Party in Colombian Politics, 1863–1899* (Tuscaloosa: University of Alabama Press, 1981), 33.

25. Feliciano Montenegro Colón, *Geografía general*, 4 vols. (Caracas: Imprenta de Damiron y Dupouy, 1834), 3: 550; AHN, Gobernación de Bogotá (hereafter cited as GB) vol. 3, fol. 844.

26. *El Constitucional de Cundinamarca*, September 15, 1832.

27. *El Constitutional de Cundinamarca*, September 22, 1833.

28. *El Constitucional de Cundinamarca*, September 15, 1832.

29. *El Constitucional de Cundinamarca*, February 18, 1837.

30. *Gaceta de la Nueva Granada*, April 15, 1838.

31. Ojeda Ojeda, *Villavicencio*, 226.

32. John Blydenstein, "Tropical Savanna Vegetation of the Llanos of Colombia," *Ecology* 48, no. 1 (Winter 1967): 13.

33. Agustín Codazzi, *Geografía física i política de las provincias de la Nueva Granada*, 3 vols. (Bogotá: Banco de la República. Archivo de la Economía Nacional, 1959) 3: 377–79.

34. In *Death by Migration: Europe's Encounter with the Tropical World in the Nineteenth Century* (New York: Cambridge University Press, 1989), Philip D. Curtin notes that the European scientific community divided into two camps to explain the causes of certain tropical diseases. The "contagionists," a minority, believed that cholera and yellow fever were transmitted from one person to another like smallpox and syphilis. The "anticontagionists" argued that epidemics grew out of local conditions of a miasmatic nature. For example, a Dr. Inglis who prepared a sanitary report for Madras, India, in 1863, declared that cholera was caused by "peculiar physical and atmospherical states operating on the decomposing vegetable and organic

products at the low fluvial level described, and the sudden cessation, to removal of all fermenting elements requiring meteorological conditions for their development" (75). Judging by his description of the causes of disease in the Llanos, Codazzi adhered to the "anticontagionist" school of thought.

35. AHN, GB, vol. 2, fol. 360.

36. The place was called "Gramalote" because the location was thickly covered with couch grass knows as *gramal*. See Raquel Angel de Flórez, *Conozcamos al Departamento del Meta*, 3 vols. (Bogotá: Fonda Rotatorio Judicial Penitenciaria Central, 1962–1963), 2: 53.

37. Flórez, *Conozcamos*, 2: 53; *El Constitucional de Cundinamarca*, January 19, 1845; Rufino Gutiérrez, *Monografías*, 2 vols. (Bogotá: Imprenta Nacional, 1920–1921), 1: 60; Joaquín Paredez Cruz, *Departamento del Meta* (Villavicencio: Cooperativa Nacinal de Artes Gráficas, 1961), 131. On May 30, 1986, the Muncipal Council of Villavicencio issued an *Acuerdo* declaring that the official date of the founding of Gramalote was April 6, 1940. See Nancy Espinel Riveros, *Otra mirada a la historia de Villavicencio* (Villavicencio: Fundación Centro de Historia de Villavicencio, 2000), 28.

38. *El Constitucional de Cundinamarca*, January 19, 1845.

39. *Gaceta de la Nueva Granada*, May 17, 1846.

40. Enrique Ortega Ricarte, *Villavicencio, (1842–1942): Monografía* (Bogotá: Prensa de la Biblioteca Nacional, 1943), 82.

41. *Gaceta Oficial*, June 23, 1850.

42. Ortega Ricarte, *Villavicencio*, 83. At the same time, the legislature erected Cumaral into a *distrito parroquial* and renamed it Serviez. The ordenanza that created Villavicencio is reprinted in Espinal Riveros, *Otra Mirada*, 16. Espinel Riveros suggests that Omar Baquero Riveros in *Villavicencio ayer y hoy, 1840–1990* (1990) has argued that the town was not named after Antonio Villavicencio y Verástegui, the Independence hero, but rather don Manuel Villavicencio who served as governor of the Llanos in 1789. (Note: I have not been able to locate this book by Baquero Riveros or find any other reference to it.) Nevertheless, Espinel Riveros concludes, after considering the various arguments pro and con, that it is more likely that the namesake of the town was Antonio Villavicencio y Verástegui, because in the nineteenth century there was a tendency to pay tribute to the heroes of Independence. See Espinel Riveros, *Otra mirada*, 48–49.

The actual date of the founding of Villavicencio has also been subject to debate. On the one hand, Espinel Riveros maintains that purchase of the Hacienda Apiay in 1797 should mark the city's founding. On the other hand, Padre Mauricio Dieres Monplaisir stated that the town was founded on December 20, 1842. Accordingly, its bicentennial was duly celebrated on December 20, 1942. Then in 1986 the Municipal Council of Villavicencio decreed that the city was founded on April 6, 1840. In 1989 the Academia Colombiana de Historia examined all three hypotheses and determined that the strongest evidence supported the date of October 21, 1850. Accordingly, it ruled that Villavicencio should celebrate is sesquicentennial on October 21, 2000. See BHA, 76: 767, 1989 and Espinel Riveros, *Villavicencio*, 172–190.

43. *El Contitucional de Cundinamarca*, August 26, 1852. Javier Ocampo López has pointed out that it was quite common in Colombia for a town to be founded initially by spontaneous colonization and then to be officially recognized by the government at a later date. In this regard he adds that Villavicencio is similar to

Manizales in that both were initially founded for economic reasons at the intersection of two key roads. Cited by Espinel Riveros, *Otra mirada*, 43.

44. Ortega Ricarte, *Villavicencio*, 96–98; Ramón Guerra Azuola, "Apuntamientos de Viaje," BHA 4: 43 (January 1907): 424; *El Constitucional de Cundinamarca*, June 26, 1852.

45. For example, in 1842 the vecinos of Cáqueza contributed COL$206 to improve the road, AHN, GB, vol. 11, fol. 426.

46. *El Constitucional de Cundinamarca*, October 1852.

47. At Guerra Azuola's death, his heirs found among his papers an album containing maps, illustrations, and accounts of his travels through New Granada between 1853 and 1860, including a report of his participation in the civil war of 1860 as aide-de-camp to Conservative General Joaquín Paris. The album was presented to the Academia Nacional de Historia and published in installments in the BHA, 1906–1907. The section dealing with his trip to the Meta River appeared in BHA 4: 43 (January 1907): 415–30.

48. Guerra Azuola, "Apuntamientos de Viaje," 416. A league is a measure of distance equal to 3.5 miles.

49. Guerra Azuola, "Apuntamientos de Viaje," 417.

50. Guerra Azuola, "Apuntamientos de Viaje," 419.

51. Guerra Azuola, "Apuntamientos de Viaje," 421.

52. Guerra Azuola, "Apuntamientos de Viaje," 420–21.

53. Codazzi, *Geografía física i política*, 3: 396.

54. Guerra Azuola, "Apuntamientos de Viaje," 421.

55. Marco Palacios, *Coffee in Colombia (1850–1970): An Economic, Social and Political History* (Cambridge, U. K.: Cambridge University Press, 1980), 29.

56. Delpar, *Red against Blue*, 13.

57. Miguel Triana, *Al Meta* (Bogotá: Casa Editorial de "El Liberal," 1913), 123.

58. *Eco de Oriente* (Villavicencio), October 15, 1918; "Los colonizadores del Llano," in *Revista Pan* (Bogotá: Imprenta Popular, 1937), 15: 149.

59. Joaquín Ospina, *Diccionario biográfico y bibliográfico de Colombia*, 3 vols. (Bogotá: Editorial Aquila, 1939), 3: 421–22; Flórez, *Conozcamos*, 2: 73–75; Luis de Greiff, *Semblanzas y comentarios* (Bogotá: ABC, 1942), 107–12.

60. Emiliano Restrepo, *Una excursión al territorio de San Martín* (Bogotá: Editorial Kelly, 1957), 9.

61. Catherine LeGrand, *Frontier Expansion*, xiv.

2

Villavicencio during the Federation Era, 1863–1888

Liberal determination to break Conservative resistance to their policies produced the previously mentioned civil war of 1859 that, after dragging on for three years, brought Tomás C. Mosquera to power. Mosquera immediately enacted a set of extreme measures that dealt a body blow to the Conservatives. In particular, he struck at the temporal power of the church, decreeing the disamortization of its property and the extinction of religious communities.[1] Remaining in effect until 1885, the Rionegro Constitution of 1863 incorporated these and other libertarian, anticlerical, and federalist reforms.

The Constitution of 1863 represented the epitome of Radical Liberal ideas, but even more important from the standpoint of Villavicencio, it transformed New Granada into the United States of Colombia. Modeled after the U.S. Constitution, it elevated the powers of the former nine departments and created the legal basis for a system of special rule for the lightly settled, peripheral regions of the country. Article 78 declared that such territories that were "thinly populated or inhabited by tribes of Indians . . . may be ceded to the general government for the purpose of colonization or making material improvements." It added that as soon as a territory had a civilized population of three thousand inhabitants, it could send a *comisario* (commissioner) to the chamber of representatives who would have a voice and a vote in discussions about laws concerning the territory and a voice but would have no vote in discussions about laws of general interest. When the population reached twenty thousand, it could elect a *diputado* (deputy) in place of a commissioner with a voice and vote in all discussions. On achieving two hundred thousand inhabitants, the territory would be eligible for statehood.[2]

Thanks to Article 78, the Federation Era (1863–1886) witnessed the emergence of the first truly national system of territories that reflected the Radical Liberals' admiration of the territorial division of the United States and became a predecessor for the *intendencias* and comisarías that were adopted at the end of the nineteenth century. With their resources sorely overtaxed, five of the nine states—Bolívar, Boyacá, Cundinamarca, Magdalena, and Santander—quickly recognized the advantages of having the federal government take control of unproductive wilderness regions.[3] Between 1866 and 1872 they turned over six territories to federal rule. The first two were San Andrés and Providencia Islands, ceded by Bolívar on September 28, 1866, and the Llanos of San Martín, ceded by Cundinamarca on September 16, 1867, both of which were formally accepted by the national government on June 4, 1868.[4] The aim of this chapter is to assess the impact of this territorial initiative on the development of Villavicencio between 1863 and 1888.

By Law 39 of June 4, 1868, by which the federal government accepted jurisdiction over San Andrés-Providencia and San Martín, Congress outlined the new system of territorial rule. In each territory, the president appointed a prefect for two years, and this person was the principal administrative officer, empowered to enforce laws, settle disputes, create towns, civilize Indians, and defend Colombian sovereignty from foreign encroachment. The prefects were to name *corregidores* to head divisions formerly known as distritos parroquiales, but now called *corregimientos*. *Corporaciones* (municipal councils) were to handle town government. Working closely with the corregidores, they could impose direct or indirect taxes to raise money for local needs. The national government pledged to pay the salaries of the prefects, corregidores, priests, missionaries, and schoolteachers. It promised to build a primary school in each corregimiento, to raise a census of the territory, and to maintain mail service and police protection. The law authorized the president to grant up to ten hectares of baldíos to any colono who would settle in the territory, and it exempted Indians who accepted civilized life from military conscription.[5] President Santos Gutiérrez's Decree of July 6, 1868, executing Law 39, described specifically the duties of the prefects, corregidores, and municipal corporations and set forth the process for adjudicating baldíos, conducting a census, providing police, and building district jails.[6] The responsibility for overseeing the territories fell to the secretary of the interior and foreign relations (a cabinet post reorganized in 1880 as the secretary of government), who reported to Congress on their progress in his annual *memoria* (report).

On August 9, 1869, Santos Gutiérrez signed a decree naming Villavicencio as the capital of the Territory of San Martín.[7] At that time the territory was divided into nine corregimientos: Boquerón, Cabuyaro, Cumaral, Jiramena, Medina, San Juan de Arama, San Martín, Santo Tomás de Upía, and

Villavicencio. It had a population of 2,090 men and 1,966 women for a total of 4,056, almost all of whom had emigrated from towns in the Andean cordillera. Medina was the largest town with 1,796 people, followed by San Martín with 717 and Villavicencio with 625.[8] The prefect, notary, and principal administrator of the *hacienda* (public finances) lived in Villavicencio where a *juez superior* (high judge), whose jurisdiction embraced all the territory, also resided. Each town elected a municipal government in December, and the territory sent a comisario as an observer to the Chamber of Representatives in Bogotá.[9]

During the administrations of Santos Gutíerrez (1868–1969), Eustorgio Salgar (1870–1872), Manuel Murillo Toro (1872–1874), and Santiago Pérez (1874–1876), in comparison to previous governments, a substantial amount of official energy and money was invested in the territorial system. These were years of relative peace and economic growth, and the Radical Liberals imbued their initiative with unbounded optimism. While all six territories received renewed attention, it was the Llanos of San Martín and Casanare that capture the popular imagination. Fully 40 percent of the COL$455,379.50 appropriated for the territories between 1868 and 1881 was invested in the eastern frontier.[10] Camacho Roldán, secretary of *hacienda y fomento* (finance and development) between 1868 and 1872, had been

Illustration 2.1.   Villavicencio and the Llanos
Source: *Geografía pintoresca de Colombia* (Bogotá: Litografía Arco, 1968), 115–22.

Illustration 2.2.   Arrival in Villavicencio
Source: *Geografía pintoresca de Colombia* (Bogotá: Litografía Arco, 1968), 115–22.

born in Nunchía, Casanare and was a tireless proponent of the region he regarded as Colombia's counterpart to the Great Plains of the United States.
Several Radical Liberals, including Santos Gutiérrez, bought land near Villavicencio, and a steady stream of travelers published accounts of their adven-
tures in the Territory of San Martín.[11] Congress passed many laws intended
to promote the development of the Llanos by building roads, encouraging
foreign immigration and domestic colonization, civilizing the Indians, making salt more readily available for human and animal consumption, and improving public administration. A brief review of these efforts will offer insight into the growing importance of Villavicencio during this era.

THE BOGOTÁ-VILLAVICENCIO ROAD

The Radical Liberals were convinced that road construction was a fundamental step in the modernization of the republic. Of the roads leading to the
territories, none was more important than the so-called Camino del Meta
that, starting from Bogotá, would pass through Villavicencio and on to Ma-
cuto, a port on the Meta River on which, it was envisioned, steamships
would soon be sailing. In December 1868, Santos Gutiérrez personally inspected the route between Bogotá and Villavicencio, becoming the first

Colombian president to visit the town and the Territory of San Martín. Camacho Roldán, his secretary of hacienda y fomento, indicated the significance of the route when he wrote in 1869:

> The Llanos Orientales have a future for us like the territory west of the Ohio has had for the U.S.A., the pampas for Argentina, and the northern tropical region for Australia. The Territory of San Martín lying twenty leagues from the capital of Colombia is the door, and the road to the Meta is the key to that vast region, our duty is to open them.[12]

Construction of the road got underway in 1869. Engineers divided the envisioned 193-kilometer route into three sections, Bogotá to Quetame (50 kilometers), Quetame to Villavicencio (53 kilometers), and Villavicencio to a port on the Meta (90 kilometers), and estimated that the entire project would cost one hundred eighty thousand Colombian pesos. In July, the government appropriated ten thousand Colombian pesos to begin work, signed a contract with Nicolás García to widen the Quetame-Villavicencio section, and ordered an iron bridge to be manufactured at a New York City factory to replace the cable and basket spanning the Río Negro at Quetame. A year later, Camacho Roldán made a careful inspection of the entire route. Dissatisfied with García's progress, he signed a new contract with Juan Nepomuceno González Vásquez in December 1870, and Congress increased the subsidy to twenty thousand Colombian pesos in 1870 and 1871.[13]

González Vásquez stayed on the job until 1876, struggling against daunting obstacles. The road that skirted around jagged mountain peaks offered little shelter for the workers at night or sources of food. Torrential rains complicated all efforts, and it was difficult to find peons willing to do such dangerous labor for a daily wage of thirty centavos, half of which had to be spent on food.[14] Their flimsy spades, pickaxes, and drills shattered against the hard rock surface, so that a blacksmith had to be available at all times to make repairs. The biggest setback was the arrival of the bridge to span the Río Negro at Quetame. Built in New York City at a cost of three thousand Colombian pesos, pieces of the bridge were boxed into twenty-two cartons, shipped by sea to Barranqulla, and then sent up the Magdalena River to Honda. Mules carried the cartons to Bogotá and on to Quetame, but when workers assembled the bridge, they discovered that it was too short to cross the chasm. Ever resourceful, González Vásquez redesigned the wooden base for an additional cost of six thousand Colombian pesos and installed the jerry-rigged structure by the end of 1871.[15] Nicolas Pardo, a Bogotá lawyer who traveled to Villavicencio in November 1874, had high praise for the work of the "intelligent and patriotic engineer González Vásquez," but he reported that at every step on the road between Bogotá and Quetame, "one finds a quagmire, a gorge, a precipice or a headlong slope," and that the section beyond Quetame between Servitá and Villavicencio was "nearly impassable."[16]

The outbreak of civil war in 1876 caused the government to default on its contract with González Vásquez. The engineer continued construction at his own expense until December 1877, when after several months without reimbursement, he gave up in disgust and went to Cúcuta to work on the San Buenaventura railroad. In 1880 the government reassessed the situation and determined that González had completed 45 kilometers at a cost of nearly COL$70,000. It settled his claims for COL$2,499.55, a sum that included interest on the funds that had been withheld. Secretary of Development Gregorio Obregón reported that an additional COL$20,000 was needed to repair war-related damage to the Quetame-Villavicencio section. He estimated that 148 kilometers remained to be built and that each new kilometer would cost COL$2,500. Thus, the total amount needed to build the road had swollen to COL$460,000 or nearly two-and-a-half times the 1869 estimate.[17]

During the next five years the highway saw little progress. The attempt to extend the road from Villavicencio to a port on the Guatiquía River, a Meta tributary, came to naught, and in 1883, the iron bridge installed at so much expense in Quetame collapsed into the Río Negro after its wooden base had rotted away. Travelers were again reduced to crossing the river via a basket suspended from a cable or fording it with their cattle at great risk to life and limb.[18] After nearly fifteen years of sporadic construction, the condition of the Bogotá-Villavicencio highway fell far short of Radical Liberal expectations, but judging from the accounts of travelers, communication between the two cities had been improved. Ernst Röthlisberger, who made the trip in December 1883, found the road between Bogotá and Quetame quite hazardous, but pronounced the section between Quetame and Villavicencio "exceptionally" well designed by the government engineers.[19]

IMMIGRATION

The Radical Liberal leaders of the Federation Era hoped to stimulate a wave of European immigration into the Llanos. Secretary Camacho Roldán launched a campaign to attract foreigners to Colombia and especially to the Llanos. He sent notes to Colombian consuls in major European and U.S. cities advertising the opportunities available in the Llanos, and in 1871 Congress appropriated twenty thousand Colombian pesos to promote immigration.[20] Despite these measures, with the exception of a number of Spaniards fleeing Cuba during the Ten Years War (1868–1878), few Europeans came to Colombia, for despite the incentives that Colombia was offering, they preferred to settle in the United States or Argentina, both of which provided more agreeable climates and employment with better wages.

The "foreigners" that did enter the Llanos at this time were Venezuelans, who were already acclimated to the heat and tropical diseases of the region.[21]

Contemporary accounts report that many people crossed over the border to escape the civil wars besetting Venezuela. The majority of these refugees settled in Arauca or Casanare, but some also made their way to the Llanos of San Martín, where they found a less than warm welcome. Prefect Rafael Vanegas wrote that in 1874 many Venezuelans had come up the Guaviare River to the port of Bolívar, a half-day's journey from San Martín. The newcomers included artisans, merchants, and ranchers, who had planned to settle in the *municipio* that was the wealthiest in the territory in terms of cattle and hatos. By 1875, however, many were leaving, having encountered little food and outright hostility from the Colombians. Vanegas explained that the *sanmartineros* regarded the arrival of any foreigner to their town as a true calamity, because such a person "threatens their traditions of semi-savage independence and lackadaisical ranching methods." Any challenge to their routine was a "tyranny" to which they could not conform.[22]

Racism was undoubtedly a factor in the Colombian attitude. Alfred Hettner, who visited Emiliano Restrepo's Hacienda Los Pavitos near Villavicencio in 1882, was deeply impressed by Restrepo's black Venezuelan *mayordomo*, whom he described as the "prototype of the Llanero" with his great stature, his physical energy, his scorn for book learning, his frivolous inclinations, and his love of pleasure. Deciphering the mayordomo's "patois dialect," Hettner learned that he had traveled all over the Llanos. The German observed:

> Notable, in general, is the penetration of the Venezuelans in the Llanos, Negros and Zambos for the most part, in contrast to the natives of the Colombian Llanos who are essentially Indians and *cholos*, or mixtures of Indian and white. It appears that this difference in the composition of the population originated in the different type of cultural development, since there [Venezuela] large haciendas were founded already in colonial times when slavery still existed, while here [Colombia] settlement only seriously began in the present century.[23]

COLONIZATION

The biggest influx of people into Villavicencio and the Territory of San Martín were entrepreneurs and campesinos from Cundinamarca and Tolima. To encourage this movement, the Radical Liberals adopted land policies designed to create a nation of small farmers and to encourage at the same time the expansion of export agriculture. Article 24 of Law 39 of June 4, 1868, empowered the president to concede ten hectares of baldíos to each family who settled in the territory. Santos Gutiérrez's decree of July 6, 1868, stated that the family head was to send a *memorial* to the prefect describing the land he or she wished to claim, supported by sworn testimony of three witnesses that the land in question was baldío. If the petition was in order, the prefect granted provisional ownership and informed the president, who made the final resolution, after which the land was to be surveyed at the cost of the petitioner and duly notarized.[24]

While these requirements may appear to be simple, they posed insurmountable obstacles to the peasants who, being poor and illiterate, could not pay for the preparation of the memorial, let along the costs of measuring the land. Those who managed to find the funds were so discouraged by the paperwork and bureaucratic delays that they withdrew from the proceedings.[25] To alleviate this difficulty, Congress passed two additional laws. Law 61 of June 14, 1874, affirmed that every individual who occupied uncultivated territory acquired ownership to the land he or she cultivated, whatever its extension, and Law 48 of 1882 stated that "cultivators squatting on public land with shelter and crops will be considered possessors in good faith and shall not be deprived of possession except by sentences handed down in civil court." Colonos raising annual crops were to receive the cultivated parcel and thirty additional hectares, while those who built fences could keep all the territory enclosed so long as it included no more than three times the area actually exploited.[26] Unfortunately, despite its good intentions, the law did not stop land usurpation in the Llanos.

The scales were weighted in favor of the wealthy, educated entrepreneurs who had two additional ways to acquire land in San Martín. The first was to use titles of concessions of baldíos given by the republic as military compensation. These titles were bought and sold on the open market and regularly quoted at thirty to forty centavos per hectare. The second method was to use *bonos territoriales* (territorial bonds) awarded to foreign creditors by Article 5 of the "Convenio" of November 22, 1860. In that year, bonos territoriales had been issued to equal 1,718,351 hectares. Parts of these bonos were amortized in different regions of the country, but by 1868 there were still more than a million and a half hectares in circulation that were quoted between twelve and fourteen pennies per hectare in the London, Paris, and Amsterdam markets. Restrepo, who explained the procedures for claiming lands under these acts in articles published in the Bogotá newspapers, *El Liberal* and *El Bien Público*, estimated that by observing these stipulations one could buy 2,500 hectares of land, sufficient for a large hacienda, for COL$1,125. Sold at public auction, the same parcel would cost less, but the title would not be clear.[27]

Although it was easier for the entrepreneur than for the colono to obtain land, there were still complications that tended to discourage large investors from moving out to the Llanos. Restrepo, for example, was critical of the decision embodied in the Código Fiscal of 1873, which stated that public land could not be sold for less than fifty centavos per hectare. The law's intent was to bring more money into the treasury, but its effect was to make it impossible to purchase baldíos through public auction. In addition, Law 61 of

1874 raised the price of land by requiring owners of cattle to fence in their herds to establish ownership, a costly procedure in the Llanos. Restrepo urged that both these measures be repealed, because if settlers were to be attracted to the territory, land must be made available to them as cheaply as possible.[28]

In the fertile Sabana de Apiay, a legal battle of awesome proportions faced potential new investors. The Sabana de Apiay consisted of seventy-five thousand hectares of farmland and pasture, forming a large triangle bounded by the northern branch of the Río Negro, the Guatiquía, and the Eastern Cordillera. As noted in chapter 1, in the eighteenth century the Jesuits had claimed much of this region for their Hacienda Apiay, and after their expulsion, the vast estate was resold a number of times. Jacinta Rey purchased it eventually, and after her death in 1792, her six children divided up the land. Soon, some sold their titles to others, so that by 1860 the number of people claiming to own shares in the so-called Community of Apiay had grown to three or four hundred. None of these claimants had clear title, and all were engaged in endless and protracted litigation. Apiay's fertility and its proximity to Villavicencio captured the interest of entrepreneurs who bought into the community or merely staked out their own claims. By 1868 there were seven substantial cattle ranches and two coffee haciendas—Ocoa and El Buque—on the savanna. In 1870, Restrepo warned that the claims of the *comuneros* were a stumbling block to the future development of Apiay, and he urged the national government to suppress the "community" and assign individual titles to the members with a clear delineation of each property. "These operations," he wrote, "already difficult today, will be much more difficult within a few years," for when large agricultural estates have been created, "the spirit of *tinterillaje* [chicanery], which is the ruin of incipient towns, will abound."[29]

According to records published by the Ministerio de Industrias, between 1860 and 1889 fifty land grants totaling 324,405 hectares were awarded to thirty-six individuals in the Territory of San Martín. The Compañía de Colombia received the most land, with 58,586.8 hectares, followed by Aparicio Escobar and associates, with 49,496.8, and Restrepo, with 23,607.6. On the other end of the scale, there were six grants of less than 500 hectares, but two of these went to Restrepo and one to Indalecio Castilla, who had other much larger grants. Only three individuals could be said to be small landholders: Eduardo Monroy, with 307.8 hectares in Medina; Sebastián Lemos, with 46 hectares; and Félix Arciniegas, with 64 hectares in San Martín. Fifty-four percent of the land awarded was in the municipio of San Martín, reflecting the huge grants made to the Compañia de Colombia and Aparicio Escobar for the exploitation of forest products, while only two men received land in Villavicencio—Restrepo and Eduardo Jaramillo R. It is clear that while hundreds of campesinos moved into the territory at this time, few achieved their ultimate goal of becoming property owners with legally registered titles.[30]

THE QUININE BOOM

The demand for land in the forests around Villavicencio was stimulated at least in part by an expanding international market for quinine, an alkaloid useful in treating malaria, which was extracted from the bark and roots of the cinchona tree. Forests growing along the slopes of the Andes from New Granada to Peru contained a variety of these trees, and rising prices for the bark spurred a frenzied rush to exploit this tropical resource. Bolivia and Ecuador were the leading exporters of the bark, but Colombian output was substantial and marked by three cycles: 1849–1852, 1867–1873, and 1877–1882. The forests of Tolima and Santander furnished the largest amount of the product, but shipments from the Territory of San Martín were also high, amounting to some 30 percent of the five thousand eight hundred tons exported by the 1880s.[31]

Three companies dominated the extraction of bark in the territory: the Compañía de Colombia in the south between the Guayabero and Ariari rivers; the Compañía del Sumapaz in the center between the Arirari and the Humadea; and the Compañía de San Martín between the Humadea and the Upía. In 1868 Restrepo estimated that the three companies employed 1,500 to 2,000 workers during the seven-month extraction season, and in addition, there were hundreds of individuals working on their own.[32]

When compared to its competitors, Colombian bark suffered from two liabilities. First, because a variety of types of trees whose bark produced different amounts of alkaloid were harvested indiscriminately, the quality of the Colombia product was inferior to that produced by Ecuador and Bolivia, and it could only be exported for profit when the world supply was unusually restricted.[33] A second liability was the haphazard methods employed by Colombians to harvest the bark. As described by Carlos Michelsen U. in 1871, once two or three peons had located a cinchona tree, they would cut the bark around the base of the trunk, and then, using axes, chop the tree down. When it was lying on the ground, they would proceed to remove the outer bark by stripping it with mallet blows and taking it off at once with knives to remove the valuable inner bark. This material they would leave to dry in the air or in ovens if it was raining.[34] The bark was then sent to Villavicencio and then on to Bogotá for shipment down the Magdalena. This wanton destruction of the trees was counterproductive, because the forests were quickly depleted. Once plantations begun by the British in India and Malaya and the Dutch in Java began to produce high quality bark in the 1880s on a predictable schedule, demand for the Colombian quinine plummeted. The boom collapsed, but the destructive method of harvesting forest products had set an ominous precedent for the rubber boom that would begin in the 1890s and continue until World War I.[35]

CIVILIZATION OF THE INDIANS AND
THE CATHOLIC CHURCH

A top priority in devising the territorial system was to transform the Indians, estimated at twenty-one thousand in San Martín and fifty thousand in Casanare, into Colombian citizens. While some sedentary tribes, such as the Achaguas and Piapocos, were relatively open to assimilation into white society, the resistance of the nomadic Guahibos grew steadily throughout the nineteenth century. To deal with this issue Congress passed four laws, Law 40 of June 5, 1868, on "the civilization of the Indians," Law 45 of June 4, 1870, "on the reduction of savage Indians," Law 11 of April 27, 1874, on the "development of colonization of the Territories of Casanare and San Martín," and Law 66 of July 1, 1874, "on the reduction and civilization of the Indians."[36] While all of these laws were well intentioned, they proved to be unworkable either because Congress failed to fund them or because they relied on missionaries to help settle the Indians, at a time when radical anticlericalism had virtually destroyed missionary activity in the country.

The forlorn hope that missionaries would be able to pacify the Indians was doomed by Mosquera's suppression of the religious communities in 1861 and the wave of repression that followed. Faced with the choice of renouncing their vows or leaving the country, several Dominicans, including Fray Antonio Acero, Dr. Simón López, Francisco Jiménez González, and José de Calasanz Vela chose exile in the Llanos of San Martín, while Padre Santiago Pinilla, Fray Juan Nepomuceno Bustamente, and Padre Justo Pastor Rincón, all Recoletos, fled to Casanare.[37]

The people of Villavicencio valued the services of Catholic priests, who since the departure of Santos Martínez in 1853, were rarely seen in their isolated town. For that reason, and despite their solidly Liberal loyalties, they welcomed the Dominican exiles. The local militia jefe, on the other hand, was eager to humiliate them. He approached Fray Acero and threatened to shoot him if he did not swear allegiance to the Law of Tuición of July 10, 1861, which stated that no cleric could exercise his ministry without permission from the national or state governments. When Acero refused, the jefe, drunk and angry, ordered his soldiers to set up a scaffold in the plaza. As the horrified townspeople looked on, Acero was marched to the place of execution. The soldiers raised their muskets, and the jefe gave the signal to fire, but wonder of wonders, the guns did not go off. The soldiers, so impressed by the courage of the priest, had loaded them without powder. Now

Illustration 2.3.   A Church in Villavicencio
Source: *Geografía pintoresca de Colombia* (Bogotá: Litografía Arco, 1968), 115–22.

beside himself with rage, the jefe ordered the soldiers arrested. He drew his sword to cut off Acero's head, but before he could reach his victim, the spectators fell on him, seized his weapon, and took him to the jail. Andrés Mesanza, the Dominican historian who recounted this incident in a biography of Fray Acero, did not omit its extraordinary denouement. Having escaped death, the priest immediately went to the prison to talk to the jefe. He obtained his release, converted his former persecutor, and heard his confession.[38]

On their arrival in the Llanos in November 1861, the Dominicans assumed assignments as parish priests to towns throughout the canton of San Martín , but during the next few months, most of them contracted malarial fevers and died. The survivors included Fray Buenaventura García, who managed to convince the local officials to allow him to transfer to the healthier climate of Cáqueza, and Vela who stayed on in Villavicencio. As the only cleric in the territory, Vela attended to the spiritual needs of the settlers and visited the Indian villages along the Humadea, Guatiquía, and Meta rivers. Isolated from Bogotá by the cordillera, he was not affected by Mosquera's renewed persecution of the church on his reelection to the presidency in 1867, but after Mosquera was exiled, Vela took advantage of the lull in clerical persecution to return to Bogotá to complete his education.

He received Holy Orders on September 26, 1870, and was ordained a priest in 1872.[39]

After serving the parish of Cájica, Santander, for a year, Vela went back to Villavicencio, where he became an important leader. He also served the adjoining parishes, traveling by horse, foot, and canoe to baptize children, perform marriages, and say mass until his death in 1895. Undeterred by fevers or rudimentary living conditions, he was enchanted by the Llanos and felt intuitively their enormous potential. As he explained to the minister of the treasury in 1890:

> Twenty-eight years ago by virtue of the ideas triumphant then and in obedience to the decrees on religious communities, I had to come, because I belonged to one of the extinguished orders, to the Llanos of San Martín. On becoming acquainted with this very beautiful region, passing though its pampas, navigating its rivers, getting to know some of its savage tribes and practicing out of necessity some uses and customs inherent to the wilderness, the idea came to me that it was and is today, the principal place for the republic to convert the savage Indians that would be a logical consequence of the colonization of its vast wilderness and the clear and stable demarcation of its borders.[40]

The Llanero priest vividly impressed visitors to Villavicencio. Röthlisberger, who met him in 1893, found a tall, robust man, with an expressive and kindly face, red cheeks, and a beautiful thick beard worn with the permission of his superiors. He wrote:

> Padre Vela, in his white and black habit, was a splendid and masculine figure. But almost never, because of the fierce heat of that region, did he wear the habit of the order; in civilian clothes he looked more like a stout miller. He liked very much to ride horseback and to share the life of the Llaneros. He was a Llanero in the best sense of the word. He also had a small hato; he raised cattle and sold them. He had to do this because the government did not pay his salary punctually and because the inhabitants of the Llanos do not show any special largess with their clergy.[41]

In 1887, Rufino Gutiérrez, a government inspector from Cundinamarca, observed that Vela combined his zeal for the propagation of the faith and the moral and material progress of the territory with fertile and unceasing activity, a great knowledge of the Llanos, and exquisite tact to counsel his baptized parishioners and to catechize the Indians along the Meta and Ariari rivers. "He is generous, hospitable, charitable, of great practical sense and no little wisdom."[42]

Reminiscent of the colonial Jesuits, Vela wrote detailed descriptions of the land and people. Archbishop Vicente Arbeláez ordered his lengthy report dated March 31, 1884, on the Meta missions published in the *Anales Religiosos*, the official periodical of the diocese.[43] In 1889, under contract

Photo 2.1. José de Calasanz Vela, 1840–1895
Source: *Trocha* (Villavicencio) 174 (July 1990): 28.

with the Ministry of Finance, Vela explored the Guaviare, Orinoco, and Vichada rivers to reach San Fernando de Atabapo, capital of the Venezuelan province of Amazonas. His account of his experiences and recommendations for the development of the Llanos south of the Meta, published in 1890, was influential in the creation of the Intendencia of Meta in 1897.[44] In 1895, Vela was thrown by his horse and died instantly. He was buried in Uribe and is still remembered today as a priest who brilliantly represented the Church when its presence elsewhere in the Llanos was in deep eclipse.

VILLAVICENCIO, 1863–1890

Many of the travelers to Villavicencio between 1863 and 1890 recorded in their memoirs or reports a vivid picture of the town. Restrepo, who arrived in 1868, described a small settlement at the foot of the cordillera with six to eight hundred inhabitants. Their houses roofed with palm leaves were located along streets laid out at right angles. To the south extended the coffee haciendas of El Buque, owned by Sergio Convers, and Ocoa, owned by Narciso Reyes and Federico Silva. The Guatiquía River lay to the north. To the east lay the extensive sabanas of Apiay. From the Guatiquia to the north and east, the land was all baldío or public land.[45] Also located in this area were the two important salt mines of Cumaral and Upín. Restrepo reported that the inhabitants of Villavicencio enjoyed modest comforts and lived in the midst of abundance. Most of the families maintained estancias outside the town along the Guatiquía where they cultivated corn, plátano, yuca, sugar cane, and rice. He added, "These products form the basis of life and are obtained without great effort. Fish abound in the Guatiquía, and salt is available for almost nothing, while fat cattle from the hatos of Apiay and San Martín can be obtained at a very low price."[46]

On February 28, 1871, the first of many fires swept through Villavicencio, reducing to ashes two thirds of the houses of the town as well as the church, casa cural, and the buildings that served as the school and jail.[47] Carlos Michelsen U. and A. Saenz, who were exploring the Territory of San Martín at this time and arrived in Villavicencio shortly after the fire, remarked that the palm-thatched houses had burned so rapidly that there was no possibility of saving them.[48]

Edouard André, a special envoy from the French government, visited Villavicencio in 1875. André reported that the population had grown to some one thousand three hundred people who lived in simple houses made of earth mixed with grass and roofed with palm leaves. On the dirt floor inside rested three stones that constituted the *tulpa* or classic kitchen stove. In some of the more elaborate houses pieces of muslin replaced the *cristales* in the windows since *vidrio* (window glass) was still not used in the territory. Citing improvements in the road to Bogotá, and the steady arrival of new immigrants, André predicted a prosperous future for the town.[49]

In his review of the notarial documents for this period, Miguel García Bustamante notes that along Villavicencio's principal *calle real* (commercial street) the typical building was a house with a *tienda* (store), a living room, two bedrooms, a wall-papered dining room, as well as a pantry, kitchen, maid's room, an oven and *pesebreras* (mangers). The store would have large counters and shelves made of wood and sold items such as anise, *panela* (unrefined brown sugar), chocolate, sugar, cinnamon, nails, herbs, packsaddles, stirrups, bits, cinches, knives, axes, and other necessities. Other commercial establishments in the town included a drugstore, an *aguardiente* distillery, several inns, a billiard parlor, and small factories that produced *teja* (roof tiles), adobe, and soap. There were also individuals who loaned money. Mule owners often rented their animals to people who needed them, and especially in the summer, mule trains regularly left town, carrying merchandise to the hatos and neighboring villages.[50]

PUBLIC ADMINISTRATION

The creation of the Territory of San Martín inaugurated the first regular system of public administration in Villavicencio, the success of which was largely dependent on the abilities of the prefects who exercised powers that in the states were divided between governors and legislators. The prefect appointed to Villavicencio had some advantages over his counterparts in the other territories in that he was within three day's contact with Bogotá, could count on fairly reliable mail service, and ruled over a small population that was concentrated along a strip of territory close to the cordillera. Nevertheless, it was difficult to find a qualified individual who would accept such a position that entailed exile to a godforsaken wilderness. As a result, the men who served as prefects varied greatly in their abilities. In the eighteen years between 1869 and 1887, the secretaries of government received only eight of eighteen required annual reports from the prefects of San Martín, and the records reveal the names of just seven of these officials: Lenard Cubillas M. (1868); Marcelino Gutiérrez (1870); Nicolas Fajardo (1873); Rafael Vanegas (1874–1875); Manuel Antonio Londoño (1879–1881); Eliseo Forero (1883); and Vicente Largarcho (1884). Nevertheless, their reports, for all their defects, offer insight into local developments in Villavicencio and in the territory as a whole.

If the president experienced trouble in finding qualified prefects, the prefects had even more difficulty in finding men to serve as corregidores. Accorded to Law 39 of June 4 and the Decree of July 6, 1868, corregidores were to be key district officials. They were to work with the municipal councils, administer funds, and serve as judges of the first instance, but except in rare cases, they were to receive no salary, and in theory, those who accepted the appointment were required to separate themselves from their private businesses for a year. Prefect Londoño reported in 1879 that in San Martín, men from other places had held the post of corregidor for the last six years because "this job is hateful and anyone who accepts it does so for a short time and with repugnance.[51]

The election of a commissioner to represent the territory in Congress proved to be the most contentious political issue in Villavicencio. In 1871 party antagonisms were heated enough to force a second ballot for the commissioner, and after the election, residual bad feeling between the two sides kept the territory in turmoil for the next five years.[52] By contrast, public apathy inhibited the activities of the local government. Prefect Vanegas wrote in 1875 that the inertia of the principal citizens of the town defeated the best efforts of the officials. If he asked one of them to be the *personero* or treasurer, the person was apt to reply rudely, "I am a foreigner in this country," or "I will do nothing, absolutely nothing; you will waste time nominating me for such a post; I will resist all legal pressures, and I will not serve."[53] Four years later, Prefect Londoño could report little progress. He wrote that all the municipal councils were functioning except in Villavicencio, where it was impossible to get people to serve because they were lacking in public spirit. Only the schoolteacher had agreed to sit on the council and that was because his job required him to do so.[54]

The most constant threat to public order was a band of outlaws based in Cáqueza that stole cattle from the surrounding ranches and sold them to people in the Llanos. Collaborators in Villavicencio who purchased these animals protected the thieves, and Vanegas pointed out that anyone who lodged a complaint against them often met with an unfortunate accident. He urged that the outlaws be brought to justice before the judge in Cáqueza, because their activities struck fear in Villavicencio and the surrounding communities. The situation seems to have improved, for the existence of the threat of cattle thieves was not mentioned in the prefects' reports after 1875.[55] In 1882 Prefect Forero wrote that, with regard to public order, "There have been no disturbances. The only enemy here to our progress is the deadly, unhealthy llanos, which are a powerful obstacle to the increase of the population."[56]

Law 39 empowered territorial municipios to levy or maintain direct, indirect, or personal taxes that had existed in the district prior to 1868 so long as the taxes were of purely local character, and the revenues were used for the benefit of the locality. Sources of income in the Territory of San Martín included taxes on *degüello* (the slaughter of cattle and pigs), on the sale and export of aguardiente, and on gambling; the sales tax; and *peaje* (road tolls), fines, and direct contributions. They were collected by the personero, who was appointed by the prefect. The money was used to improve roads, subsidize salaries of national employees, and to buy office supplies and furniture for the schools. In 1874, for example, the budget for the territory was COL$2,440. Villavicencio's share was COL$890 pesos of which COL$410 pesos were spent on road improvement. In 1875, Prefect Vanegas wrote that some levies charged by the municipios, such as the tax imposed by Villavicencio on cattle exported to Cundinamarca, were technically illegal because they had not existed before 1868. But all of his predecessors had tolerated this abuse because the vecinos did not object to the tax, and the revenue it generated was needed to finance the local government. Such taxes, he argued, were justified because they were practical, did not fall on agricultural or forest products, and penalized only such pernicious vices as gambling and drinking.[57]

In 1879 tax revenues had increased to COL$5,986.35 of which COL$2,107.50 were raised by Villavicencio. Three years later the total figure showed a substantial reduction to COL$3,203 with Villavicencio's share at COL$971. Prefect Londoño explained that the decline was due to the fact that he had not included the tax Villavicencio imposed on the export of cattle at

COL$0.20 a head, because that money was now being invested in a fund to improve roads and was controlled by the Junta de Caminos.[58]

By the 1880s, the Municipal Council of Villavicencio regularly collected taxes on liquor, gambling, and degüello, as well as requiring men between the ages of eighteen and sixty, who resided in the town, to contribute *servicio personal subsidiario* (personal labor). The council levied a charge on cattle that passed through San Martín from Casanare on their way to Bogotá and taxed residents for the construction of a public aqueduct to bring water to the main plaza.[59]

Roads

Building roads was a perennial concern of the prefects. Having the highest priority were roads connecting Villavicencio with San Martín; Villavicencio with a port on the Meta River; and Villavicencio with Medina. Although congress repeatedly voted subsidies for all three roads, the money was never forthcoming, forcing the prefects to rely on local tax revenues and the contributions of the wealthier vecinos, such as Restrepo. Although a few kilometers were constructed, progress was insignificant. The sole exception to this gloomy picture was a trail connecting the municipio of Uribe with Tolima, which was completed in 1870, because of the efforts of Nazario Lorenzana, Francisco A. Uribe, and Bernardo Herrera, founders of the Compañía de Colombia, who had acquired considerable land on the eastern slopes of the cordillera for breeding mules and cattle and for exploiting cinchona forests. The Compañía de Colombia planted improved pasture and food crops at intervals of twenty to twenty-five kilometers to serve as overnight rest stops, and thanks to this road, the trip from Tolima to Uribe took three or four days. Although the road continued in service until the early twentieth century, it remained a secondary route to the territory, perhaps because of its remoteness from Bogotá.[60]

Salt

Reinvigorating exploitation of the salt mines of Upín and Cumaral was another priority of the prefects, because ranchers depended on the mines to get salt for their cattle. During this period the central government still retained the colonial monopoly on the production and sale of salt. The government auctioned off the right to operate a mine to private investors, who agreed to produce a certain amount of salt each year to be sold at a fixed price in an *almacén* (official store). Although inhabitants of the territories were exempt from other national taxes, they still had to pay the salt tax.

In the past, the potentially rich deposits at the Upín Salina had been exploited in the most primitive fashion. The contractor, selected by the national government, hired ten or twelve peons, who came to the mine when the rains ended in November and cleared off the layer of earth that had fallen on top of the salt. They used gunpowder charges to blow up chunks of salt and dirt from the bank, hacking the giant fragments into *vijua* (smaller pieces), with pick axes. The peons carried the vijua over a rickety wooden bridge that spanned the Upín River and stacked it in a miserable hut, grandly called the almacén. The mine closed when the rains returned in March. Any unsold salt was left to disintegrate in the humidity. Worked in this manner for four months, Upín produced an average of six thousand arrobas (units of weight equivalent to about twenty-five pounds) of vijua a year.[61]

In October 1868, the first prefect of San Martín, Leonard Cubillos M. inspected the *salina* (salt mine) and described its ruinous state. The contractor's agent could not produce his account book. The inadequate buildings were small and badly constructed. Earth completely covered the mine. The road between Upín and Villavicencio was a hazardous footpath, and the official *resguardo* (guard unit) hired to prevent contraband consisted of two men, neither of whom lived at the mine and were completely ignorant about how to stop theft. Cubillos recommended that the government close the salina, or better yet, reorganize it so that it could produce compacted salt that was much preferred over vijua.[62]

During the next twenty years, presidents signed extraction contracts with a number of individuals. While some were more honest than others, the basic conditions of the salina outlined by Cubillos remained the same. The poor quality salt that it yielded was suitable only for cattle. Demand always exceeded supply, and the price was often as high as four Colombian pesos an arroba. In 1886, Rufino Gutiérrez accused the government of artificially maintaining a high price on Upín salt so that it could not compete with the salt from the Cundinamarcan mine at Zipaquirá.[63]

Education

In Law 39, Congress pledged to build a school in each territorial corregimiento and to pay salaries for the teachers. The school reform initiated by the Organic Decree of Public Primary Instruction of November 1, 1870, reinforced the national effort to proliferate primary schools throughout the country. In 1873 Prefect Fajardo reported that there were five schools for boys and three for girls in the territory (one of each in Villavicencio) with a combined enrollment of 430 pupils. He added that all the schools were supplied with necessary equipment and furniture, but diseases that attacked the population and the reluctance of parents to send their children to school severely reduced attendance.[64] Unfortunately, the condition of the schools seems to have declined over the next ten years. The prefects continually complained about the lack of school supplies—books, pens, paper, pencils, and chalk—and the difficulty of finding qualified teachers because of the bad climate and low salaries. By 1882 Prefect Forero reported that public instruction "was in a state of prostration and decadence." Only six schools were in operation. The teacher at the school in Cabuyaro had served for six months without receiving his salary. Still worse, in San Martín, end-of-term exams could not be held, because the teacher had committed suicide.[65]

SUMMARY

Between 1868 and 1886 the population of the entire municipio of Villavicencio had increased from 625 to 3,315 inhabitants, with 650 inhabitants living in the *cabecera* (capital).[66] Its elevation as territorial capital had made it the principal town in the Llanos of Meta, outpacing its rivals in San Martín and Medina. In addition to its role as a place where cattle were brought to be fattened before making the trip up the road to Bogotá, Villavicencio had become the home base for the wealthiest entrepreneurs in the region, who either were producing rice and sugar cane as well as cattle on their large estates or were exploiting the forests for valuable cinchona bark to be used in the production of quinine.

Despite these advantages, the town was not attractive. Rufino Gutiérrez, who visited the region in 1886, reported that the municipio contained the districts of Cumaral, Apiay, Campoalegre, and Rionegro y Ocoa, while the urban area, "dominated by the cerros del Alto and La Estanzuela, occupied the space between the caños Pararado and Gramalote." The town had one hundred thirty houses, eleven streets, and a plaza surrounded by fruit trees. "It lacks public buildings almost completely. There are two dilapidated *ranchos* [huts] that are called the *consistorial* [government house] and the school. Another rancho, now abandoned, belongs to the Nation, and there is a larger one, much neglected, that becomes, at times, the parish church. There is no *sacristía* [sacristy], but they are building it, and it contains nothing that merits attention." [67]

On September 19, 1887, following the recommendation of Gutiérrez, the Municipal Council issued an *acuerdo* (accord) to define definitively the urban limits of the municipio.[68] The new acuerdo drew up the following boundaries: the wooden bridge over the caño Parrado that served as the entrance of the national road to Villavicencio from Bogotá, the property of Ricardo Rojas known as El Triumfo, water under the caño, the El Jicalido pasture of José Liborio Rubio, the road that went to Cumaral, the El Caney pasture owned by Alcides Cubides, the roads that led to the cemetery, the headwaters of the caño Gramalote, the El Porvenir pasture owned by Celestino Suárez, the land between the two roads that went to San Martín, the El Barzal pasture of the Hacienda El Buque owned by Sergio Convers, lands owned by Baronio and Eudosia Arciniegas, the gate to the pasture of Leonardo Cubillos, the pasture of Juan Herrera, the pasture called Moreno owned by Ricardo Murcia, the property of the heirs of Dionisio Mora, the road that led to El Alto, and the La Cabaña pasture owned by Obdulio Pardo until it reached the national road and the bridge over the caño Parrado. This document, notarized in Villavicencio on September 22, 1887, served as the basis of the limits of the urban area until 1937.[69]

The End of the Radical Regime

By the early 1880s, the Radical Liberals who had ruled Colombia under the Constitution of 1863 were losing their hegemony. Between 1868 and 1874 they had launched many ambitious projects including the territorial initiative, but a disruptive election of 1875 weakened their consensus, and in April 1877 they crushed a revolution begun by Conservatives in 1876 but only at great cost. With the election of Rafael Núñez in 1880, the national government began to dismantle the work of the Radical Liberals, reestablishing relations with the Vatican and allowing the federal government to assume a more dominant role over the states. Secretaries of government began to point out that the special territorial administration had not produced the progress that had been hoped for. Beginning in 1881, the national government started a process of returning jurisdiction of the territories to the states. Five years later, the adoption of the Constitution of 1886 reduced the states to departments and reincorporated all of the national territories into the departments to which they had formerly belonged. As a result, in September of that year the territory of San Martín once again became a district ruled by Cundinamarca. The Regeneration Era had begun.

NOTES

1. Charles W. Bergquist, *Coffee and Conflict in Colombia, 1886–1910* (Durham, N. C.: Duke University Press, 1978), 7.

2. William M. Gibson, *The Constitutions of Colombia* (Durham, N. C.: Duke University Press, 1948), 292–93.

3. The remaining four states were Antioquia, Cauca, Tolima, and Panama.

4. *Diario Oficial* (Hereafter cited as DO), 4: 1,254, June 15, 1868. The other territories were Casanare (ceded by Boyacá, September 5, 1868, and accepted March 29, 1869); Bolívar (not the state but the southwest portion of Santander, which included all of Carare and part of Opón) ceded by Santander September 30, 1870, and accepted November 18, 1870; La Nevada y Motilones ceded by Magdalena March 24,

1871, and accepted August 17, 1871; and Goajira ceded by Magdalena September 25, 1871, and accepted January 24, 1872.

    5. *Codificación nacional de todas las leyes de Colombia desde el año de 1821.* 34 vols. (Bogotá: Imprenta Nacional, 1924–1955) (hereafter cited as *Cod. Nac.*) 23: 375–81.

    6. *Cod. Nac.* 23: 414–25.

    7. DO, 5: 1,657 (August 9, 1869): 945.

    8. Anibal Galindo, *Anuario estadístico de Colombia, 1876* (Bogotá: Imprenta de Medardo Rivas, 1878).

    9. Galindo, *Anuario estadístico de Colombia, 1876,* 112.

    10. *Memoria del Ministerio del Gobierno* (hereafter cited as MMG), 1881, 78.

    11. Among them were Carlos V. Michelsen, Nicolas Pardo, Antonio Muñoz, Ernst Röthlisberger, Edouard André, Alfred Hettner, and Emiliano Restrepo.

    12. *Memoria del Ministerio de Hacienda y Fomento* (hereafter cited as MMHF), 1869–1870, 53.

    13. DO, March 14, 1871.

    14. DO, January 13, 1870; March 6, 1971.

    15. A North American engineer named Hurbult, the son of the U.S. minister to Bogotá in 1869, drew up the original specifications for the bridge. See Albelardo Ramos, "Puente de Fierro sobre el Río Negro," *Anales de Ingeniería* (Bogotá) 1: 9 (April 1, 1888), 258.

    16. Nicolás Pardo, *Correría de Bogotá al Territorio de San Martín* (Bogotá: Imprenta de Gaitan, 1875), 4–12.

    17. *Memoria del Ministerio de Fomento* (hereafter cited as MMF), 1881, 37–38.

    18. Miguel Triana, *Al Meta* (Bogotá: Casa Editorial de "El Liberal," 1913), 22.

    19. Ernst Röthlisberger, *El Dorado* (Bogotá: Banco de la República, Archivo de la Economía Nacional, 1963), 228–29.

    20. Salvador Camacho Roldan, *Escritos varios,* 3 vols. (Bogotá: Editorial Incunables, 1983), 2: 259–69; *Cod. Nac.* 25: 450–54.

    21. In 1882, Felipe Pérez wrote, "We must not expect that people from the Andes will come to the Llanos knowing that they will die of fevers as soon as they arrive. . . . The immigrants will have to be Venezuelans, savages, or Africans who will dominate the plains." *Geografia general, física y política de los Estados Unidos de Colombia* (Bogotá: Imprenta de Echeverría Hermanos, 1883), 304.

    22. *Informe,* Prefect of San Martín, 1875, in MMG, 1876, 15.

    23. Alfred Hettner, *Viajes por los andes colombianos (1882–1884),* trans. Heinrich Henk (Bogotá: Banco de la República Archivo de la Economía Nacional, 1976), 279.

    24. *Cod. Nac.* 23: 414–25.

    25. Pérez, *Geografía general,* 332–33.

    26. *Cod. Nac.* 27:119–22; LeGrand, *Frontier Expansion,* 213, footnote 38.

    27. Restrepo, *Una excursión,* 111.

    28. Restrepo, *Una excursion,* 179–82.

    29. Restrepo, *Una excursion,* 41; Gutiérrez, *Monografías,* 1:62. *Eco de Oriente* (Villavicencio), October 15, 1918. LeGrand notes that the dispute over the Apiay community was not unique, because hacendados wishing to expand their domain often resorted to *juicios de partición* (partition suits). Juicios de partición were iniciated by a number of comuneros who owned a tract of land in common (an *indiviso*) as the consequence of a land grant inheritance or the purchase of shares. The object

of the suit was to divide the property legally and to mark the individual portions of each part-owner, *Frontier Expansion*, 54.

30. "List of Public Land Grants, 1828–1931," in *Memoria del Ministro de Industrias al Congreso Nacional en las sesiones ordinaries de 1931*, vol. 5, 326–27.

31. Omar Baquero, *Departamento del Meta: Historia de su integración a la nación, 1536–1936"* (thesis, Universidad Nacional of Bogotá: 1986), 49.

32. Restrepo, *Una excursión*, 325–26.

33. Frank Safford, *The Ideal of the Practical: Colombia's Struggle to Form a Technical Elite* (Austin: University of Texas Press, 1976), 188.

34. Carlos Michelsen U., *Suplemento. Estudio sobre las quinas esplotadas en el Territorio de San Martín*, July 19, 1871.

35. José Antonio Ocampo, *Colombia y la economía mundial, 1830–1910* (Bogotá: Siglo Veintiuno, 1984), 282–85.

36. *Cod. Nac.* 23: 381–82; 25: 61–62; 27: 36–40; 134–38.

37. Gutiérrez, *Monografías*, 1:71; Ganuza, Monografía de las misiones vivas, 2: 323.

38. Mesanza narrates this incident that originally appeared in the obituary of Fr. Antonio Acero published in the Bogotá journal, *La Unidad Católica*. See Andrés Mesanza, *Apuntes y documentos sobre la orden dominicana de Colombia (de 1680 a 1930): apuntes o narración*, (Caracas: Editorial Sur America, 1936), 245–46.

39. José de Calasanz Vela, "Desde Villavicencio hasta San Fernando de Atabapo" in *América Española (Cartagena)*, (1935) 2: 225.

40. Vela, "Desde Villavicencio," 227.

41. Röthlisberger, *El Dorado*, 250.

42. Gutiérrez, *Monografías*, 1:61.

43. Vela, "Visita de las poblaciones del Meta," *Anales Religiosos* (Bogotá) 1 (1884), 351–53.

44. Vela, *Desde Villavicencio*.

45. Restrepo, *Una excursión*, 36.

46. Restrepo, *Una excursion*, 39.

47. DO VII #2180 (March 6, 1871), 214.

48. Michelsen U., and A. Saenz, *Informe de los exploradores*, 41.

49. Edouard André quoted in Paredes Cruz, *Departamento del Meta*, 144. André, a special envoy of the French government, visited Villavicencio in 1875 and published an account of his travels in *Tour de Monde* in 1878.

50. García Bustamante, *Un pueblo de frontera*, 109–10.

51. *Informe*, Prefect of San Martín, 1979, in MMG, 1879, 78.

52. *Informe*, Prefect of San Martín, 1873, in MMG, 1874, 3.

53. *Informe*, Prefect of San Martín, 1875, in MMG, 1875, 4.

54. *Informe*, Prefect of San Martín, 1879, in MMG, 1879, 75.

55. *Informe*, Prefect of San Martín, 1875, in MMG, 1875, 3.

56. *Informe*, Prefect of San Martín, 1882, in MMG, 1882, 100.

57. *Informe*, Prefect of San Martín, 1875, in MMG, 1876, 7-8.

58. *Informe*, Prefect of San Martín, 1881, in MMG, 1881, 4.

59. García Bustamante, *Un pueblo de frontera*, 149.

60. Rausch, *The Llanos Frontier*, 95.

61. Röthlisberger, *El dorado*, 237; Hettner, *Viajes*, 285.

62. DO, December 21, 1868.
63. Gutiérrez, *Monografías*, 1:64.
64. *Informe*, Prefect of San Martín, 1873 in MMG, 1873, 6.
65. *Informe*, Prefect of San Martín, 1882 in MMG, 1882, 100.
66. Gutiérrez, *Monografías*,1:58.
67. Gutiérrez, *Monografías*, 1: 59.
68. An earlier attempt in 1866 had been declared invalid by authorities in Bogotá because it included private lands. See García Bustamante, *Un pueblo de frontera*, 150.
69. García Bustamante, *Un pueblo de frontera*, 151.

3

Villavicencio during the Era of Regeneration, 1886–1899

The victory of Rafael Núñez, the Independents, and their Conservative allies in 1886 signaled the rejection of the Radical Liberal doctrines that had dominated Colombia since 1849 and the triumph of a clear set of principles known as Regeneration. Centralism, strengthened institutional authority, and close church-state cooperation—key elements of the program—were enshrined in the Constitution of 1886, which restored the authority of the central government by reducing the states to departments ruled by governors nominated by the president. The acts of *alcaldes* and municipal councils were subject to review by the governors, a measure that extended the centralization of authority to the local level. Under the new charter, the president and senators were elected indirectly for six-year terms and representatives were elected for four-year terms. Qualifications for voting included literacy or property ownership, and restrictions were placed on civil rights. The central government alone had the right to import, manufacture, and possess arms; the death penalty was restored for serious crimes, and censorship imposed on the press held it responsible for injury to personal honor and attacks on the public peace. Finally, Roman Catholicism was declared the religion of the nation, and a concordat signed in 1887 with Pope Leo XIII granted further concessions and guarantees to the church. This document, amended several times in the twentieth century, remained the fundamental charter of the republic until 1991 when it was replaced with a new constitution.[1]

The Constitution of 1886 abolished the territories that had been created by the Constitution of 1863. As a result, executive decrees of September 1886 returned Casanare to Boyacá and San Martín to Cundinamarca.[2] The new arrangement lasted only four years, because neither Cundinamarca nor Boyacá had budgets large enough to sustain these vast, largely undeveloped

47

areas. Bad weather, horrendous roads, and difficult topography prevented highland authorities from visiting the Llanero villages, holding elections scheduled there, or even providing them with adequate judicial services. To make matters worse, on January 28, 1890, a disastrous fire destroyed Villavicencio, the most populous town east of the Andes. By June 1892 the assemblies of Cundinamarca and Boyacá had each petitioned congress for an annual subsidy of one hundred thousand Colombian pesos for the "protection, development, and administration" of their Llanos regions, and on July 28 the Boyacense legislators passed a resolution asking that the national government take over the administration of Casanare completely.[3] Two weeks later, on August 9, the municipal council of Villavicencio, citing the region's decline under Cundinamarcan rule, petitioned congress to restore the region as a national territory.[4]

On September 17, 1892, the legislators responded by reestablishing the territories of San Martín and Casanare. Decree 392 of January 17, 1893, designated both regions as "National Intendancies" and set forth a series of dispositions regarding their organization. This mandate was further implemented by Decree 392 of July 26, 1897, "On the Administration of the National Intendancies." For Villavicencio, Conservative hegemony during the Regeneration Era brought a slow reconstruction of the town, new administrations marked by heightened political wrangling, renewal of missionary activity by Salesians, improved transportation along the Meta River, and modest economic growth.

THE 1890 FIRE

In Villavicencio at 12:30 AM on January 28, 1890, fire broke out in a house owned by Francisco Rojas. Because nearly all the buildings had palm-leaf roofs, the fire spread quickly, reducing the town to a "pile of ashes."[5] Included among the losses were stores owned by José Bonnet, Emiliano Restrepo, and Juan Fanegra. Although Villavicencio in the past had experienced other fires, the magnitude of this disaster prompted the Cundinamarcan secretary of government, Jaime Córdoba, to send two thousand Colombian pesos in departmental funds to aid in reconstruction of a town he deemed to be "the most important for the colonization of that vast territory."[6] A committee composed of Fr. José de C. Vela, Bruno Restrepo, and Sergio Convers was organized to supervise distribution of this money, and the task of rebuilding got underway. The municipio passed regulations restricting construction materials to adobe, cement, *teja de barro*, or zinc, and also forbid the storing of gunpowder and the setting off of fireworks in or near the town.[7]

Reconstruction did not go smoothly, however. In the first place, some vecinos wanted to take advantage of the occasion to move the town to a site known as La Grama owned by Ricardo Rojas. This flat pasture had the advantage of a beautiful view of the river, but owners of houses, which had not been destroyed because they had zinc roofs, opposed the plan, and the transfer fell through. Second, a conflict arose between the organizing committee members fueled by the determination of Padre Vela to control the outflow of aid. The problem grew worse after congress approved Law 18 of October 17, 1890, authorizing a contribution of eight thousand Colombian pesos to the municipio of Villavicencio to help in the rebuilding of the church and the casa cural. According to a memorial sent to Tobías Hernández, the Intendant of San Martín, dated December 28, 1893, and signed by members of the municipal council of Villavicencio, Vela was refusing to work with the council and insisting that he should have exclusive control over the money awarded by congress. Hernandez responded that because the money had been awarded to rebuild the church and the casa cural, neither the council nor Vela should determine its dispersal because that responsibility fell to the Archbishop of Bogotá, Bernardo Herrera Restrepo. On July 12, 1894, the archbishop concurred. Noting that Vela was no longer the cura of Villavicencio, he recommended that the money be handed over to the current *párroco* (parish priest) and the president of the *junta especial* that had been established for its disbursement.[8] The death of Vela on December 6, 1895, removed from the scene this extraordinary priest whom Carlos Cuervo Márquez described as "the center around which moves all the religious, political and social organization of the immense territory contained between the Meta and the Guaviare Rivers."[9]

Against the wishes of the local authorities, when the first Salesian missionaries arrived in January 1895, they set up their headquarters in the town of San Martín, because there still was no church in Villavicencio; eventually the rebuilding effort was begun.[10] Workmen using bricks and stones started constructing the façade. The sanctuary was made of *bahareque* (wall construction using sticks interwoven with reeds and plastered with mud) and covered with a ceiling of thatched palm leaves (later replaced with zinc) that was supported by wooden columns. An iron cross hung from the ceiling, a gift from Antonio Rojas R. Likewise, a special donation from Críspulo Burgos paid for the intricately elaborate wrought ironwork of the main door, but the windows on both sides of the building were simply large, empty holes. The creation of a more beautiful and functional church did not occur until 1909 when R. P. Juan Bautista Arnaud, a "true artist and able architect," took charge of its renovation.[11]

POLITICAL UNREST

Most of the intendants, who served in the Intendancia Nacional de San Martín during the 1890s, were capable individuals, and some, such as Elisea

Medina and Marco Antonio Torres, had a deep attachment to the region. Nevertheless, as Conservatives and representatives of Rafael Núñez, Carlos Holguín, and Miguel Antonio Caro, presidents whose governments openly repressed their political opponents, they found themselves isolated in a population with firmly established Liberal sympathies. As a result, they were constantly requesting soldiers not only to capture the outlaws that infested the region but also to control their Liberal adversaries. Decree 392 of January 17, 1893, stated that the nation should provide police to keep order in each territory, but because of lack of funding, the intendants found themselves without sufficient men and weapons to capture outlaws, settle local feuds, or put down rebellions.

The need to station soldiers in Villavicencio was a recurrent theme in the correspondence between the intendants and Bogotá. In April 1894, Intendant Jorge Novoa telegraphed the Ministerio de Gobierno: "Insist absolutely on the necessity of sending at least ten or fifteen soldiers here, since there is no police. There are many wanted criminals, and the authorities have no means to apprehend them."[12] This request was reiterated by Pioquinto Márquez C., who as acting intendant, telegraphed the ministerio in November 1894:

> Last night Joaquín Rojas was murdered. They called me at one o'clock in the morning, and although I was completely alone, I went to help. Last night there was trouble between employees of the liquor monopoly and revolver shots. I am looking for the criminals. . . . you understand that in our country and even in those more civilized, bayonets are the basis of every stable system.[13]

Liberal antagonism only exacerbated the activities of nonpolitical outlaws. On July 12, 1894, Intendant Habacuc Beltrán wrote to the ministry of government:

> In many towns of the intendancy one observes movements against the authorities and a certain kind of social unrest that if it is not remedied, it is possible that this region will become the center of a revolutionary organization or undisciplined forces which are inclined to protest against what the government does even with the best intentions. . . . I believe it is necessary to base a force (of soldiers) in this town while the police are [being] organized. . . . [14]

Apparently some soldiers were sent to Villavicencio, but their deployment there must have been brief. In a letter dated November 5, 1894, the secretary general of the intendancy implied that the soldiers had been removed and offered four reasons why their return was absolutely vital:

> In the first place, most of the inhabitants of these regions are of an opinion contrary to that of the few employees who are with me. In the second place, our opponents believe in absolute liberty and resent all monopolies. . . . In the

third place, being this [Bogotá-Villavicencio] road is a favorable way for the introduction of all kinds of arms, vigilance is necessary, and the permanent presence of a detachment would inspire fear in those who are trying to do it. In the fourth place, the municipio does not have police of any kind, and consequently the authorities are vulnerable to any type of crime and disorder.[15]

In January 1895, the war faction of the Liberal party—a closely knit coalition of regional leaders—sent out a call for revolution. Devised by Eustacio de la Torre Narváez, a wealthy Cundinamarcan coffee grower, and Juan Félix de León, a law professor and newspaper editor from Santander, the plan was to seize the presidential palace and imprison Vice President Caro in a coup seconded by *pronunciamientos* in several departments. Warned in advance, Caro arrested de La Torre before he could act, but other conspirators, undeterred, "pronounced" on January 23 in Facatativá, Cundinamarca. Soon there were rebel armies in Santander, Boyacá, Tolima, and Casanare, but the revolution, opposed from the start by many important Liberal and dissident Conservatives, was doomed. Government troops led by General Rafael Reyes defeated the insurgents at La Tribuna, Cundinamarca, on January 29, and won other battles in Tolima, Boyacá, and Panamá. On March 15, Reyes delivered the decisive blow by vanquishing General Pedro María Pinzón at Enciso, Santander. Two days later, the rebels capitulated. Caro's preventive measures, his excellent choice of military commanders, and his ability to print money to pay for the war proved to be too much for the divided Liberal efforts.[16]

In Casanare General Gabriel Vargas Santos joined the revolution, overwhelming the government garrison in Arauca and confiscating the customs revenues. Other rebels took Orocué and Támara. Within the Intendancy of San Martín, only Medina joined the insurrection, although some Liberal guerrillas fled to Uribe after their defeat in Tolima. By February 2, Intendant Hernández had assembled fifty men, who pledged to defend the government but had no weapons. A few days later, General Rufino Gutiérrez arrived to take charge as *jefe civil y militar*. On learning that Orocué had fallen, Gutiérrez dispatched the "Ospina Camacho" regiment on March 15 to retake the town, unaware that the enemy had already abandoned it. By April Gutiérrez had restored peace in Medina and throughout the territory, while in Casanare General Vargas Santos had withdrawn his troops to Venezuela.[17] By October resistance throughout the country was over, and Vice President Caro lifted the state of siege.[18]

The Liberal Revolt of 1895 caused little material damage in Villavicencio or the surrounding territory, but it did heighten political tensions. Intendant Hernández, following orders from Bogotá, removed officeholders sympathetic to the rebellion and replaced them with friends of the government. This purge was more intense in Uribe, San Martín, and especially Medina because the entire town had been compromised by the revolution.

Hernández was afraid to hold an election for the municipal council there, because the people who would win would not support the government. For that reason, Medina remained without any local officials until June, when Hernández appointed men he could trust.[19]

Liberals in Villavicencio continued to resent this continued Conservative repression. On May 11, 1896, Intendant Aristides Novoa wrote to the minister of government:

> Radicals from here, turbulent and revolutionary, keep the town and territory in constant alarm. They form political groups, circulate false notices, denigrate the government, write articles and scandalous telegrams against the intendancy employees. . . . There is much speculation and unrest about when the next pronunciamiento will take place. We only have ten rifles and 250 shells. Even when we can count on our friends, we lack arms to organize a force.[20]

The results of the election of December 5, 1897, confirmed Novoa's contention that government workers were a besieged group in the territory. In Villavicencio, there were 140 votes for the Liberal candidates for president and vice president, Miguel Samper and Foción Soto; 22 votes for Independent Rafael Reyes, who had withdrawn from the election; and only 18 votes for Manuel A. Sanclemente and José Manuel Marroquín, the government-supported Nationalist candidates who were declared the winners on February 1, 1898.

Even more revealing is Intendant Francisco Duarte's account of behavior on election day in the territory. He informed Secretary of Government Antonio Roldán that Judge Nicasio Anzola voted for the Nationalists and did all he could to get other votes for them, but the *fiscal* of the court voted with the Liberals; the administrator of the Salina of Cumaral supported the *oposicionistas* and kept his employees from voting; and the administrator of the liquor monopoly "worked with much enthusiasm and activity with the Liberals" to defeat the government. Duarte suggested that the latter should forfeit his job with the liquor monopoly because of his disloyalty. "The oposicionistas are not only political enemies but also personal enemies, insulting the nationalist employees, forming threatening and suspicious circles, so that I have had to call together the new *nationalistas* to reinforce the police in certain cases." In Duarte's view, the situation was untenable. "I beg you to send me an army contingent for otherwise it will be impossible for me to continue performing this job, and I will irrevocably submit my resignation."[21] Secretary Roldán recommended that military forces be stationed in the intendancy, because the Llaneros lacked sufficient "discipline and character" to serve as policemen; but as usual no action was taken.[22] On the eve of the War of the Thousand Days, the intendancy, like neighboring Casanare, was a whirlpool of political hatreds and popular resentment against the Conservative government in Bogotá.

MISSIONS

Regeneration governments were eager to reestablish the missions in the Llanos. Núñez began the reconciliation process with the Vatican during his first administration by negotiating with special papal envoy Monseñor Juan Bautista for the restoration of the religious orders. In 1882, the Dominicans, Recoletos, Franciscans, and other communities were reincorporated in Colombia. Congress repealed most of the anticlerical regulations enacted after the civil war of 1876–1877. In addition to declaring Roman Catholicism as the national religion, the Constitution of 1886 stated that civil authorities could enforce respect for the church, that public education was to be conducted in accord with Catholic teachings, and that the church would be considered a juridical person in civil matters.

In the Concordat of 1887, the government pledged to provide an annual subsidy to the church and compensation for losses suffered from the 1861 disamortization decree. It guaranteed its independence from civil interference and granted it substantial influence over education. In Article 25, the government assigned to the church an annual subsidy of one hundred thousand Colombian pesos in perpetuity for the support of dioceses, chapters, seminaries, missions, and other church activities. Reassured by this civil support, in 1893 Pope Leo XIII approved the creation of a *vicariato apostólico* (apostolic vicariate) for Casanare based in Tame, and in 1897 a vicariato apostólico for San Martín based in Villavicencio.[23] The actual labor of founding missions fell to three religious orders: the Salesians in San Martín, and the Recoletos and the Hermanas de la Caridad in Casanare.

The first members of the Society of St. Francis de Sales, popularly known as the Salesians, arrived in Bogotá in February 1890. Led by Padre Evasio Rabagliati, they purchased the former convent of the nuns of Carmen and opened the Colegio Salesiano de Leon XIII in September. Soon afterward, they began a home for vagrant boys and took over management of the Agua de Díos leper hospital in Tocaima, Cundinamarca. Shocked by the large number of lepers in Colombia and the lack of facilities to help them, Padre Rabagliati proposed to Vice President Caro in 1895 that the Salesians found a national leper hospital at a place where all the afflicted could be brought together. Caro approved the project, and Rabagliati began searching Santander and Boyacá for an appropriate site for the hospital. Then in January 1895, while traveling with Dr. Gabriel Castañeda in the Llanos of San Martín, he discovered what appeared to be an ideal location between the Meta and Nare rivers. It was on this trip that Rabagliati became convinced that the Salesians should develop missions in the intendancy. He was still in Villavicencio when the outbreak of the Revolution of 1895 postponed further action on either project.[24]

Early in 1896, after the conclusion of the conflict, Rabagliati accepted responsibility for Villavicencio, San Juan de Arama, Uribe, and Jiramena. On

February 3, he left for the Llanos accompanied by two priests, Leopoldo Ferraris and Ernesto Briata; an acolyte, Carlos Silva; and Antonio Pérez, brother coadjutor. Notwithstanding the truly horrible state of the road, they arrived in Villavicencio after three days to find that the church still had not been reconstructed since the 1890 fire.[25] Much to the dismay of the townspeople, the Salesians continued on to San Martín and decided to base their headquarters there until the church could be rebuilt in Villavicencio. Rabagliati then returned to Bogotá for the start of Lent, while the others settled in to begin the missions.[26]

In 1897 Pope Leo XIII declared the Intendancy of San Martín a vicariato apostólico, and the Salesians expanded to three houses: Padre Briata, with coadjutor Jeremías Fernández and two acolytes, was assigned to Uribe; Padre Leopoldo Ferrari, coadjutor Antonio Pérez, and two acolytes remained in San Martín, and Padre Tomás Tallone, brother Jesús Martínez, and acolyte Bernardo Romero lived in Villavicencio.

Letters written by the Salesians during this period suggest that they were generally well received in the intendancy. An exception was Tomás Tallone, an Italian priest whose brusque, arrogant manner put him at odds with his Villavicencio congregation. The situation came to a head on Holy Saturday, April 10, 1898, when several vecinos asked and received permission from Tallone to take a saint from the still-uncompleted church and hold a procession in its honor. The priest did not participate in the ceremony, which ended normally enough with devotions held in a private home, but when the celebrants tried to return the saint to the church, they found the door locked on Tallone's orders. Not wishing to leave the image outside, they broke the door open *sin fuerza ni escalamiento* (without force or scaling) and left it in its accustomed place. Tallone condemned this action as desecration; the vecinos maintained that they had intended no disrespect and demanded that the priest be expelled. Archbishop Restrepo Herrera endorsed Tallone's decision and also advised Intendant Elisio Silva to support him. By that time, however, Padre Rúa had ordered Tallone to return to Bogotá, and the incident was closed.[27] In his annual informe, written just after the crisis, Silva reported that the people sincerely wanted a new priest but only if he was Colombian. Father Tallone was virtuous and self-denying, but "he did not have well-developed the necessary traits to exercise his ministry in this region, where more than anything, it is indispensable to have good will and tact in dealing with the people."[28]

IMPROVING COMMUNICATION

Economic growth in and around Villavicencio depended on facilitating communication with Bogotá. After Law 140 of 1888 called for improvements on the Bogotá-Villavicencio road and its extension to the Meta River, vecinos of Gachetá and Chocontá sent separate petitions to congress, each asking that the highway be rerouted from its present course so that it might pass through their towns. Finding merit in their requests, Secretary of Development Leonardo Canal recommended that the government begin work on all three routes simultaneously, but given the limited funds that were appropriated, this initiative proved totally impractical.[29] In spite of the fact that many of its sections were impassable in the rainy season, the existing Bogotá–Villavicencio route continued to provide the principal access to the Llanos.

Building a railway between Bogotá and Villavicencio was a second alternative that sparked considerable interest. Railway fever was engulfing Colombia when Rafael Núñez took office with work proceeding on eight different lines. Although Juan de Díos Tavera had put forward a plan in 1879 to build a railroad from Bogotá to the Unete River, a large tributary of the Meta, his plan was defeated by opponents who believed the departments of Santander and Cundinamarca would profit more from rail connections with the Magdalena River.[30]

The idea refused to die, however, and in 1893, Secretary of Development J. M. Goenaga, who had succeeded Canal, signed a contract with the London firm of Punchard, McTaggard, Louther, and Company to design plans for a railroad that would connect Bogotá to a port on the Meta navigable at all times to ships of three-foot draught. In due course, a team of English engineers arrived to examine possible routes. On completing their survey, they recommended paralleling the Bogotá-Villavicencio highway by running the railroad through the Boquerón de Chipaque and along the Río Negro. This plan would require one hundred ninety kilometers of track to connect Bogotá with Puerto Banderas on the Humadea River (the present-day Metica River), a tributary of the Meta. The government appointed its own experts, Diódoro Sánchez and Manuel Ponce de León, to study this plan. When the Colombian engineers discovered several flaws—the most important being that the Humadea did not have a depth of three feet during the dry season—the project was shelved and not revived again until 1916.[31]

Perhaps the greatest communication success of this era was the establishment of steam navigation along the Meta and Orinoco Rivers linking Villavicencio with the Atlantic Ocean. Governments in Bogotá had long envisioned such a route but had been stymied by boundary disputes with Venezuela and the latter's steadfast refusal to allow Colombian ships free access to the Orinoco. After the election of Núñez in 1880, relations between the two republics took a turn for the better. Renewed negotiations produced an agreement in 1881 to refer the boundary dispute to King Alfonso XII of Spain for arbitration.

A beneficiary of this thaw in tensions was José Bonnet, a Frenchman born in 1846 who came to Colombia in 1865. Bonnet founded a commercial house in Bogotá in 1875. Soon afterward, he opened branch offices in Orocué and Villavicencio and acquired coffee plantations in the Territory of San Martín. In 1881, Venezuelan president Antonio Guzmán Blanco agreed to let Bonnet introduce goods into Colombia, via the Orinoco and Meta, without paying duty at Ciudad Bolívar. The Frenchman began at once to ship merchandise into Orocué and Villavicencio, intending to reship the goods to Bogotá, but he was forced to stop this commerce when the Colombian Congress passed Law 61 on September 13, 1882, prohibiting the importation of foreign merchandise from territories into states that had no *aduanas* (customs houses). Bonnet protested vigorously, and eventually in August 1884, President Núñez granted him a new contract guaranteeing him the right to bring goods into the states via the territories without paying duty.[32]

In 1890 Bonnet signed a contract with the Holguín government to recommence steam navigation on the Meta and Orinoco. He pledged that his ship, *Libertador*, would make six round trips each year, traveling between Ciudad Bolívar and Orocué in the dry season and between Ciudad Bolívar and Cabuyaro in the rainy season. He also agreed to build a warehouse in Orocué and to transport, at prices equivalent to those charged on the Magdalena River, mail, missionaries, government officials, and soldiers. In exchange, the government promised Bonnet a subsidy of three thousand Colombian pesos for each round trip and to press Venezuela to grant free trade along the river permanently. Finally, it awarded him thirty thousand hectares of baldíos along the Meta on which he was to found three agricultural colonies, each consisting of at least ten families who would cultivate coffee, cacao, and other products suitable for export.[33]

Undoubtedly the most elegant ship to sail the Meta, the *Libertador* left Ciudad Bolívar on her maiden voyage on November 1, 1893. A miniature replica of the steamboats plying the Magdalena but without their cabins and other amenities, she was 24 feet wide and 124 feet long, including the rear paddle wheel. Her average speed was nine miles an hour, but she could go as fast as twelve. With a crew of nineteen, she could carry one hundred and ten cattle and up to one hundred tons of cargo.[34] On this first trip the *Libertador* carried cloth, hardware, wine, and foodstuffs on which no duty had been paid, a concession that provoked heated protests from local Venezuelan merchants. After she had anchored at the port of Barrigán on November 7, Habacuc Beltrán telegraphed the minister of justice asking him to inform Vice President Caro of the "general enthusiasm" that greeted her appearance, for "all see that this, added to the measures taken by the government, will redeem the rich eastern region."[35] On her return voyage, the *Libertador*, carrying passengers, coffee, cacao, hides, and rubber, took only five days to reach Ciudad Bolívar from Orocué.

Steam navigation quickened the economic pulse of both the territories of San Martín and Casanare with the chief beneficiary being the port of

Orocué. On his visit there in 1894, Jorge Brisson noted that the well-built houses placed along wide, clean streets were illuminated by kerosene street lamps. In addition to Bonnet, Ramón Real and Franzius Aguilar founded commercial firms exporting coffee and cattle and importing foreign goods. Thanks to the aduana, trade was brisk, and in 1894 the exchange of commercial paper totaled eight hundred thousand Colombian pesos, rivaling the volume of one million fifty thousand Colombian pesos for that year in Arauca.[36]

To a lesser degree, Villavicencio also profited from this new outlet for trade. Between 1891 and 1897, four new *sociedades comerciales* were begun, "stimulated initially, by the possibilities of navigation along the Meta, and later by the growth of the city and its influence in the territory."[37] These companies, which were not legally incorporated, included Sergio Convers y Ricardo Murcia with a capital of COL$12,250 (1891); Cesáreo Pardo y Marco A. Pardo with a capital of COL$5,590 (1893); Aristides Ortega y Santiago Guayacán with a capital of COL$120 (1893); and Leonidas Márquez y Marco A. Pardo with a capital of COL$3,500 (1897).[38] Their relative short existence, which varied from two to five years, was probably influenced by the failure of Venezuela and Colombia to ratify the 1894 Treaty of Navigation and Commerce. From the beginning merchants in Ciudad Bolívar and Colombian rivals had protested that Bonnet's government contract had given him an unfair advantage, and in 1899, the secretary of finance canceled the land grants that had been awarded him on the grounds that he had not fulfilled his obligations. In that same year, Cipriano Castro seized power in Caracas and banned free trade on the Meta and Orinoco. Bonnet was ruined, and it was not until the 1920s that there was another proposal to provide regular steamboat service on the Meta.[39]

ECONOMIC GROWTH

Although these commercial establishments contributed to the economic development of Villavicencio, the growing wealth of the city was firmly based on the expansion of agriculture, cattle ranching, and participation in the rubber boom. As early as the 1870s, entrepreneurs who had settled in the Territory of San Martín began to participate in the coffee bonanza that had replaced tobacco as Colombia's principal export. Of the eight largest haciendas in 1875, El Buque, owned by Sergio Convers, and La Virginia, owned by Diego Suárez and Vicente La Faurie, produced coffee, and Ocoa, owned by Narciso Reyes and Federico Silva, combined coffee with cacao, sugar cane, and cattle. With its 80,000 to 100,000 coffee trees, El Buque was said to outstrip any coffee *finca* in Cundinamarca, and Ocoa, with 70,000 trees, was almost as large. All three estates had machines to hull, wash, and

Illustration 3.1.   Growing Coffee in the Llanos
Source: *Geografía pintoresca de Colombia* (Bogotá: Litografía Arco, 1968), 115–22.

dry the beans, and El Buque had a hydraulic water wheel, *ventolina* (wind-mill), water tanks, and several workshops. In 1874, thanks to the output of these three haciendas, the Territory of San Martín exported 90.4 metric tons of coffee valued at COL$20,642.[40]

After a sharp price decline in 1882 to 1883, coffee produced in the Llanos could no longer compete with that grown in other areas of the country due to the high cost of transportation. Throughout the 1890s it continued to be an important crop in Medina, a piedmont town in the territory, but the for-ward-looking owners of the larger estates began to replace their coffee trees with other crops. Sergio Convers traveled to Cuba to determine the most ef-ficient methods to produce sugar, and modern machinery to process sugar cane and rice began to appear on the estates. By the end of the century, corn, rice, and honey had replaced coffee as the chief agricultural products ex-ported from San Martín territory.[41]

Despite these adjustments, until the twentieth century agriculture played a secondary role to cattle raising in the Llanos. While ranches in the north-ern territory of Casanare continued to operate using the same methods de-veloped during the colonial era, ranchers based around Villavicencio were more innovative. Restrepo, Convers, Reyes, and Nicolás Castro experimented with crossbreeding and improved pasture. They regularly gave salt to their animals and urged their neighbors to do the same, though without much success. Records from 1892 reveal that, on the average, 45 cattle from Villavicencio were sacrificed each month in Cundinamarca, for a total of 549 during that year.[42] In 1898 Benito Rondon estimated that there were around 25,000 head of cattle in the intendancy divided among one hundred hatos, "being very few those persons who owned more than four hundred animals."[43] Although the precarious road to Bogotá continued to be a liability, cattle production remained steady until the War of the Thousand Days.

Rubber, rather than coffee, was the export from the Llanos most closely associated with the Regeneration Era, for after 1890 it replaced quinine as the principal product harvested from the forests of San Martín and Casanare. As early as 1870 Hilario Ibarra was extracting high quality latex from rubber trees near Villavicencio, but his enterprise failed because the trees did not give off enough sap to make the exercise profitable. Restrepo, writing in 1875, postulated that forests lying farther to the east and south of Villavicencio might prove more lucrative because they received more rain.[44] The Compañía de Colombia, owner of some sixty thousand hectares around the town of Uribe, began producing rubber in the 1880s. In December 1886, the original founders—Francisco Antonio Uribe, Bernardo Herrera, and Nazario Lorenzana y Montoya—dissolved the company, and after the death of his father on June 4, 1887, Carlos Uribe divided the assets between two new partnerships. The Compañía Herrera y Uribe took two-thirds of the original holdings, and the Compañía Lorenzana y Montoya got the rest.[45] Both firms continued to produce rubber from their lands. In 1886, Carlos Uribe along with two other men received an additional fifteen thousand acres of national forests in the district of Uribe. The following year, the *Gaceta de Cundinamarca* announced that three grants, each of ten thousand hectares, had been awarded to three sets of partners in the municipio of Villavicencio. All grants were awarded for five years for the purpose of extracting rubber and *copaiba* (balsam). The recipients could only work five thousand hectares at a time and were required to take care of the trees to preserve their abundance and quality.[46]

According to the ministry of industry, there were fifty-eight land grants awarded to forty-five individuals totaling 149,022.6 hectares in the Intendancy of San Martín between 1887 and 1899. Over one third of this land, or 58,649 hectares, was in Medina, followed by 29,024.5 in Villavicencio, 25,948.7 in San Martín, and 20,488.3 in Uribe. Cabuyaro lagged behind with 13,711.5 hectares, and there was a single grant in Cumaral of 1,200 hectares. In contrast to the period between 1860 and 1885, no grant larger than 5,000 hectares was awarded; however, José Bonnet received ten separate grants that totaled 43,867.6 hectares in Medina, Villavicencio, and Cabuyaro, while Sergio Convers added three new grants or 7,396 hectares to his already considerable holdings. There were six awards of 5,000 hectares; seventeen between 3,000 and 4,999 hectares (of which eight went to Bonnet); and sixteen from 1,000 to 3,999 hectares (including one to Bonnet). At the other end of the scale, there were eleven grants under 499 hectares, and eight between 500 to 999 hectares.[47]

These records do not indicate the use to which the land was put. While some of the grants over one thousand hectares might have been for cattle, it is a safe assumption that the majority of the recipients intended to collect rubber, with the action centered especially in Uribe, Medina, and Villavicencio. In addition, scores of independent colonos were searching for rubber in the baldíos without attempting to apply for ownership.

The Colombian government authorized rubber extraction on the condition that the trees not be destroyed, but companies and independent collectors routinely ignored this prohibition and felled the trees rather than tapping their sap in the Brazilian fashion. In 1887, Lisandro A. Moreno complained to the secretary of finance that the Compañía Herrera y Uribe was violating the terms of its grant by cutting down trees in the *aldea* of Uribe. Local authorities were doing nothing to stop the "numerous outrages," and the inhabitants of the isolated town acted "like savages even though they belong to social classes of some consideration."[48] Moreno was especially concerned that the loss of trees would leave many of the collectors without work, but the government was powerless to halt the practice. On July 18, 1898, Intendant Eliseo Silva assured the secretary of finance that he would "immediately give the order to the authorities of my jurisdiction so that they will stop the felling of the rubber tree forests," but his orders were ignored as easily as those of the local officials in Uribe.[49]

By that time, some attempt was being made to grow rubber on plantations. Enrique Cortés and Ismael José Romero published manuals explaining cultivation techniques and describing ways to counteract the more destructive forms of rubber collection.[50] The Compañía Herrera y Uribe began a plantation, La Mariana, with fifty thousand trees along the Guayabero River, but it was destroyed by the War of the Thousand Days. In 1910, Luis Convers Codazzi and Enrique Mistral started La Mistralia with twenty-five thousand trees near Villavicencio. They hired guards to keep the trees from being cut down by colonos, but they had to abandon the effort when low-cost Malaysian rubber drove prices down.[51]

SUMMARY

For Villavicencio and the Territory of San Martín, the Regeneration Era proved a mixed blessing. Administrative centralism, fundamental to Núñez's political agenda, brought down the territorial system developed by the Liberals over a forty-year period, but after a brief period of incorporation with Cundinamarca, the territory was reconstituted as an intendancy, implying continued federal attention. Reconciliation with the Catholic Church brought a resurgence of missionary activity that was welcomed by officials and residents alike. The Salesians, who established themselves in the territory, laid the groundwork for their more substantial activities after the end of the War of the Thousand Days. José Bonnet's steamship service along the Meta and Orinoco Rivers opened up a new outlet for commerce, and the innovative practices of leading entrepreneurs brought improvements in ranching and agriculture.

Despite these positive developments, as Omar Baquero has pointed out, the territory remained a backwater. Although the road to Bogotá gave Villavicencio a favored position as the gateway to the Llanos, its lamentable condition deterred large-scale trade or economic development. With a few notable exceptions, cattle ranching remained primitive, and agriculture was primarily produced for local consumption. The exploitation of rubber in the territorial forests had some importance for Villavicencio in terms of trade, but the unregulated nature of the harvesting of trees was ultimately destructive.[52] Finally, from a political standpoint, the policy of exclusivism endorsed by Regeneration governments weakened Bogotá's ability to rule effectively over the fervently Liberal Llaneros. Nationalist employees sent to administer Villavicencio and the territory became a kind of occupation force that was largely resented by the local elites. The general undercurrent of unrest, which erupted during elections and the Liberal revolt of 1895, would rise to a new level of violence with the outbreak of the War of the Thousand Days.

NOTES

1. James Park, *Rafael Núñez and the Politics of Colombian Regionalism, 1863–1886* (Baton Rouge: Louisiana State University Press, 1985), 269; Malcolm Deas, "Colombia, Ecuador and Venezuela, c. 1880–1930," in *The Cambridge History of Latin America*, ed. Leslie Bethell, 5 vols. (Cambridge: Cambridge University Press, 1986), 5: 645.

2. Humberto Plazas Olarte, *Los territories nacionales con una introducción al estudio de su geografía y de su historia* (Bogotá: Editorial Pax, 1944), 138. The other territories were also returned to the departments that had originally ceded them.

3. *Ordenanzas expedidas por la asamblea departmental de Boyacá en sus sesiones de 1892* (Tunja, 1892), 82, 89; *Gaceta de Cundinamarca*, July 28, 1892.

4. Archivo del Congreso, Bogotá (hereafter cited as AC), Cámara, "Asuntos Despachados," vol. 10, fol. 34.

5. José de Calasanz Vela, *Dos viajes por la orinoquia colombiana, 1889–1988* (Bogotá: Fondo Cultura Cafetero, 1988), 24; *El Heraldo* (Bogotá) Series II, No. 31, February 5, 1890.

6. *Gaceta de Cundinamarca* 4: 300, February 4, 1890.

7. *Gaceta de Cundinamarca* 4: 307, March 4, 1890, 522.

8. Ministerio de Gobierno (hereafter cited as MG), Tomo 48, fol. 359–63.

9. Carlos Cuervo Márquez, *El Llano* vol. 7, (Bogotá: Banco de la Republica. Archivo de la Economía Nacional, 1955), 326. Vela was buried under the main altar of the church in Uribe, and the tomb was marked with a marble stone inscribed "Fr. José C. Vela was born August 27, 1840. He received Holy Orders on September 28, 1870. He served disinterestedly the parishes of the Llanos of San Martín for twenty-four years. R.I.P." This stone can now be seen in the principal cemetery of Villavicencio, where it was moved along with Vela's remains in the 1950s by Colombian authorities during La Violencia.

10. José Joaquín Ortega Torres, *La obra salesiana en Colombia; Los primeros cincuenta años: 1890–1940* (Bogotá: Escuelas Gráficos Salesianas, 1941), 167.

11. Mauricio Dieres Monplaisir, *Lo que nos contó el abuelito: El centenario de Villavicencio, 1842–1942* (Villavicencio: Imprenta San José, 1942), 74.

12. AHN, MG, vol. 48, fol. 378.

13. AHN, MG, vol. 48, fol. 420.

14. AHN, MG, vol. 47, fol. 406.

15. AHN, MG, vol. 47, fol. 314.

16. Bergquist, *Coffee and Conflict*, 48–49.

17. AHN, MG, vol. 49, fols. 376–89, 438–50.

18. AHN, MG, vol. 49, fol. 118.

19. AHN, MG, vol. 49, fols. 391, 396.

20. AHN, MG, vol. 51, fol. 690.

21. AHN, MG, vol. 50, fol. 889.

22. Memoria de Ministerio de Gobierno (hereafter cited as MMG), 1898, 54.

23. J. Lloyd Mecham, *Church and State in Latin America*, Rev. ed. (Chapel Hill: University of North Carolina Press, 1966), 126.

24. Ortega Torres, *La obra salesiana*, 6, 144.

25. Ortega Torres, *La obra salesiana*, 166.

26. Ortega Torres, *La obra salesiana*, 195.

27. Ortega Torres, *La obra salesiana*, 192.

28. *Informe*, Intendant of San Martín, 1898 in MMG, 1898, 5.

29. Memoria de Ministerio de Fomento, 1890, xxiv.

30. Juan de Dios Tavera B., *Eco de Oriente* (Bogotá: Imprenta Popular, 1879), 1–11; Safford, *Ideal of the Practical*, 191.

31. Peregrino Ossa Varela, *Geografía de la intendencia nacional del Meta* (Bogotá: Ministerio de Agricultura y Comercio, 1937), 81.

32. José Bonnet, *Comercio oriental por el Río Meta* (Bogotá, 1884); *Anales del Senado*, Series 2, no. 107, August 7, 1884.

33. DO, January 16, 1891.

34. Jorge Brisson, *Casanare* (Bogotá: Imprenta Nacional, 1896), 130–31.

35. AHN, MG, vol. 47, fols. 110, 111.

36. Brisson, *Casanare*, 154.

37. García Bustamante, *Un pueblo de frontera*, 110.

38. García Bustamante, *Un pueblo de frontera*, 114–15.

39. In February 1923, the ministry of public works signed a contract with José Nieto, by which the latter promised to establish navigation on the Meta and adjoining

rivers with ships having a capacity of three to five tons. There is no evidence that Nieto was able to fulfill this commitment. See *El Espectador*, February 11, 1923.

40. Restrepo, *Una excursión*, 115; Flórez, *Conozcamos*, 75.

41. René de la Pedraja Tomán, *Los llanos: colonización y economía* (Bogotá: CEDE Documento 072, June 1984), 64–65; García Bustamante, *Un pueblo de frontera*, 84.

42. Ortega Ricaurte, *Villavicencio*, 11.

43. Benito Rondon, *Descripción geográfica del Llano de San Martín* (Bogotá, 1898), 9–15 cited by Baquero, *Departamento del Meta*, 89.

44. Restrepo, *Una excursión*, 213.

45. *Gaceta de Cundinamarca*, December 14, 1886; *Informe*, Intendant of San Martín, 1898, in MMG, 1898, 3.

46. *Gaceta de Cundinamarca*, June 7, August 16, and October 18, 1887. One of these grants was awarded jointly to Emiliano Restrepo and Manuel Restrepo H.

47. *Memoria del Ministro de Industrias*, vol. 5, 326–28.

48. AHN, Baldíos, vol. 8, fol. 71.

49. AHN, Baldíos, vol. 18, fol. 364.

50. Ocampo, *Colombia*, 388.

51. "Los colonizadores del Llano," 172.

52. Baquero, *Departamento del Meta*, 88–89.

4

War and Dictatorship, 1899–1909

The decade between 1899 and 1909 marked a turning point in Colombian history, for the War of the Thousand Days (1899–1902), the separation of Panama in 1903, and the dictatorship of Rafael Reyes (1904–1909) known as the Quinquenio provided the economic and political basis for the consolidation of the modern republic.[1] This era was no less pivotal for Villavicencio as violence, driven by the Liberal revolt against the government of Manuel Antonio Sanclemente and José Manuel Marroquín, engulfed not only the city but all three Llanos territories: San Martín, Casanare, and Arauca. The accession of Reyes to power in 1904 presaged a new territorial governmental system that would lay the groundwork for the modern development of the "Gateway to the Llanos." After a brief overview of the major battles of the war, this chapter will focus on the course of the insurgency in Villavicencio and the Territory of San Martín. It will then assess the legacy of the struggle within the region as it became apparent during the rule of Reyes.

THE WAR OF THE THOUSAND DAYS—AN OVERVIEW

The grievances of the Liberal party on being shut out from public office during the Era of Regeneration was the principal cause of the War of the Thousand Days, but the fighting was also prompted by an economic crisis created by a sharp fall in coffee prices that was severely aggravated by official economic policies. Fighting in the highlands broke out on October 17, 1899, when militant Liberals fielded an army to topple the Conservative government headed by the aged and ailing Sanclemente. "A Liberal defeat at Bucaramanga on November 13, 1899, was followed in December by a decisive

Liberal victory when forces led by Generals Rafael Uribe Uribe and Benjamín Herrera prevailed over a larger government army in the battle of Peralonso."[2] In May of 1900, the Conservatives countered by vanquishing their enemies in the battle of Palonegro, a conflict that lasted two weeks and left in its wake four thousand casualties. After this defeat the Liberals were reduced to waging an irregular war of guerrilla fighting marked by outbreaks of brutality and banditry on both sides.

In the meantime, dissident Conservatives deposed Sanclemente on July 31, 1900, in the hope that his successor, José Manuel Marroquín, would be conciliatory to the revolutionaries. Marroquín soon indicated, however, that he would prosecute the war with even greater vigor than his predecessor. After three years of fighting, sheer exhaustion probably contributed to the decision of Uribe Uribe and Herrera, who had emerged as the principal Liberal generals, to sign peace treaties in which the Marroquín administration promised to institute political reforms. As many as eighty thousand men may have died in combat or of disease; the damage to property was extensive and the value of the Colombian peso plummeted as a result of uncontrolled currency emissions by the government. The secession of Panama in 1903 was the final blow that underscored the debilitation into which Colombia had fallen.[3]

THE WAR IN VILLAVICENCIO AND
THE INTENDANCY OF SAN MARTÍN

The war came to Villavicencio even before it broke out in the highlands. On September 30, two hundred men attacked the town, easily overpowering jefe civil y militar Juan Campela, the alcalde Pedro Obando, and their force of eight policemen. Liberal rebels also seized Uribe, Medina, and San Martín to control much of the intendancy. Learning on November 30 that General Mariano Ospina Chaparro was on his way from Bogotá with several hundred soldiers to restore order, the rebels decided to evacuate Villavicencio, taking Campela and Obando with them. During the march to Cabuyaro, the two prisoners managed to escape, returning to Villavicenio in time to see Ospina Chaparro's triumphant entry into the city. The general reinstated Campela as jefe civil y militar and dispatched 350 soldiers to retake San Martín. Led by Colonel Eduardo Gómez, fifty of these men marched along the short, difficult path through the forest to San Martín, while the rest, mounted on horseback and carrying supplies, took the longer road that required fording several rivers. The larger force caught up with a group of revolutionaries eight leagues from Villavicencio and overpowered them, seizing three hundred horses and two hundred cattle. Flushed with victory, they returned with their booty to Villavicencio, leaving Gómez and his fifty men to face alone more than six hundred rebels in San Martín. Gómez waited for a week, but when the rest of the army did not come, he decided to return to Villavicencio without challenging the rebel stronghold, taking with him four Salesian missionaries who were no longer safe in San Martín. The rebels sniped away at the retreating soldiers, but by December 12, Gómez was back in Villavicencio with only one casualty.[4]

Ospina Chaparro kept a firm hold on the capital of the intendancy, but the plains outside the city were in enemy hands. In late December, the rebels were joined by more Liberals fleeing Tolima, where they had been defeated on December 9 at the battle of El Playón near the town of Colombia. Led by Tulio Varón, a fierce guerrilla fighter whose obsession was to kill Conservatives, they made their way to San Martín, and from there to Surimena, stopping at last in Santa Elena de Upía. At Upía they met General Gustavo Sánchez Núñez, who told them that the government had mounted strong outposts on the roads leading to Cundinamarca and Boyacá.

Buoyed by "a very Colombian hope, that any day the situation would change," Varón resolved to stay in Upía.[5] Life in the camp was miserable. Beset by disease, the rebels were reduced to a diet of unsalted meat and plátanos, but they concentrated on keeping their horses healthy, for without mounts they knew they would be helpless in the Llanos.

In January 1900, the arrival in Upía of General Avelino Rosas, who had sailed with a handful of followers up the Meta River from Arauca to Orocué, revived the spirits of the guerrillas who claimed him as their new commander. Rosas organized two new cavalry squadrons. In one, he put the numerous generals, colonels, and other high officers, and in the other, the ordinary soldiers. Some members of the first group, becoming disenchanted, deserted and returned to Tolima, but the rest followed Rosas enthusiastically. By the end of the month he had carried out a successful strike against the government garrison at Medina, seizing a large supply of weapons.

From Medina, Rosas marched his men swiftly toward Villavicencio, sweeping over numerous government outposts set up to defend the road. Outside the capital, the rebels exchanged shots with some government soldiers and tried to ascertain the size of the force inside the city. As soon as Rosas realized that he was facing more than two thousand soldiers, he began a retreat for San Martín. Ospina Chaparro followed, but despite the numerical superiority of his army, he could not disperse the rebels. On the contrary, Rosas inflicted losses on government forces by ambushing soldiers at every clump of trees or narrow gap in the road. In March, at a place called Las Peñas, between the Mestas de Guéjar and Uribe, Rosas won a decisive victory over Ospina Chaparro. This encounter effectively stopped the government offensive and allowed Rosas to continue his march over the cordillera to Tolima.[6] A few days later five hundred Liberals commanded by

General Crispulo Burgos attacked Villavicencio, forcing General Eliodoro Moyana, head of the local Conservative Party and *alcalde vitalicio* (mayor of the town), and his seventy men to surrender. Burgos then briefly dominated Villavicencio and the surrounding region as jefe civil y militar.[7]

During the second or guerrilla phase of the war, the Conservatives regained control of Villavicencio, while irregular bands of Liberal rebels roamed freely through the plains. When Liberal leaders fled from Tolima and Cundinamarca to the Intendancy of San Martín, they found compatriots ready for action. One such leader was Cesáreo Pulido, a seasoned, committed warrior from Cundinamarca who joined the rebels in San Martín in March1901. Pulido spent five months in Uribe, rebuilding his treasury and his army. Aided by General Gabriel M. Calderón, he raised money to buy weapons by exacting "voluntary" contributions from all of the wealthy people in the district, "without distinction of political colors."[8] He bought a large quantity of rubber harvested from the forests around Uribe and sold it at a good price in Orocué, a transaction managed with puritanical scruples by General Calderón. Pulido also expropriated cattle and rubber from the Compañia de Herrera y Uribe, eventually putting the owners out of business.

In early August, Alejandro Villoría led one thousand government soldiers over the cordillera from Colombia, Tolima, to attack Pulido. The guerrilla leaders with only 120 men evacuated Uribe, but the timely arrival of twenty cases of weapons, brought down the Meta River by General Emilio Santofimio, abruptly changed the balance of power. On August 24, 1901, Pulido soundly defeated Villoría at "Las Peñas," notwithstanding the disparity in numbers. After retaking Uribe, he went on to occupy Villavicencio and Quetame. Now firmly in control of much of the intendancy, he opened up contact with the rebel Ejército de Oriente, commanded by General Foción Soto, and accepted a position as Soto's subordinate. Meanwhile in San Martín, Plácidos Castro organized another band of 190 Liberals and moved into Villavicencio in January 1902.[9]

In February 1902 General Soto ordered Pulido to march to Medina and from there to occupy Gachalá. The conflict with government forces was going badly until the arrival of Uribe Uribe who took over direction of the combat supported by an army of two thousand men. Eventually the government soldiers fled, leaving behind much equipment that the rebels seized on their entry into Gachalá on March 13.[10]

Victory now seemed assured as Uribe Uribe took part of the army to Chocontá, while Pulido and Juan MacAllister led the rest to Guasca, but luck deserted them on March 17. At a place called El Moladero, General Ramón González Valencia, the most able among the Conservative officers, fell on Uribe Uribe, with a large, well-equipped army and completely routed his force. Four days later, an army led by General Nicolás Perdomo annihilated Pulido and MacAllister at El Guavio, ending Uribe Uribe's hope of replicating Bolívar's victory at the Battle of Boyacá.[11]

In full retreat, the remnants of the shattered Liberal United Army gathered in Medina. On April 2, the officers signed the Act of Medina, in which they agreed to go their separate ways. Pulido would return to Tolima; the guerrillas from Santander and Boyacá would go back to Boyacá, while MacAllister and the Cundinamarca Division would stay in the piedmont zone either to threaten Villavicencio or to penetrate Oriente Province. In the meantime, Uribe Uribe and Soto would travel to Curaçao to discuss with Gabriel Vargas Santos, the most senior Liberal leader, the possibility of opening up a campaign on the Atlantic coast to gain control of the Magdalena River.[12]

But the rebel cause was already lost. Two thousand government troops reconquered Villavicencio and San Martín, soon after Pulido started back to Tolima, and by the time he had ascended the cordillera to the Páramo of Sumapaz, many of his men had deserted, disillusioned and torn by jealous rivalries.[13] Pulido was captured on August 6 and executed at El Espinal, Tolima, on September 13. With Pulido's death, rebels in the Llanos of San Martín knew that further resistance was futile. By October 1902, there were only two Liberal armies of any size in the field—one in the Department of Magdalena, led by Clodomiro Castillo and Uribe Uribe, and the other in Panama, commanded by Herrera. On October 18, Castillo and Uribe Uribe accepted an armistice with the government. Six days later they signed the Treaty of Neerlandia, ending the war on the coast. On November 21, Herrera met with government leaders on a U.S. warship to sign the Treaty of Wisconsin, and officially at least, the War of the Thousand Days was over.[14]

THE IMPACT OF THE WAR ON VILLAVICENCIO AND THE TERRITORY OF SAN MARTÍN

In his thesis, "Departamento del Meta: Historia de su integración a la nación, 1536–1936," Omar Baquero argues that the War of the Thousand Days did not have a negative effect on Villavicencio.[15] The census of 1904 tends to support this conclusion for while the Intendancy of Casanare revealed a population of 12,555, or less than half of the official figure listed in 1870 as 26,055, in the Intendancy of San Martín, the population was reported as 4,957, a 14 percent increase over the 1870 census figure of 4,056. Especially noteworthy was Villavicencio's growth from 625 in 1870 to 3,315 in 1904, for it had now replaced Medina as the largest town in the region.[16]

A closer reading of the evidence, however, does suggest that the prolonged conflict did raise havoc in the Llanos of San Martín in at least four ways. First, the continuous hostilities brought normal government functioning to a standstill. In December 1899, Juan Campela, jefe civil y militar in Villavi-cencio, complained to the secretary of government that General Ospina Chaparro was usurping his prerogatives by issuing his own passports and re-fusing to recognize those authorized by Campela. The general ordered two of Campela's aides to march with his army to San Martín, and when they re-fused, he threw one of them in jail. Already he had seized from the inten-dancy twenty-eight steers, fifteen *cargas* (unit of measure equal to about six bushels) of panela, salt, iron, and nails, and declined to give any receipt. Campela assured the secretary that as "a Conservative by tradition and con-viction and as an agent of the government," he would not put up with this kind of behavior, and he asked that a new commander be sent who would be faithful to his legal obligations, because Ospina Chaparro was not fulfill-ing his mission with honor.[17]

Political confusion was intensified when President Marroquín issued De-cree 97 of September 20, 1900, separating from the intendancies of Casanare and San Martín, the area encompassing present-day Vichada, Vaupés, Caquetá, and Putumayo to form a new "Intendencia Oriental," with its capital in Maipure. Rafael Reyes abolished this intendency in 1905, but its brief existence provided a precedent for organizing the Comisaría Es-pecial del Vichada in 1913.[18]

A second consequence of the war was that both government and rebel troops indiscriminately plundered property owned by the inhabitants of Meta. Campela alleged that Ospina Chaparro's soldiers had appropriated one hundred mules and horses from hatos without making any account to him and without giving receipts to their owners, many of whom were "for-eigners, women or neutral persons."[19] In another case, rebels seized sixty-seven mules from Baptiste Broughter, a French citizen, some of which were subsequently recovered by government troops. When Campela ordered the officer who had found the mules to return them to Broughter because "the government cannot be responsible for reimbursing owners who do not sell them willingly," the man refused.[20] For their part, the rebels extorted money from the *ganaderos* and missionaries and took from the hatos whatever they needed. Troops on both sides sacrificed cattle without any consideration; disease decimated the herds still further; and the forest invaded extensive regions formerly cultivated.[21] As previously noted, Pulido, when he was in Uribe, took such a quantity of cattle, rubber, and money from the Com-pañía de Herrera y Uribe that he effectively put it out of business.

To protect their interests, the ganaderos played the two sides against each other. Such was the strategy adopted by Sergio and Luis Convers, owners of El Buque, the largest hacienda in the intendancy. With its rich sugarcane fields, coffee trees, and cattle, El Buque was a tempting prize. Sergio, who was still a French citizen, charted a neutral course between the government and the rebels for several months. He supplied cattle to both on demand

and aided all deserters who sought refuge at El Buque, regardless of their political affiliation, but eventually both sides accused him of treachery. Fearing for their lives, Sergio and his son, Luis, fled to Bogotá, as government soldiers took over the hacienda. When the two Convers returned in 1902, they found that all their workers had run away and that there was no one to harvest what remained of the coffee crop.[22]

Third, the fighting paralyzed trade. The insecurity of mountain trails to Cundinamarca disrupted annual cattle drives to the interior. The government created a monopoly on the salinas of Cumaral, Upín, and Chámeza. This monopoly was broken for three months, when revolutionary forces commanded by General Avelino Rosas seized the mines, but throughout the war, the acquisition of salt for domestic purposes was virtually impossible, transforming this necessary item into a luxury.[23]

Finally, the war disrupted the missions. In December 1899, rebels forced the Salesians to leave San Martín and to close their house there the following month. Soon afterward, they terminated their mission in Uribe but continued to work in Villavicencio, where government troops were in control. In August 1901, the Salesian superior, Dom Miguel Rúa, made the difficult journey to Villavicencio from Bogotá and was agreeably surprised to find that reconstruction of the church after the 1890 fire was progressing satisfactorily and that both morning and evening services were well attended. With few exceptions, the faithful received holy sacraments, and in eleven days there were no less than thirteen hundred confessions and communions. The situation changed abruptly, however, after Rúa had returned to Bogotá and rebels led by Pulido occupied the city. Padre Ernesto Briata stayed on for a few months, but when rebels sacked his house and took away whatever they wanted, he realized the mission was no longer viable.[24] In 1902, the Salesians closed their residence in Villavicencio and regretfully relinquished their mission field in the Llanos, defeated by revolutionary violence and the insistence on the part of the papal apostolic delegate, Monseñor Vico, that Salesians must be at least thirty-five years old before they could work in the missions, a provision that the order could not meet.[25]

VILLAVICENCIO AND THE INTENDANCY OF SAN MARTÍN DURING THE QUINQUENIO

Tobías Hernández's annual report of 1904 was the first to be written by an intendant of San Martín since 1898. In it he described a devastated, neglected region plagued by violence and a stagnant economy. To improve the situation, he asked the national government for mounted police to maintain order, to resume regular payments of the intendancy's subsidy, to overhaul the judicial system, to restore the missions, to improve the roads and bridges, and for a colonization plan that would award free land to families willing to settle in the Llanos. As Hernández concluded:

> These regions need a paternal government that will give them a *modo de vivir* [way to live], encourage immigration and colonization, and open land and river communication. If the government cannot do this, it should return the territories to the departments and see if they can provide enough money so that each of the municipios at least can have a primary school.[26]

This report, submitted in April, received little attention from the politicians in Bogotá, who were in the midst of a hotly contested presidential campaign that pitted ultra-Conservative Joaquín Vélez against General Rafael Reyes—the man who had urged ratification in 1903 of the Hay-Herrán Treaty acknowledging U.S. control over the proposed Panama Canal and who had tried to put down the Panama revolution but without success. Initial balloting by electoral assembly showed Vélez with a slight edge, but the final tabulation gave Reyes the victory with 994 votes to 982 for his opponent. Vélez supporters immediately challenged twelve votes cast for Reyes by the Guajira Peninsula, where the election had take place in a notoriously irregular fashion. In the end, the Gran Consejo Electoral decided the disputed votes in Reyes's favor just three days before the president was to be inaugurated.[27] On August 7, 1904, Reyes took office, calling for a program of national restoration.

For the next five years, Reyes created a virtual dictatorship by dissolving Congress in 1904 and creating his own bipartisan but extralegal National Assembly to stamp his presidential decrees with a seal of legitimacy. He extended his term of office from four to six years and exiled or imprisoned critics who protested his policies too loudly. Surviving several assassination attempts, Reyes persevered until June 13, 1909, when an unraveling financial system combined with public outrage over his campaign to win approval of tripartite treaties signed with the United States and Panamá, forced his resignation. The general sailed for Europe and spent the next ten years traveling through Africa, the Middle East, the United States, and Latin America. He died on February 18, 1921, the man who, in the words of Darío Mesa, drew a line between the old and new Colombia.[28]

Reyes's policies toward the Llanos are difficult to assess because there are few official reports, the subject is ignored in secondary works, and the primary sources, if they exist, have yet to be fully uncovered. On the basis of what can be ascertained, it appears that, besides supporting the missions and using Meta as a place to exile his opponents, he proposed no new ideas for modernizing the plains and his determination to divide the departments into small administrative units had the unfortunate effect of dismantling the national territorial system which had been evolving for several decades.

In 1902 Marroquín signed with the Vatican a Convention on Missions. In accord with this agreement, Colombia gave religious orders absolute authority to govern, police, educate, and control the Indians in wilderness areas or about 75 percent of the republic. Missionaries had jurisdiction over primary education for all people in these territories—white and Indian—as well as unlimited access to public lands to promote colonization. Even more importantly, church authorities had the right to reject nominees for positions in civil government if they regarded the individuals as unsuitable or as threatening to the Indians or the missionaries. The government pledged to provide seventy-five thousand Colombian pesos annually to underwrite these activities, of which two thousand five hundred Colombian pesos were allotted to the Apostolic Prefecture of the Llanos of San Martín and Vichada. The Vatican awarded this region to the Company of María (also known as the Montfort Fathers).[29] Throughout the Quinquenio the government subsidized the missionaries financially and supported their work in education through the ministry of public instruction.

The Montfort Fathers along with their female counterparts, the *Hijas de la Sabiduría* (Daughters of Wisdom) entered the Llanos of San Martín after the Salesians had withdrawn. Both traced their origins to the Society of Mary, founded in France in 1705 by St. Louis Marie Grignion de Montfort, which expanded rapidly after the beatification of its founder in 1888. Dedicated to restoring the reign of Christ through the reign of Mary, at the turn of the century, the Montfort Fathers were founding missions in Ireland, Denmark, Haiti, and Africa as well as South America. In August 1903, the first of their number, Eugenio Morón, arrived in Bogotá to assume his duties as Apostolic Prefect of the double prefecture of Vichada-Vaupés and the Llanos of San Martín. The following January he left for Villavicencio accompanied by three Montfort Fathers, who had been transferred from Peru, and by the Salesian Ernesto Briata, who introduced them to the people of the prefecture and shared with them his past experience. Five more missionaries came in 1905; two more in 1906; and the Hijas de la Sabiduría began schools for girls in Villavicencio and Medina in 1905.[30]

Morón administered the dual prefecture until 1908, concentrating on organizing the parishes of Villavicencio, San Martín, and Medina. He founded the vice parish of Surimena and visited Uribe on several occasions. In 1907, he undertook an expedition to Vichada, but illness forced him to stop at San Pedro de Arimena. In 1908, after learning that the Pope had elevated the prefecture to a vicariato apostólico , he resigned his post because, not being a bishop, he could no longer continue to head the province. It was under the regime of his successor, Don José María Guiot, who ruled from 1908 until his retirement in 1939, that the most significant expansion of the Montfort Fathers took place. Indeed, as Baquero concludes, these missionaries would have "a notorious influence on the political and ideological development of Villavicencio and the neighboring towns at least until the era of La Violencia."[31]

Reyes's decision to exile his opponents to Meta was not without precedent for, as we have seen, in the 1850s Father Manuel Santos Martínez proposed a plan to transport beggars from Bogotá to begin a settlement in Jiramena, a short distance south of Villavicencio, and in 1861, following the suppression of religious communities by T. C. Mosquera, several Dominicans sought refuge in the Llanos of San Martín to avoid expulsion from New Granada.[32] Reyes, however, was the first to silence his critics by sending them to a newly created penal colony on some land donated by Emiliano Restrepo near the salinas of Cumaral and Upín.

The first prisoners arrived on June 22, 1907. Most of them had been convicted of political crimes. Under the direction of Lieutenant Benjamín Ferro, they built a camp and then began to work in the salt mine. Father Dionisio LeTendre, a former cura of San Martín, served as chaplain at the settlement known as La Colonia, which at its height had eighty inmates and forty guards. In 1905 Reyes exiled another group of his opponents to Orocué. Both of these prisons were disbanded in 1910 after his fall from power, but at La Colonia, enough colonos coming from Cáqueza and Guayatá, Boyacá, joined with the ex-convicts who had remained to enable the settlement to be incorporated as a municipio in 1912, later to be renamed Restrepo.[33]

If Reyes did little to promote the growth of Villavicencio, his subdivision of the nine traditional provinces into thirty-four departments and reorganization of the national intendancies in 1905 was clearly counterproductive. Designed to cripple the power bases of his enemies and to encourage economic growth in the subregions of the highlands, his decision to combine the former intendancies of Casanare and San Martín into a single "Intendencia Nacional del Meta," and to create two new intendancies of Alto Caquetá and Putumayo only heightened the administrative confusion that remained after the War of the Thousand Days. At least four other decrees were passed in the next two years that tinkered with the jurisdictions of the various intendancies. As Victor M. Salagar, secretary of government in 1922, commented, Reyes eliminated with a stroke of the pen the territories that had evolved between 1892 and 1905 and created others without giving them the administration they required to justify separating them from the departments.[34] The dictator's policies may have laid the foundation for the twentieth-century Colombian state, but they left Villavicencio and the Llanos far behind. It remained for the Conservatives who came to power in 1909 to create the conditions that would set Villavicencio on the road to modernization.

NOTES

1. The best account of this period is Bergquist's *Coffee and Conflict*. For general surveys, see Deas, "Colombia, Ecuador and Venezuela"; Dario Mesa, "La Vida Política después de Panama" in MANUAL, 3: 83–176; and Javier Ocampo López, *Historia básica de Colombia* (Bogotá: Playa & Janes, 1987), 257–72.

2. David Bushnell, *The Making of Modern Colombia: A Nation in Spite of Itself* (Berkeley: University of California Press, 1993), 149–50.

3. Bushnell, *Colombia*, 150–51; Helen Delpar, "Thousand Days, War of the (1899–1902)" in *Encyclopedia of Latin America*, ed. Helen Delpar (New York: McGraw-Hill, 1974), 582.

4. AHN, MG, vol. 54, fol. 794; Ortega Torres, *La obra salesiana en Colombia*, 352.

5. Gonzalo Paris Lozano, *Guerrilleros del Tolima*, 2nd ed. (Bogotá: El Ancora Editores, 1984), 35.

6. Paris Lozano, *Guerrilleros*, 36–37. Rosas then continued his trek to the highlands unmolested, arriving in Tolima in early March to join the army of General Aristóbulo Ibáñez.

7. Ojeda Ojeda, *Villavicencio*, 178; Florez, *Conozcamos*, 2: 54.

8. Bergquist, *Coffee and Conflict*, 186–87; Tulio Arbeláez, *Episodios de la Guerra* (Manizales: Tip. Caldas, 1904), 37–38.

9. Arbeláez, *Episodios de la Guerra*, 6–32. Ojeda Ojeda, *Villavicencio*, 178.

10. Rafael Serrano Camargo, *El General Uribe* (Bogotá: Tercer Mundo, 1978), 204–6.

11. Serrano Camargo, *El General Uribe*, 204–6.

12. Rafael Uribe Uribe, *Documentos politicos y militares*, 4 vols. (Medellín: Beneficencia de Antioquia, 1982), 4: 343–44.

13. Ojeda Ojeda, *Villavicencio*, 178.

14. Bergquist, *Coffee and Conflict*, 185; Arbeláez, *Episodios de la guerra*, 37–38.

15. Baquero, *Departamento del Meta*, 90.

16. MMG, 1904, 210–27.

17. AHN, MG, vol. 54, fols. 799–801.

18. AHN, MG, vol. 55, fol. 676; MMG, 1922, xliii.

19. AHN, MG, vol. 54, fol. 799.

20. AHN, MG, vol. 54, fol. 803.

21. "Los colonizados del Llano," *Revista Pan* (1937), 15: 149.

22. Flórez, *Conozcamos*, 2: 77.

23. Informe del Inspector de las Salinas de Cumaral y Upín en 1904 in *Diario Oficial* (No. 12,262) January 19, 1905, cited by Baquero, Departamento del Meta, 90.

24. Ortega Torres, *La obra salesiana*, 299–300.

25. Ortega Torres, *La obra salesiana*, 353.

26. *Informe*, Intendant of San Martín, 1904, in MMG, 1904, 159.

27. Bergquist, *Coffee and Conflict*, 223; Jesus María Henao and Gerardo Arrubla, *Historia de Colombia*, 5th ed. (Bogotá: Librería Colombiana, Camacho Roldán, 1929), 763.

28. Mesa, "La vida política después de Panamá," 3, 117.

29. Mecham, *Church and State*, 133; Antonio José Uribe, *Anales diplomáticos y consulares de Colombia*, 6 vols. (Bogotá: Imprenta Nacional 1920), 6: 432–39.

30. Ortega Torres, *La obra salesiana*, 354; *Bodas de plata misionales de la Compañía de María en Colombia: 1904–1929* (Villavicencio: Imprenta San José, 1929), 116; Flórez, *Conozcamos*, 1: 104.

31. *Bodas de plata* misionales, 112; Baquero, *Departamento del Meta*, 92.

32. Ortega Ricaurte, *Villavicencio: 1842-1942*, 96–98. Although Santos Martínez's project failed after four years, the idea of using vagrants or even prisoners to populate the frontier did not die.

33. MMG, 1910, 19; Paredes Cruz, *Departamento del Meta*, 195; Oscar Pabón Monroy, "Restrepo," in *Trocha* (Villavicencio), no. 168 (December 1989), 18–19.

34. MMG, 1922, lxix.

5

Capital of the National Intendancy of Meta, 1909–1930

The twenty-one-year period between 1909 and 1930 is sometimes called the Conservative Republic, or the Era of National Harmony. On June 13, 1909, a few days before going into exile, Rafael Reyes presided over a congressional election that gave a majority to a newly organized party, the Republican Union. Led by Liberals and Historical Conservatives, this party was committed to a program of strict republicanism, bipartisanship participation in government, and laissez-faire economics. Its members dominated the National Assembly that was installed on July 20. After choosing General Ramón González Valencia to complete Reyes's term of office to August 7, 1910, the delegates proceeded to dismantle most of the repressive measures of the Quinquenio. Within a few months they approved laws that reduced the presidential term to four years, prohibited immediate reelection, provided for annual meetings of congress, restored direct presidential election, and made provisions for minority representation.

The National Assembly elected Carlos E. Restrepo, an Antioqueñan Conservative and leader of the Republican Union, as president from 1910 to 1914. The next four presidents were also Conservatives because the Liberals were in disarray, struggling to recover from their catastrophic defeat in the War of the Thousand Days. Despite the predominance of a single party, elections were held, public order was maintained, and upper-class civil liberties were generally respected. The government continued the policies of promoting export growth and selective protectionism for domestic industry while repudiating measures that might threaten the interests of the large landowners.[1] Fueled by the expansion of an export economy in coffee, bananas, and petroleum and the influx of foreign capital, the Conservative administrations spent millions of Colombian pesos to develop railroad and highway networks and to complete other public works projects. By 1930 Colombia had moved into the modern age with the arrival of automobiles, the first aviation company, the first radio transmissions, motion pictures, and the formation of a national system of communication.[2]

Despite its geographic isolation, the town of Villavicencio was not unaffected by these developments. The national government reestablished the Intendancy of Meta, designating Villavicencio as its capital. With its prestige further bolstered by the presence of the Montfort missionaries, the city slowly extended its authority over the white and native inhabitants of the territory. Its influence increased thanks to improvements in the Bogotá-Villavicencio road, the influx of spontaneous immigration from eastern Cundinamarca, growing cattle production for the highland market, and the emergence of rice as a major cash crop. Although truly rapid growth did not take place until the decade of the 1930s, the foundation for Villavicencio's emergence from small town to metropolis was laid during the Conservative Republic.

THE RESTORATION OF THE INTENDANCY

By Decree 238 of September 23, 1909, the Conservatives restored the Intendancy of Meta to include the municipios of Villavicencio, Orocué, and San Martín, but until 1928, Congress continued to tinker with the boundaries of the territory. In 1910, it awarded the municipio of Medina (formerly part of Meta) to Cundinamarca; in 1912 it reassigned Orocué to Casanare; and in 1913 it separated the eastern portion of the intendancy to form the Comisaría Especial of Vichada. Thus by 1928 the National Intendancy of Meta consisted of four municipios—Villavicencio, Restrepo, San Martín, and El Calvario—and six corregimientos—Uribe, Surimena, San Juanito, Cumaral, Acacías, and San Pedro de Arimena.[3]

According to the system adopted by the National Assembly in 1909, the intendant appointed by the president controlled territorial government from Villavicencio. He was responsible for maintaining order, overseeing the budget, inspecting local municipal councils, and working with the missionaries to promote public instruction, colonization, and economic development. Assisting him were two circuit judges from Cundinamarca—one for criminal and the other for civil cases—and a police force of twenty-five men. Each municipio had an alcalde and a five-member council. In Villavicencio there was also a *junta de caminos* (road committee) to oversee repair of national roads, using funds collected from tolls.[4]

Historian-archaeologist Miguel Triana, who spent several weeks traveling throughout the territory in 1912, described the intendant as a nominal official "without real initiative, without funds and nearly without subordinate employees to transmit his authority."⁵ Between 1909 and 1931, nineteen men held the post. Judged by their *informes*, published annually with the *memorias* of the ministers of government, they were men of varied ability, but they were all Conservative political appointees who had the disadvantage of ruling a region populated predominantly by men and women of Liberal sympathies. Frequently they would request special laws to administer the Llanos, arguing that conditions there differed radically from the rest of the nation. While Pablo V. León wrote in 1913 that the Llaneros were "a good sort, easy to govern, hardworking, and respectful of authority," other intendants reported that there were many crimes and registered their dissatisfaction with the size and organization of the police.⁶ Court records for 1912 show that there were forty-seven blood crimes (homicides, injuries, quarrels, and attempted assaults), thirty crimes against property (rustling, robbery, swindles, and contraband), fifteen crimes against honesty (cohabitation, incest, rape, and forced adultery), and twenty-seven miscellaneous crimes (perjury, slander, and vagrancy). Triana attributed most of the violence to abuse of aguardiente, and added that given the weakness of the authorities, the number of crimes was relatively insignificant.⁷

THE MONTFORT MISSIONARIES

The intendant, at his headquarters in Villavicencio, was the chief political officer, but it was the Montfort missionaries who dominated developments in the town and surrounding territory that formed the apostolic vicariate of the Llanos of San Martín in 1908. The spiritual leader of this enormous domain, which encompassed three hundred fifty thousand square kilometers of plains and jungles (or the contemporary departments of Meta, Vichada, and Caquetá), was the Illustrious Señor Doctor Don José María Guiot, a French citizen and Montfort Father, who was consecrated Bishop *in partibus* of Augustópolis and served as apostolic vicar from 1908 until 1939. The masculine and feminine orders of the Society of Mary, founded by St. Louis Marie Grignion de Montfort, had begun arriving in Villavicencio in 1905. By 1930 some thirty Montfort Fathers, most of them originally from France or Holland, had served in the Llanos as *párrocos* in towns of the intendancy or as missionaries to the Indians in Vichada and Vaupés. The Hijas de la Sabiduría had houses in Villavicencio, San Martín, El Calvario, and Vichada. They taught boys and girls in schools and staffed the hospital founded in 1912. The Montfortian monopoly in the vicariate was not broken until 1921, when some Christian Brothers started a boys' school in Villavicencio.⁸

Because no more than ten or twelve religious were working in the vicariate at any one time, their presence in the outlying districts was as tenuous

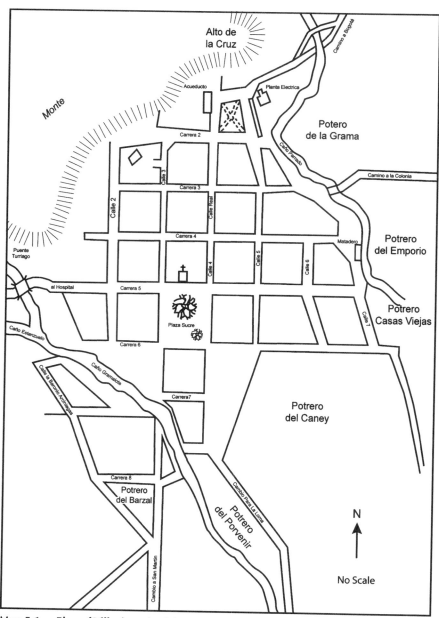

Map 5.1. Plan of Villavicencio, July 19, 1916

as that of the national officials. As Triana observed, "The immense extension of these parishes make their administration very difficult if not impossible with so few ecclesiastical personnel during the winter season which lasts for two-thirds of the year."[9] On the other hand, within Villavicencio the Montfort Fathers were powerful figures. Assisting Bishop Guiot and residing in the capital were Juan Bautista Arnaud, who served as párroco before leaving in 1912 to colonize the upper Guatequía River district; Gabriel Capdeville, who replaced Arnaud as párroco and served as apostolic provicar; and most important, Mauricio Dieres Monplaisir, first coadjutor, ecclesiastical notary, secretary of the vicariate, director of various social works, and school inspector in the absence of the bishop. Capable and energetic, these three men left their mark on life in the capital and in the settlements beyond.

When Bishop Guiot arrived in Villavicencio, there was no episcopal residence, and the church dedicated to Nuestra Señora del Carmen had only partially been rebuilt after the devastating 1890 fire. Fortunately, Juan Bautista Arnaud was a competent architect and drew up plans for both buildings. Antonio Camargo, a local resident, supervised their construction. Thanks to their efforts the bishop was able to move into his residence, and the church was nearing completion. Arnaud also collaborated with the alcalde of Villavicencio, Colonel Heliodoro Moyano, to raise money for a hospital by holding Sunday bazaars. On July 20, 1910, they laid the cornerstone of the new facility. On November 1, 1911, the Montfort hospital opened its doors, managed by the Hijas de la Sabiduría with an annual government subsidy of eight hundred Colombian pesos (decreased to four hundred Colombian pesos in years of penury). Hamilton Rice, an American geographer, who was delayed in Villavicencio in February 1912 by bad weather while on an expedition to the northwest Amazon Basin, inspected the hospital and wrote the following in his field report:

> It was [an] aviary as well as hospital such as would delight a Frank Buckland, for countless pigeons, fowls, ducks, and parrots roosted on the patients' beds or solemnly paraded on the mud floors. A brave and noble-hearted little *Soeur de Sagresse* did what she could to alleviate the sufferings of the wretched patients, but the absence of proper medical attendance and the pitiful stock of supplies made her task a discouraging and hopeless one.[10]

In 1912 Gabriel Capdeville left his post in San Martín to become párroco of Villavicencio, replacing Arnaud who had embarked on a colonization project along the upper Guatequía. Although Capdeville had been born in France, his parents were Spaniards, and he spoke Spanish without an accent, a talent that made him more acceptable to the Llaneros. Capdeville assisted the bishop and monitored the repairs on the church and episcopal residence. He organized the Santa Cecilia Boys Band, whose nineteen members, outfitted with handsome uniforms, played on patriotic occasions. He started the San José Bank, which by 1917 boasted a capital of COL\$4,006.41 and three hundred thirty-three depositors. In that year, there were six primary schools in Villavicencio taught by the Hijas de la Sabiduría and inspected by Padre Dieres Monplaisir.[11]

As secretary of the vicariate, Dieres Monplaisir worked with Capdeville on social projects and edited the diocesan newspaper, *Eco de Oriente*, bringing out two mimeographed issues a month between May 15, 1913 and March 15, 1916. The installation of a printing press brought from France permitted the expansion of the operation, and beginning on April 12, 1916, (2nd Epoca) the newspaper made its weekly appearance as an elegantly printed periodical, featuring national and local news. Dieres Monplaisir used the newspaper to propagate his political, moral, and social views and to promote progress in the intendancy.[12] He supported several bills introduced in congress to build a railroad between Bogotá and the Meta River and encouraged the introduction of improved pasture to nourish the local cattle.

Photo 5.1. Mauricio Dieres Monplaisir, 1887–1947
Source: *Bodas de plata misionales de la Compañía de María en Colombia, 1904–1929* (Villavicencio: Imprenta San José, 1929), 117.

The years between 1908 and 1917 brought improvements in the city's infrastructure. Before 1908 water was brought into Villavicencio by an arrangement of ditches, which sluiced streams from the caño Gramalote to fountains on the street corners. In that year, however, galvanized pipes were introduced that improved the water quality and allowed it to be piped into the interiors of the houses.[13] In 1915 entrepreneur Francisco Arango presented the municipal council with a memorial soliciting permission to establish an electric plant for the city.[14] Having gained approval, Arango hired Jorge Bejarano to build the plant that began generating power the following year. On November 24, 1916, Padre Mauricio showed the first motion pictures in Villavicencio, using a silent projector brought from France. Some ninety people assembled in the open-air Teatro Verdun, while Dieres Monplaisir, using a small pointer, interpreted the pictures that flashed across the screen.[15]

THE EARTHQUAKE OF AUGUST 31, 1917

In 1917 Villavicencio had 418 houses, twenty-eight *manzanas* (blocks of houses between two streets), seven *calles*—two of which were Calles Reales—eight *carreras*, two plazas—Sucre and Ricaurte—and approximately three thousand inhabitants. It had a municipal jail, the Hospital Montfort, an electric plant, water service, and six schools (four urban and two rural) with a combined attendance of four hundred children.[16] Unfortunately, these positive developments received a serious setback on Friday, August 31 of that year. At 6:30 AM, a powerful earthquake shook Villavicencio and the surrounding area for fifteen seconds. The episcopal residence, the cathedral, and the roof of the hospital collapsed, killing eight people and injuring six others. Nearly all the adobe houses in the town were destroyed. Damage was also severe in San Martín, where tremors toppled the church and most of the houses.[17]

Recovery was slow. Bishop Guiot went to France to raise money, but rebuilding the cathedral in Villavicencio was a monumental task, because the rear wall and part of the lateral nave had collapsed. By 1921 the church was again functional, but it was not until 1956 that Nuestra Señora del Carmen was fully restored based on a series of plans developed by Padre José Ramakers.[18] A new residence was built to house the Hijas de la Sabiduría, who previously had been confined to a miserable wooden hut. The hospital was expanded and in 1923 received a new zinc roof paid for by the government.[19] In the meantime, Father Gabriel Capdeville, stricken with dysentery, retired to a monastery in Italy. As Bishop Guiot gradually withdrew from diocesan affairs, Father Mauricio, who was now párroco of Villavicencio in addition to his other duties, emerged as the most influential ecclesiastical figure in the town.

POLITICAL CONFLICTS

Dieres Monplaisir did much to foster progress in Villavicencio, but he was not uniformly revered. In the first place, he was a foreigner who spoke Spanish with a marked accent.[20] Secondly, in a region where most inhabitants identified themselves as Liberals, there was smoldering resentment against the priest's unabashed championing of Conservatives. The tense political climate was revealed in an article published on April 25, 1923, by Bogotá's Liberal daily newspaper, *El Tiempo*, which described a bazaar held in Restrepo during the previous week that was sponsored by Liberals to raise money to buy a printing press and to start a school. The anonymous local reporter explained that a press and a school were the most urgent needs of Liberalism in the intendancy because the Marist Fathers monopolized the media with their political-religious newspaper "saturated with the most odious of policies," and because the government had unconditionally delivered public instruction "to a foreign community that does not permit official inspection or a review of its programs." He added that the bishop, in an effort to stop the event, had ordered a notice affixed to the church door stating that

> we, José María Guiot, Apostolic Vicar of the Llanos of San Martín, warn our faithful that they all commit mortal sin if they take part in the Liberal bazaar, whether directly or indirectly, donating, buying or serving at tables.[21]

Despite this attempt at sabotage, the bazaar was a huge success. The Liberal Party had raised five hundred Colombian pesos "to acquire the decisive elements that it needs for future struggles."[22]

Finally, while only Conservatives were appointed intendants, not all of them found it easy to work with Padre Mauricio. As early as February 1919, a Liberal from Meta, writing under the pseudonym CELASP, published an article in *El Diario Nacional* accusing Bogotá of neglecting the intendancy and alleging that the efforts of the intendants were overpowered by the missionaries, who had all the moral and material advantages. "The Maristas," he charged, "make a crude war on the work of the intendants obstructing every project."[23]

The most sweeping indictment came from Colonel Aristides Novoa who served as intendant from May 22, 1922, to April 23, 1923. In a report to his successor, Jorge Luna Ospina, that he later published in *El Tiempo*, Novoa alleged that Padre Dieres Monplaisir had forged an intolerable dictatorship over Meta and that during the past twelve years that Novoa had lived there,

> all, absolutely all the gentlemen, who have served this intendancy with independence of character and civil dignity and most of the circuit judges, hacienda administrators, police chiefs, and mayors have had friction and more or less serious disputes with the missionary that I am talking about, because they did

not let him have his own way, because they did not give in to his demands and whims, because they did not servilely humble themselves before his dictatorial impositions and before his rough and uncivil treatment.[24]

A series of conflicts with Padre Mauricio marked Novoa's term of office, despite that the colonel described himself as "a Conservative and a Catholic, by principle, by deep-seated conviction, and by constant practice." The first confrontation came on October 12, 1922, when Novoa gave a speech during the celebration of the Fiesta de la Raza. Padre Mauricio objected to the tone of his remarks and complained to Bishop Guiot, who sent a telegram to the minister of public instruction requesting that he censure Novoa. The feud escalated during the celebration of the Fiesta de la Paz on November 21. Novoa gave a patriotic speech to a large and respectable group of Liberals and asked them to join with the Conservatives and himself in singing the national hymn. Padre Mauricio left the plaza in disgust, returning later to pull down all the decorations and flags. On Dieres Monplaisir's instigation, Bishop Guiot sent another telegram to the minister of public instruction, accusing Novoa of not respecting the ecclesiastical authorities and of being the cause of "an extremely delicate situation that is getting worse by the moment."[25] On December 9, *El Tiempo* published both the telegram and Novoa's response, with this comment:

> We are astounded: Villavicencio and the Meta region, in appearance a section of the republic is, in reality, an ecclesiastical colony, in which civil power is neither respected nor attended to, and which is ruled by the imperious orders of R. P. Maurice Dieres Monplaisir, párocco of Villavicencio, secretary of the episcopate, inspector of public instruction and French citizen who for some time has resided among us.[26]

The inevitable explosion came as preparations for congressional elections, set for May 12, 1923, were raising political temperatures, and Novoa was ending his term of office and arranging to turn over the government to Jorge Luna Ospina. On the evening of April 22, three weeks before the elections, Oliverio Reina, part-time rancher and part-time bandit leader of a group of ultraconservative thugs, who enjoyed the patronage of Padre Mauricio, got into a bitter argument with a young Liberal, Efraín Chalarca, while they were drinking beer in a popular Villavicencio bar. Reina left the bar in a rage only to return quickly with some friends and the obvious purpose of beating up Chalarca. As his assailants drew their pistols, Chalarca fired first, killing Reina instantly. Seeing their leader fall, Reina's companions shot Chalarca in both legs and proceeded to beat him to death, while the men who had come to Chalarca's aid fought back, killing Antonio Ibagón. By this time an infuriated mob had gathered. Led by Rómulo Reina, nephew of Oliverio, they shouted, "Death to Liberalism," and went on a rampage, throwing stones at houses, breaking doors and windows. Informed of the uproar, Colonel Novoa rallied his force of six policemen, but they could not restore order. In the early hours of April 23, he telegraphed Minister of Government José Osorio for help, fearing that the enraged Conservatives would seize what arms were available in Villavicencio and make war on the Liberals.

While he waited for Osorio to reply, Novoa held a meeting of concerned citizens. He divided the men into two groups. To the first, made up of eight "honorable and clear-sighted Conservatives," he gave weapons belonging to the government and instructions to convince their copartisans to lay down their arms. The second group, consisting of unarmed Liberals and Conservatives, was to go through the streets to get those on both sides to stop fighting. As the two groups set out, Novoa sent a second telegraph to the minister of government asking him to appoint a special investigator to conduct an impartial inquiry into the incident.[27]

The unrest continued until April 27 when the new Intendant Jorge Luna Ospina, a nephew of President Ospina Pérez; the special investigator, Dr. José María Dávila Tello; and a squadron of cavalry arrived. As Novoa left for Bogotá under military protection to tell his side of the story, Ospina offered ample guarantees to gain public confidence, and after a few days the presence of the cavalry restored peace. By June Dr. Dávila Tello had charged six Liberals and two Conservatives with criminal actions and remanded them to Bogotá for trial. The cavalry soldiers remained for several months to prevent further unrest. After they were recalled to their regiment, many people threatened to leave the city, because they feared that the local police were insufficient to guarantee their security. In October 1923, the national government expanded the police force to twenty-five uniformed men. Luna Ospina stationed these officers in Villavicencio and the other municipios. In his annual report of 1924, he stated that they had carried out their duties well and were adequate for the normal needs of the intendancy.[28]

The violence in Villavicencio had national repercussions. The Liberal press of Bogotá gave full coverage to the events, and after his arrival in May, Colonel Novoa's account of the incident was printed in full in *El Tiempo.* Novoa accused Padre Dieres Monplaisir of deliberately obstructing his work as intendant. The priest, he charged, had used the *Eco de Oriente* "not only to criticize bitterly and unjustly the actions of the authorities but also to insult, jeer, and cowardly slander them." Moreover, he had a willing tool in Oliverio Reina. "Whenever he was hatching some political-religious problem or it was necessary to obtain some goal or to impede the fulfillment of some disposition," Dieres Monplaisir would summon Oliverio to his residence, and afterward the man would leave "in an angry mood to call together his gang, to drink, to shout threats and insults, and to spread panic throughout the town."

The intendant's implication was clear. The events of April 22, 1923, may have gotten out of hand, but they had been orchestrated by the French priest.[29] The editor of *El Tiempo* accepted the colonel's account, exclaiming that a travel-adventure novel could not include more interesting scenes of tropical life than those he had described. It was obvious that Padre Mauricio aspired to be lord and master of the intendancy, and the riot showed how a gang leader, "favored by friendships with important people, instills terror, ignores the authorities and finally falls by the violence he himself provoked." The Liberals lived under the threat of being attacked by bands incited by the missionaries from which the intendant was forced to defend himself "as if he were in the desert, revolver in hand and risking life at every step." "The danger is latent," the editor warned. "At any moment, an event could occur of the most serious consequence."[30]

Remarkably, the elections, which had contributed to the crisis, were held in complete calm on May 13, 1923. According to *El Tiempo*, in Villavicencio there were 192 votes for the Liberals and 475 for the Conservatives with a large number of the former abstaining. *El Espectador* reported the totals for the intendancy as 906 votes for Liberals and 1,200 for Conservatives and Dissidents. Noting that the municipios of Cabuyaro and Uribe, "both completely Liberal, abstained from voting," it concluded that "with all, the Conservative triumph is truly Pyrrhic."[31]

The events of April 22 are important, because they suggest that the influence exercised by the Montfort Fathers in Meta was consistent with the powerful role played by the Catholic Church everywhere in Colombia in the 1920s. The extreme personal animosity between Novoa and Dieres Monplaisir, however, appears to be unique. The other intendants were able to accommodate themselves to the priest's domineering personality, and for the most part, civil and religious authorities cooperated to promote missions, public instruction, public health, and colonization.

PUBLIC SCHOOLS

In accordance with the Convenio of 1902, the principal responsibilities of the Montfort Fathers were to civilize the Indians and establish schools throughout the vicariate. Although in 1913 Congress estimated that nearly thirty thousand "savages" lived along the banks of the rivers in the eastern plains, few unconverted tribes still lived within the boundaries of the National Intendancy of Meta where most of the parishes, though poor and isolated, were populated by mestizos. Given the lack of potential converts in Meta, the Montfort Fathers directed their missionary forays toward Vichada and Vaupés, a subject that has been well explored by Gabriel Cabrera Becerra in *La iglesia en la frontera: misiones católicas en el Vaupés, 1850–1950*.[32]

Under the watchful eyes of Bishop Guiot and Padre Mauricio opportunities for primary education expanded in the intendancy. By 1926, the vicariate was administering thirty-four schools—twenty-five in the Intendancy of Meta that enrolled 1,103 children, two in Medina, three in Vaupés, and four in Vichada. There were still no secondary schools, although the order did found a seminary for its novices in the town of San Juanito on the Guatiquía River. A night school planned for adult workers and servants in Villavicencio did not materialize, but Bishop Guiot did begin a school for deaf mutes in San Juanito that became the model for a similar school started later in Bogotá.[33]

The Hijas de la Sabiduría instructed the children in the municipios, while local women, often only barely able to read and write themselves, taught in the rural areas. Their salaries, when they were paid, ranged from twenty to fifty Colombian pesos a month. The curriculum included religious doctrine, sacred history, Colombian history, reading, writing, geography, Spanish, arithmetic, deportment, calisthenics, drawing, singing, natural history, and for girls, sewing and embroidery. All the schools lacked textbooks and maps of Colombia.[34]

The course of instruction in the Villavicencio schools was six years but only three years in the rural schools. In the latter, boys and girls attended school on different days in accordance with the recommendation of the Vatican, and approximately 4 percent of the students actually completed the course of studies. The rural school buildings were simple houses made of *bahareque* with straw or zinc roofs. Generally they had one door and two small windows. The lack of light in the room made reading and writing difficult, and during rainy days, the lessons had to consist of learning some songs or prayers. As Tomás Ojeda Ojeda points out, the teachers and students accommodated themselves to these difficult conditions because they were little different from the circumstances of their own homes.[35]

Even in urban Villavicencio, where the schools were marginally better, many parents kept their children home to put them to work in the fields or at domestic chores. Generally speaking, more boys than girls attended classes, and only the sons of the elite, who were fortunate to finish the six-year curriculum, had the possibility of attending secondary school in Bogotá.[36] In 1928, only 80 of 250 enrolled children in Villavicencio actually finished the entire course. According to Intendant José Jesús Angel, 50 percent of those who dropped out did so because of their parents' poverty and "the lack of a solid diet that makes it difficult for them to concentrate or because when they go home for lunch, the rain prevents them from returning."[37] To address these problems, in 1927 the sisters began serving breakfast and lunch in the schools. They also distributed clothes to the poorer children so that lack of decent apparel could not be an excuse for parents to keep them at home.

PUBLIC HEALTH

Surely, many children missed classes because they were sick. The deplorable state of public health in the intendancy was a matter of concern for visitors and the authorities. According to Triana, mortality was especially high in Villavicencio because of excessive humidity and sharp temperature drops between day and night. Mosquitoes bred abundantly in stagnant pools, spreading malaria and yellow fever. Inadequate sanitary facilities, scarcity of potable water, and lack of sewers intensified the dangers, particularly for immigrants from the temperate valleys of eastern Cundinamarca, who were experiencing a tropical climate for the first time. While the mortality rate for the intendancy as a whole was 30 people per 1,000, (or less than the rates for Mexico City, Lima, and Caracas), in Villavicencio it was a frightening 63.8 people per 1,000.[38] Dr. Hamilton Rice, who visited the city about the same time as Triana, was impressed by the number of corpses that passed by his lodgings every day, carried by prisoners from the town jail, in rough uncovered coffins. "Villavicencio is no place for persons of nervous temperament," he observed, "nor are the people one begins to meet a day before the town is reached pleasant to look at, with their lemon-tinted, gaunt, emaciated faces and hands of horribly lethal thinness."[39]

Improvement of public health was the responsibility of the *médico official* (official doctor), a post created when the intendancy was organized in 1910. In 1913, the first man to hold this position, Dr. Isaac Flórez, informed the intendant that malaria and yellow fever were present in various forms, especially in rural areas infested by anopheles mosquitoes. Diseases of the liver and spleen were common. Syphilis, tuberculosis, and dysentery occurred in alarming proportions, but the most serious problem was uncinariasis (tropical anemia), or hookworm, which affected virtually every resident over a year old.[40]

While doctors had been aware for many decades of the dangers posed by malaria and yellow fever in tropical climates, the identification of tropical anemia as a parasitic disease was relatively recent. Unlike the other two, which are spread by mosquitoes, tropical anemia is caused by the larvae of the hookworm that live in the soil of hot, moist regions and enter the human body by penetrating the soles of bare feet. The larvae move into the bloodstream and pass by way of the lungs, throat, and stomach to the small intestine. There they make their home, feasting and copulating, laying eggs that pass out with the stool and contaminate the soil so that other bare feet can pick up the new larvae, which hatch eggs. The host produces an anemia that saps vitality, cripples and kills, or leaves people emaciated with protruding shoulder blades, bloated stomachs, and swollen joints. By the beginning of the twentieth century, scientists had realized that hookworm was a disease that plagued millions of people in tropical and semitropical areas throughout the world. They had discovered that doses of thymol salts were effective in treating and eliminating the symptoms, and they recommended attacking the causes by disinfecting the soil, building sanitary privies, and educating people to wear shoes and practice good hygiene.[41]

The médicos oficiales of Meta repeatedly asked the national government to send them thymol capsules for individuals incapacitated by hookworm, and they did what they could to eliminate the unsanitary conditions that spawned it and other diseases. For example, in 1917, Dr. Teodosio F. Acero asserted that lack of sewers were causing inadequately drained water to seep into the houses of Villavicencio, forming breeding grounds for microorganisms that produced typhoid fever, dysentery, cholera, and tetanus. He recommended that the streets be cleared and the drains inspected; that the city ban the selling of meat in the streets, a practice which bred flies and mosquitoes; and that it widen the perimeter around the cemetery, because decomposition and putrefaction of corpses lying in shallow graves was contributing to the epidemics.[42] In 1919 Dr. Flórez published in Villavicencio a book entitled *Enfermedades dominantes en los llanos de la region oriental de Colombia*. He formed a committee on hygiene to deal with ongoing health problems, and with the cooperation of Padre Mauricio, published information on disease prevention in *Eco de Oriente*.[43]

News that the Rockefeller Foundation was beginning a five-year campaign to eradicate hookworm in Colombia raised expectations that faster progress might be made in the future. In 1919, President Marco Fidel Suárez signed an agreement with Dr. Louis Shapiro, a representative of the foundation. Shapiro promised to send medical personnel and laboratory equipment sufficient for treating up to fifty thousand cases of hookworm annually and to direct public information indoctrination throughout the country. Suárez pledged to provide one hundred thousand Colombian pesos each year to subsidize these activities and to assign an official in the ministry of agriculture to coordinate the campaign. The Rockefeller Sanitary Commission began by conducting a hookworm survey throughout the country. Soon afterward, it started the first eradication centers in the Tequendama Province of Cundinamarca and along the Magdalena River in Tolima.

The campaign did not reach Villavicencio for another six years. In the meantime, local authorities with scant resources struggled to control the disease. In May 1925, Intendant Rubén Santacoloma informed Minister of Government Ramón Rodríguez Diago that he was planning, with the aid of his son, Dr. Nestor Santacoloma, and two other doctors, to finance a sanitarium where the sick would receive care and attention. He asked for Rodríguez Diago's approval, "since negligence will bring a fatal degeneration of the race," and also urged him to send the sanitary commission which, with its knowledge and experience, could help "to broaden this campaign against that disease which decimates the towns of the Llanos."[44] When members of the sanitary commission finally did arrive in Villavicencio later that year, they dosed hundreds of people with thymol salts, but their plans to build sewers and privies were delayed for want of materials. In 1928, the médico official, Dr. José Antonio Concha, reported that malaria, yellow fever, tuberculosis, and venereal diseases such as syphilis were still exacting a heavy toll, and he called for a renewed effort against hookworm in the countryside. His successor in 1931, Dr. Gustavo Ruiz Mora, could only observe, "There is still a terrifyingly high rate of infant mortality and an alarming advance of malaria and hookworm."[45]

COLONIZATION

Despite the menace of disease and high mortality, the population of Villavicencio and the intendancy grew by leaps and bounds. Between 1904 and 1918 the number of inhabitants of Villavicencio expanded from 3,315 to 4,774, an increase of 44 percent. At the same time, the regional population more than doubled, going from 4,957 to 11,671.[46] Some of the migrants were seasonal, coming from eastern Cundinamarca to earn high wages during planting and harvesting and then returning home, but most streamed into the intendancy with every intention of remaining permanently. There were two organized colonization projects—the settlement of the upper Guatiquía River, led by Padre Juan Bautista Arnaud and the founding of a penal colony in Acacías by the national government. In addition, congress reformed the laws regulating baldíos to make it easier for small farmers to claim their land.

The Guatiquía River Basin stretches north of Villavicencio to the Cordillera de Peñas Blancas and contains more than thirty thousand hectares of land. In the 1870s colonos from Fómeque began exploring the area for cinchona trees. Founding a *caserío* or small village at El Baldío, they managed to thrive despite their isolation from other towns in Cundinamarca and Meta. In 1910, when they asked the authorities to help them build a road between El Baldío and Villavicencio, Bishop Guiot decided to send Padre Arnaud to reconnoiter the area. Arnaud returned brimming with enthusiasm about its development potential, so Guiot authorized him to begin a mission in the upper Guatiquía.[47]

Arnaud set out for the second time in December 1911, with a subsidy of four hundred Colombian pesos. He worked with the people of El Baldío to build a new town, El Calvario, clearing the forests with machetes and axes. Progress came swiftly. By 1917 there were 533 inhabitants, twenty-six houses, a chapel, a priest's house, an inn and store, an *alcaldía* (mayor's office), a prison, a market, and a school taught by the Hijas de la Sabiduría. In addition, Arnaud founded San Juanito further up the Guatiquía, and when El Calvario was elevated to municipio status, San Juanito was designated as a corregimiento. Here, the Montfort Fathers began their seminary and a school for deaf mutes. He also used four thousand five hundred Colombian pesos and colono labor to build a camino de herradura to Villavicencio. By 1929 the municipio had grown to three thousand inhabitants, and Arnaud was at work on a new road that would unite Bogotá with the Llanos by passing through El Chingaza, San Juanito, Villavicencio, Restrepo, and Medina.[48]

The national government also wanted to encourage rapid settlement of frontier areas by peasant families to provide an agricultural base for the industrialization that engulfed the country after World War I. After 1917, congress, in association with the ministry of industries, began a program to sponsor government-financed colonies that would become poles of attractions for other settlers. The legislators agreed to aid people accepted into the new colonies with transportation, loans for food and tools, and free surveys of the land. In addition they authorized several penal colonies, one of which was located in Restrepo.

In 1905 President Reyes had sent prisoners to Restrepo, but President Carlos E. Restrepo closed it in 1910 on the grounds that it was not cost effective. In November 1918 congress passed Law 60 creating the Penal and Agricultural Colony of Meta and locating it once again in Restrepo. The law stipulated that men convicted of stealing or cattle rustling in Tolima, Cundinamarca, Boyacá, Arauca, Vichada, and Vaupés would be sent to the colony, where they would be put to work on public projects and farming the land. Six months after they had completed their sentences, they would receive title to seven hectares of land. In addition, Law 60 offered seven hectares of land to volunteer colonists, who would receive their titles within a year so long as they were actually cultivating at least half of their claims.[49]

This second facility was no more successful than the first. In 1922 congress suppressed it, and passed Law 105 authorizing a new penal colony to be located in Acacías, just outside Villavicencio. On June 2, 1924, President Pedro Nel Ospina issued Decrees 1130 and 1131, which inaugurated the Acacías Penal and Agricultural Colony and designated it as a place of incarceration for vagrants and convicted criminals of Cundinamarca, Boyacá, and Atlántico.

This new facility has survived until the present although it has undergone several transformations. Between 1924 and 1932 its population fluctuated between 130 and 220 men supervised by fifty to sixty guards. Working in gangs, they planted sugarcane, tobacco, and cotton. They improved one road leading from Acacías to San Miguel and another that went toward Bogotá through Caño Acacitas. They repaired the bridge over the Guayuriba and began work on a hydroelectric plant and a telegraph line between

Acacías and Villavicencio. A town grew up around the prison, and by 1928 there were eight hundred inhabitants primarily engaged in cultivating rice. In 1932, The *dirección general de prisiones* of the ministry of government took over the administration of the Penal and Agricultural Colony, which remained the only penitentiary in Meta.[50]

In her study of land policy, Catherine LeGrand has shown that the Colombian government in the 1920s adopted a position that was vigorously pro-colono, as opposed to encouraging large entrepreneurs. Contributing to this change in focus were two new laws and a historic Supreme Court decision. In 1917, congress passed Law 71, which exempted settlers with holdings of twenty hectares or less from having to hire a surveyor, buying official paper, or paying postage in applying to Bogotá for their titles— all requirements that had made grants costly. In 1926, Law 47 simplified grant procedures for colonos even more and promised that the government would give them credit, tools, and seed. Then, in that same year, the Colombian Supreme Court handed down a landmark decision ruling that "henceforth all land in Colombia would be presumed public land unless proven differently. Only by showing the original title by which the state had alienated a given tract of land from the national domain could a landowner sustain his or her legal right to that property."[51] The ruling's effect was to withdraw legal sanction from many of the large estates consolidated in frontier regions in early years, because most landlords did not have the first titles that the court required. It also enabled the government to recover public land illegally appropriated from the national domain. Finally, until 1926 anyone could contest a settler's grant application by saying that the land was private property, but after 1926 this ploy was no longer possible. These changes meant that "so long as a small cultivator filed the correct paperwork, he or she was assured of legal title to the land."[52]

The impact of these reforms in the Intendancy of Meta is not completely clear. Only six grants were registered between 1908 and 1917—three in Villavicencio and three in San Martín, all ranging from 800 to 1,000 hectares. Between 1918 and 1931, thirty-seven grants were awarded of which twenty-seven, or 73 percent, were for 20 hectares or less—nineteen in San Martín, eight in El Calvario, and one in Uribe. These figures suggest that it was easier for small settlers to gain title after 1918 than before, yet when one considers the hundreds of colonos who were relocating to the intendancy, only a few of them actually did become legal owners.

The comments made by the intendants suggest that many individuals were frustrated despite the reforms. In 1924, Luna Ospina reported that he was enforcing Law 71 of 1917, but there was great confusion over the rights of colonos who had been occupying land without formal title.[53] In 1926 Rubén Santacoloma stated that fourteen of forty-four applications for land submitted that year had been abandoned, while the rest were pending. He added that only a few people possessed titles, and many of those who did pretended to own much larger tracts, "not permitting that anyone occupy them, which disturbs the development of agriculture and cattle." Another problem giving rise to constant lawsuits was that "former possessors have sold their small improvements with rights to thousands of hectares that have not been cultivated nor occupied with cattle as the government requires."[54]

Still pending was the dissolution of the Community of Apiay. In 1918, Sergio Convers signed a contract with more than two hundred comuneros, by which they agreed to cede him their titles in exchange for a certain number of hectares to be awarded based on years and extent of occupancy once the land had been measured. Convers planned to deliver the land by September 1919, but the division apparently did not take place. In 1928, Intendant José Jesús Angel wrote that the existence of the Community of Apiay continued to block the development of "the most beautiful portion and best cultivated area of land in the intendancy."[55]

In 1929, geographer and engineer Peregrino Ossa Varela published an article in the *Revista Nacional de Agricultura*, in which he argued, "Ownership of property is not known in the Llanos because all of the plains are baldíos, and even if some of them have been legally awarded, the documentation does not exist or is incomplete so that all is reduced to the right of possession [or who is actually living on the land]." Because of the extraordinary floods and droughts, cattle in Meta need a great extension of land, and ranchers occupy the plains without stability, moving from place to place. Alongside the *fundaciones* that show genuine growth is an "infinity of individuals who, like parasites, squat on the baldíos and steal the cattle, keeping the industry from advancing." Ossa called for special legislation that would take into account the unique conditions of the Llanos and allow for greater flexibility and more liberality in adjudication. As it stands, he concluded, "Acquisition of land here by our present laws is virtually impossible."[56]

ECONOMIC GROWTH

Undeterred by legalities, colonos moved into the intendancy and began cultivating plots of land. The road between Bogotá and Villavicencio was little better than a hazardous mule trail; yet trade between the two cities doubled between 1913 and 1925. Exports of coffee declined because the Llanos could no longer compete with harvests from other regions, but shipments of corn, yuca, and plátano grew steadily, and the widespread cultivation of rice sparked an agricultural revolution. The town and the intendancy were beginning to assume their contemporary role of providing foodstuffs for the large highland market.

The newcomers who cleared land around Villavicencio, Restrepo, and El Calvario soon discovered that rice grown without irrigation and with the most rudimentary care would give yields of five hundred to one in four months. Individual farmers could harvest and sack the crop by hand and transport it by pack mule to be milled. By 1920 there were three hydraulically powered mills to choose from: one in Villavicencio, owned by Jorge Bejarano, which also produced electricity; another on the Convers' Hacienda El Buque; and a third in Restrepo owned by Francisco Arango U. At the mills the rice was dried, threshed, hulled, and sacked. Its high quality was appreciated in Bogotá, where it brought a good price. In 1923, the intendancy produced 103,500 *arrobas* of rice grown on 2,250 hectares and valued at two hundred seven thousand Colombian pesos. Total exports from the territory doubled from 51,255 arrobas (including rice, corn, and plátanos) in 1913 to 118,295 arrobas in 1925, including 91,840 arrobas of rice, 21,530 arrobas of plátanos, and 4,925 arrobas of corn.

Dramatic changes were also taking place in cattle production—still Villavicencio's principal resource, notwithstanding the poor quality of grass in the intendancy, and the difficulty of driving the steers up the cordillera to market. As early as 1869 Emiliano Restrepo had urged fellow ranchers to plant improved pasture called *pasto gordura*, or *yaraguá*, so that they could fatten steers on their own land. Few ganaderos had followed his lead, preferring to sell their emaciated animals at a low price to other ranchers who would take them to Magdalena or Tolima and fatten them for a year before selling them for beef at a substantial profit. Then in 1919, Plácido Castro L., a ganadero from San Martín, presented a report to the Sociedad de Agricultores de Colombia in Bogotá describing his three-year effort to cultivate pasto gordura on his land using seeds provided by José María Uribe. Castro found that, with irrigation, the pasto gordura had readily substituted itself for the native grass. He predicted that if it were introduced on a large scale, the Intendancy of Meta might become a new Argentina.[57] Castro's success encouraged others to experiment, and the number of hectares of improved pasture increased from 500 in 1921 to 2,104 in 1922. In that year, the intendant jubilantly reported that ranchers in Casanare and Arauca, who used to take their cattle to Sogamoso, were sending the animals for fattening in pastures outside Villavicencio. Between 1922 and 1925 annual cattle fairs were held in Villavicencio, and the number of animals in the intendancy increased from 49,196 to 77,045. Exports grew as well. In 1913, 3,630 cattle left Villavicencio for Bogotá. By 1925 the number had quadrupled to 16,235, of which 74 percent, or 12,000, had been fattened on improved pasture.[58] Ojeda Ojeda asserts that between 1920 and 1936 Villavicencio sent between 1,000 and 1,500 cattle by foot up the Andes to the capital every week.[59]

Quickening trade transformed Villavicencio from a sleepy village to a bustling entrepôt. Rice, corn, plátanos, cattle, and hides produced in the intendancy passed through the town to the highlands in exchange for flour, soap, food, beer, oil, wire, machines, and domestic and foreign manufactured goods. Bogotá traders came with their merchandise to Villavicencio, and from there they supplied surrounding towns as far away as Orocué. They sold hats, textiles, hammocks, *bayetones* (large woolen ponchos), *alpargatas* (sandals), and other *chucherías* (gewgaws) that appealed to the Llaneros. Venezuelan merchants arrived bringing goods and money. By 1928 there were two *casas de primer orden* (commercial houses of the first order) in Villavicencio, with capital of forty thousand Colombian pesos—Echeverría Brothers and Rueda Sierra and Company. Factories included Jorge Bejarano's electric plant, which had been milling rice and making ice since 1915; Uribe and Arango's soft drink plant; and others that produced soap and tobacco. Still lacking was a bank, but Intendant Angel wrote in 1928 that the city was perfectly capable of supporting one and suggested that a branch of the Banco Agrícola Hipotecario be opened there soon.[60]

TRANSPORTATION DEVELOPMENTS

During Colombia's railway boom in the late nineteenth century, there were many schemes to build a line to connect Bogotá to Villavicencio. Padre Dieres Monplaisir was among several individuals who energetically campaigned to have a railroad built. Between August 21 and December 1917, he published *Ferrocarril del Meta*, a bimonthly periodical featuring articles and manifestos by local citizens in support of the project. In one typical article, Padre Dieres Monplaisir wrote that the railroad would foster "intimate, close, cordial, and rapid ties between Cundinamarca and the Llanos," for while it was true that the Llanos needed supplies from Bogotá, it was equally true that the capital could not overlook the Llanos as its *granero* or *dispensa natural* (fruitful, grain-producing country or natural pantry). When one considered the importance of the Meta River, he argued, it was evident that Bogotá was the head and Villavicencio the heart of an organic system that encompassed all of the Llanos Orientales. In Padre Dieres Monplaisir's view, the *Ferrocarril de Oriente* was indispensable from a national as well as a regional viewpoint.[61]

Despite the persuasiveness of these points, the only project to gain the approval of the Cundinamarca Assembly was a contract to build an electric trolley line connecting the Parque de los Mártires in Bogotá with Tunjuelito in the Municipio de Usme, which might, in the future, serve as the first leg of a railroad to the Llanos. Construction began on August 15, 1917, and by 1930 twenty-six kilometers were in service, carrying 106,569 passengers and

5,161 tons of freight in that year. The onset of the Great Depression postponed any hopes of extending the line to the Llanos. After decades of dreams and hopes, the Ferrocarril de Oriente was abandoned forever.[62]

Fortunately, endeavors to modernize the Bogotá-Villavicencio highway had a happier outcome. In 1922, the ministry of public works began upgrading the 125-kilometer road. By 1926, five hundred prisoners had rebuilt the 30-kilometer section between Bogotá and Chipaque at the expense of COL$142,488. By 1929, 17 additional kilometers to Cáqueza had been improved, costing COL$994,548. The remaining 78 kilometers were completed between 1930 and 1936, at a cost of COL$749,893. The final cost of the highway was COL$15,895 per kilometer, for a total of COL$1,886,929, including maintenance during construction, feasibility studies, and bridges over the Cáqueza, Sáname, and Negro rivers and the quebradas of Susumuco and Pipiral.[63] Although by 1930 these improvements had only reached Cáqueza, leaders in Meta were optimistic. As Intendant Santacoloma wrote, "Today we are still limited by lack of labor and the high cost of transport, but when we can count on a road to this region from the populated centers of Cundinamarca, the rice industry and others will develop on an unimagined scale."[64]

Internal transportation within the intendancy was still quite difficult. In 1923, the national government did launch a steamboat on the Meta, but it provided no money to maintain local roads that were annually disrupted by flooding rivers. The bridge over the Guatiquía that connected Villavicencio with Restrepo, the Salina of Upín, and Casanare required constant attention. In 1918, excessive humidity rotted its floor and the cables sustaining it, and a year later the bridge collapsed, not to be rebuilt until 1929.[65] The other principal bridge over the Guayariba that linked Villavicencio with San Martín was located, for some obscure reason, in an overgrown area away from the road so that it was not convenient to travelers. The lack of a telegraph line between the two cities further isolated San Martín; wire that had been strung in the 1890s had been cut during the War of the Thousand Days and was not repaired until the 1930s.[66]

The most dramatic event in transportation occurred on March 26, 1928, when Lieutenant Camilo Daza and Lieutenant Colonel Fidel Abadía Méndez landed an airplane in Villavicencio twenty minutes after taking off from Bogotá. The enormous possibilities presented by easy air communication between points long isolated by mountains and flooding rivers were not lost on local officials. Using a motion picture camera that Lieutenant Daza had brought with him, Padre Mauricio began to make films of the Llanos that could be shown in Bogotá to encourage highlanders to live and invest in Meta. A *Sociedad Anónima de Aviación Llanero* was founded with a capital of one hundred thousand Colombian pesos divided into one hundred shares at eight thousand Colombian pesos each to promote aviation, and Intendant Angel urged the minister of government to support the company, which could take over the duty of carrying mail between Bogotá, Arauca, Vaupés and Vichada.[67] With the arrival of the airplane, a new age had begun—an age that would see its fulfillment under Alfonso López and his Revolution on March of the 1930s.

NOTES

1. Christopher Abel, *Política, iglesia y partidos en Colombia* (Bogotá: FAES-Universidad Nacional de Colombia, 1987), 19. Good summaries of this era can be found in Deas, "Colombia, Ecuador and Venezuela," 641–84; Mesa, "La vida política," 33–178; and Jorge Orlando Melo, "La república conservadora," in *Colombia: Hoy*, 9th ed. (Bogotá: Siglo Veintiuno, 1985), 52–101.

2. See Carlos Uribe Celis, *Los años veinte en Colombia: ideología y cultura* (Bogotá: Ediciones Aurora, 1984) for an excellent social history of the 1920s.

3. *Informe*, Intendant of Meta, 1928 in MMG, 1928, 499; MMG, 1921, 217.

4. Triana, *Al Meta*, 40. The two circuits were combined in the 1920s, with a single magistrate from the Bogotá judicial district residing in Villavicencio. See *Informe*, Intendent of Meta, 1928, in MMG, 1928, 402.

5. Triana, *Al Meta*, 38.

6. *Informe*, Intendant of Meta, 1913 in MMG, 1913, 75.

7. Triana, *Al Meta*, 41.

8. This information has been gathered from several reports included in *Bodas de plata*.

9. Triana, *Al Meta*, 44.

10. Hamilton Rice, "Further Exploration in the Northwest Amazon Basin," in *Geographical Journal* (August 1914) 44: 2,140. The Englishman Francis Trevelyan Buckland (1826–1880) wrote about natural science for the general public. His book *Curiosities of Natural History* (New York, 1859) was widely read and included such topics as "A Hunt in a Horse-Pond," "Bats," and "The Cobra de Capello."

11. Dieres Monplaisir and Capdeville, *Las misiones católicas en Colombia: Informes 1919, 1920, 1921, 1922, 1923* (Bogotá, 1921–1923), 76.

12. *Eco de Oriente*, January 26, 1919. Dieres Monplaisir was a man of many talents. Before being assigned to the Llanos, he had just completed a doctorate in theology magna cum laude at the Universidad Anglicum of Rome.

13. Ojeda Ojeda, *Villavicencio*, 306.

14. García Bustamante, *Un pueblo de frontera*, 157–58.

15. *Eco de Oriente*, November 30, 1916.

16. García Bustamante, *Un pueblo de frontera*, 161–62.

17. *Eco de Oriente*, September 2, 1917; *El Diario Nacional*, September 20, 1917.

18. Gregorio Garavito Jiménez, *Historia de la iglesia en los llanos* (Villavicencio: Imprenta Departamental del Meta, 1994), 80.

19. Mauricio Dieres Monplaisir, Lo que nos contó el abuelito: El centenario de Villavicencio, 1842–1942 (Villavicencio: Imprenta San José, 1942), 50.

20. Raquel Angel de Flórez interviewed Padre Mauricio when she was gathering material for her history of the Department of Meta. When she remarked on his no-

ticeable French accent, he curtly responded, "Why do you say that I have a French accent when I am sure that it is now complete llanero?" Flórez wrote, "Intelligent, energetic, frank, psychologist, and honest, he himself told us, 'My tongue stings!'" *Conozcamos*, 2: 72.

21. *El Tiempo*, April 24, 1923.

22. *El Tiempo*, April 24, 1923.

23. *El Diario Nacional*, February 15, 1919.

24. *El Tiempo*, May 8, 1928.

25. *El Tiempo*, May 8, 1928.

26. *El Tiempo*, December 1923, as cited in Jorge Villegas and José Yunis, eds. *Sucesos colombianos, 1900–1924* (Medellín: Universidad de Antioquia, 1976), 432.

27. *El Tiempo*, May 8, 1925; *El Espectador*, April 25, 1923.

28. *El Espectador*, June 21, 1923; *Informe*, Intendant of Meta, 1924 in MMG, 1924, 158.

29. *El Tiempo*, May 8, 1923.

30. *El Tiempo*, May 8, 1923, as cited in Villegas and Yunis, *Sucesos*, 450–51.

31. *El Nuevo Tiempo*, May 15, 1923; *El Espectador*, May 21, 1923.

32. Gabriel Cabrera Becerra, *La iglesia en la frontera: misiones católicas en el Vaupés, 1850–1950.* (Bogotá: Universidad Nacional, sede Leticia, 2000); see also Garavito Jiménez, *Historia*, for information on the missions in Vichada and Vaupes.

33. *Informe*, Intendant of Meta, 1928 in MMG, 1928, 408; *Informe*, Intendant of Meta, 1926, in MMG, 1926, 79.

34. *Informe*, Intendant of Meta, 1928 in MMG, 1928, 410.

35. Ojeda Ojeda, *Villavicencio*, 72–73.

36. Ojeda Ojeda, *Villavicencio*, 72–73.

37. *Informe*, Intendant of Meta, 1928, in MMG, 1928, 410.

38. Triana, *Al Meta*, 42.

39. Rice, "Further Explorations," 140.

40. *Informe*, Intendant of Meta, 1913, 84–86.

41. Raymond B. Fosdick, *The Story of the Rockefeller Foundation* (New York: Harper Brothers, 1952), 31.

42. *Informe*, Intendant of Meta, 1917, in MMG, 1917, 277.

43. *Informe*, Intendant of Meta, 1919, in MMG, 1919, 2: 111.

44. *Informe*, Intendant of Meta, 1925, in MMG, 1925, 38–39.

45. *Informe*, Intendant of Meta, 1928, in MMG, 1928, 486; *Informe*, Intendant of Meta, 1931, in MMG, 1931, 89.

46. Baquero, *Departamento del Meta*, 94.

47. Padre Arnaud was a trained engineer who designed four roads and drew plans for several churches in Bogotá. See Garavito Jiménez, *Historia*, 77.

48. *Bodas de Plata*, 104–6.

49. AC, Leyes, 1918, vol 5, fol. 239.

50. *Informe*, Intendant of Meta, 1928, in MMG, 1928, 499; *Informe*, Intendant of Meta, 1932, in MMG, 1932, 106–8.

51. LeGrande, *Frontier Expansion*, 97–100.

52. LeGrande, *Frontier Expansion*, 101.

53. *Informe*, Intendant of Meta, 1924 in MMG, 169.

54. *Informe*, Intendant of Meta, 1927, in MMG, 1927, 76.

55. *Informe*, Intendant of Meta, 1928, in MMG, 1928, 479.

56. Ossa Varela, "La ganadería en los llanos orientales," 96.

57. *Eco de Oriente*, June 10, 1919.

58. *Informe*, Intendant of Meta, 1925, in MMG, 1925; 41; *El Tiempo*, November 19, 1922.

59. Ojeda Ojeda, *Villavicencio*, 128.

60. *Informe*, Intendant of Meta, 1928, in MMG, 1928, 469–71.

61. *Ferrocarril del Meta* (Villavicencio), August 21, 1917.

62. Roberto Velandía, *Encyclopedia histórica de Cundinamarca*, 5 vols. (Bogotá: Cooperativa Nacional de Artes Gráficas, 1979), 1: 325; Alfredo Ortega Díaz, *Historia de los ferrocarrilles colombianos*, 3 vols. (Bogotá: Imprenta Nacional, 1932), 3: 260.

63. *Memoria del Ministerio de Obras Públicas*, 78–80.

64. *Informe*, Intendant of Meta, 1925, in MMG, 1925, 41.

65. *Informe*, Intendant of Meta, 1918, in MMG, 1918, 354–55; *Lo que nos contó*, 58.

66. *Informe*, Intendant of Meta, 1933, in MMG, 1933, 67.

67. *Informe*, Intendant of Meta, 1928, in MMG, 1928, 507.

6

Villavicencio during the Liberal Republic, 1930–1946

Enrique Olaya Herrera's election to the presidency in 1930 was a pivotal event in the twentieth-century history of Colombia. The accession to power by a candidate supported by moderate factions of both Conservative and Liberal parties ended the long era known as the Conservative Hegemony (1886–1930) and began the sixteen-year period called the Liberal Republic (1920–1946). Olaya and his successor, Alfonso López Pumarejo responded to the crisis created by the worldwide depression by attempting to modernize Colombia through groundbreaking social and nationalistic policies designed to encourage industrialization. Pledging his government to *"Concentración Nacional"* (National Unity), Olaya initiated these reforms by revitalizing the fiscal structure, stimulating coffee production, launching major public works, pressing for revision of the civil codes, and calling for the integration of Colombia's peripheral frontier regions, which included, in addition to the Llanos, Amazonia, the Pacific Lowlands, the Guajira Peninsula, and the islands of San Andrés and Providencia.

Upon this base López Pumarejo built his *Revolución en Marcha* (Revolution on March) by pushing through congress legislation regarding the constitution, church and state, land, elections, taxes, and education that won him the title of "the nation's greatest twentieth-century reformer."[1] Like Olaya, López Pumarejo was determined to extend national rule over Colombia's far-flung frontier lands, but while Olaya's interest was concentrated on Amazonia prompted by war with Peru over Leticia (1932–1934), López Pumarejo revealed a special preference for developing Villavicencio and the Llanos of Meta. The fact that the policies he set forth regarding Colombia's eastern frontier slowed under his successor, Eduardo Santos (1938–1942) and during his own disastrous second term (1942–1946),

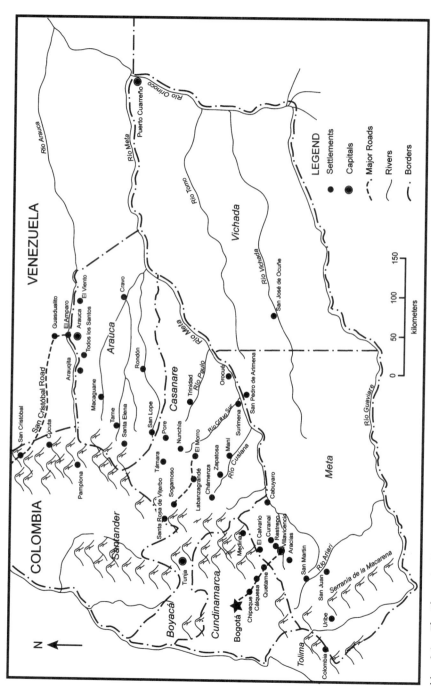

Map 6.1. The Llanos in 1930

which was completed by Alberto Lleras Camargo, does not negate the fact that during the Liberal Republic, Villavicencio and the surrounding Llanos entered a period of exceptional growth.

COMPLETION OF THE BOGOTÁ-VILLAVICENCIO HIGHWAY

López Pumarejo was not the first Colombian president to recognize the potential of the Llanos of San Martín. In December 1868, Santo Gutiérrez personally inspected the route between Bogotá and Villavicencio, and a year later his secretary of finance and development, Salvador Camacho Roldán, declared, "The Llanos Orientales have a future for us like the territory west of the Ohio has had for the U.S.A., the pampas for Argentina, and the northern tropical region for Australia. . . . The territory of San Martín lying twenty leagues from the capital of Colombia is the door, and the road to the Meta is the key to that vast region. Our duty is to open them."[2] López Pumarejo, however, was the first president to make the development of Meta the centerpiece of his territorial policy. In his biography, *El presidente López*, former minister of education Eduardo Zuleta Angel recalls that López Pumarejo kept a map of Colombia in his office and often pointed to it to underscore his belief in the bright future of the Llanos. He conceded that in the past, when it had taken three days to reach Villavicencio from Bogotá, it had not been unreasonable to downplay the region's position; but, he observed, times were different now:

> When one can travel to Villavicencio in forty minutes and to Orocué in two or three hours; when cattle can be carried by truck; when one can use fertilizers and weed killers; when a tractor can do in an hour, work that takes many people to do in a day, when it is known that one can plant cacao and African palm—to continue believing that the Llanos are not good for anything is simply one of so many manifestations of the cloudy thinking of Colombians.[3]

Without doubt the opening of the Bogotá-Villavicencio highway to motor traffic in February 1936 was the key to the quickening growth of the "Gateway to the Llanos." When Lieutenant Camilo Daza and Lieutenant Colonel Fidel Abadía Méndez landed their airplane near Villavicencio on March 26, 1928, twenty minutes after taking off from Bogotá, they demonstrated that the Cordillera Oriental was no longer an insurmountable barrier to rapid communication between the interior and the Llanos. Within five years there were regularly scheduled flights between the two cities. Nevertheless, it was obvious that it was the highway that offered the most practical access for commerce and colonos. Already in 1922 the Ministry of Public Works had begun work on the road to make it accessible to cars and trucks. Five hundred prisoners had rebuilt the thirty-kilometer section between Bogotá and

Chipaque by 1926. Seventeen kilometers were added by 1929, and between 1930 and 1936, the remaining seventy-eight kilometers were completed. The final cost of the highway, including feasibility studies, maintenance during the construction period, and the erection of bridges over three rivers and two quebradas, was COL$1,886,929 or COL$15,895 per kilometer.[4]

Excitement grew in Villavicencio as the road neared completion. Although trucks had been coming down the mountain for some months, the first cars reached the town at the beginning of February 1936. On February 16, Minister of Government Alberto Lleras Camargo arrived to inspect the highway and to consider the feasibility of extending it to Puerto López and beyond. On his return to Bogotá, he described the road as "an excellent work" that passed through "jungle regions of singular natural beauty" and was "no more or less dangerous than other roads that the Bogotá tourist travels on Saturdays such as that to Fusugasugá.[5] Four days later when the highway was officially opened, Padre Maurice Dieres Monplaisir wrote in *Eco de Oriente*:

> It is a fact. The last dynamite blast had exploded; picks, spades, and shovels had stopped, and then came a dump truck, and then another truck, and then buses and automobiles—some of which belonged to the aristocracy and were of modern makes. It is an avalanche.[6]

The celebration was completed on February 24, when President López Pumarejo arrived by automobile accompanied by the ministers of war and agriculture and by his sons, Hernando and Pedro López Michelsen. Before a crowd, who had gathered at the government house, Intendant Eugenio Campo Sarría hailed López Pumarejo as the "savior of the Llanos" and then carried him off to a reception and lunch at the Hotel Meta. During the evening the president met with local Liberal leaders and was serenaded by a typical Llanero *conjunto* (trio). The next day he went to the airfield at Apiay for a traditional *mamona* (barbecue).[7]

COLONIZATION

Even before the paving of the highway, Villavicencio along with the Intendancy of Meta was one of the fastest growing regions of Colombia. Between 1918 and 1938 the population of Villavicencio increased from 4,736 to 24,315 while that of the Intendancy grew from 11,671 to 51,674.[8] To encourage this continued growth, the Director of National Territories, Bernardo Rueda Vargas, pledged to implement policies that would extend roads, make land more accessible, improve health and education facilities, and expand the agricultural and ranching base of the economy.

Between 1934 and 1938 construction continued on the road between Villavicencio and Puerto López on the Meta River to provide a land route to connect the territory to riverboats sailing west from the Atlantic via the Orinoco and Meta River system. A plan was drawn up for a metal bridge four hundred forty meters long to cross the Guatiquía River and open up the way from Villavicencio to Apiay, Acacías, and San Martín. Other bridges receiving attention spanned the Guayuriba River and the Caño Parrado. Repairs were made on the roads linking Villavicencio to Cabuyaro, to Restrepo and Cumaral, and to El Calvario, and about 50 percent of the road connecting the town with Acacías and San Martín was completed.[9]

To encourage colonization and resolve conflicts between squatters and landlords, in 1936 congress passed Law 200, which allowed individuals to gain title to land either by deed or by proof of having worked a plot for five years. It also stated that land that was claimed but not developed would revert to the state after ten years. It is difficult to determine the impact of Law 200 on the Intendancy of Meta. The records of the public land office show that in the five years before the law was passed (1931–1935), 98 titles were registered for a total of 13,966 hectares, while between 1936 and 1940, the five years after the law went into effect, 124 titles were registered for 16,893 hectares. This small increase suggests that it was still difficult for colonos to obtain legal ownership in a territory dominated by large cattle ranchers—a conclusion confirmed by historian Reinaldo Barbosa E., who has demonstrated that in Meta as well as Casanare and Arauca, authorities routinely favored ranchers and denied applications on the grounds that the land in question was already owned by someone else.[10]

The year 1936 also saw some progress toward resolution of the Community of Apiay dispute that continued to block the expansion of Villavicencio and its environs. In 1936 Jorge Campillo as attorney for the Republic of Colombia took advantage of a newly adopted fiscal code to initiate a suit against the Community of Apiay in the Superior Court of the Judicial District of Bogotá. After reviewing the history of the case, he argued that a large part of the land claimed by the comuneros was really baldío, and he asked the court to declare it as such. On April 30, 1936, the judge agreed to his request, handing down a determination that prejudiced five hundred thirty proprietors, whose titles Convers Codazzi had recognized in 1920, as well as a large number of squatters without titles. The ruling generated two kinds of litigants: those who claimed to have title to land that had initially been private property and had only later been converted to communal land, and those who had title to land, which the nation now declared to be baldío.

The decision satisfied no one, and the case came up again before the court in 1940; but it took an act by congress to finally resolve it. In 1943 the legislators approved Law 51, which stated that comuneros, who had possessed portions of the common lands as owners and who had occupied and exploited the land, could bring their cases to court and become owners of the plots they had occupied. In the opinion of Nancy Espinel Riveros, who has chronicled the history of the Apiay Community, this law, which applied not only to Apiay in Meta but also to other regions of the country where communally owned lands were in dispute, "settled the issue with justice for those who had possessed the land and incorporated it into the economic activity of the country."[11]

The penal colony at Acacías presented a different kind of obstacle to colonization. After a town of 800 inhabitants grew up around the colony, it was clear that the prison was too close to the free population and no longer fulfilling the goal of using prisoners to colonize remote frontiers. Rueda Vargas recommended that it be transferred to a new site. His suggestion was seconded by a group of merchants, ranchers, and farmers, who urged the minister of government on January 29, 1938, to move the prison to a more isolated location, because it presently stood in the midst of fertile land suitable for development and also because, as the number of inmates had increased, so had thefts, murders, and assaults committed by escapees in the surrounding community. Unmoved by these arguments, the minister refused to act, and the penal colony remained in Acacías.[12]

With the completion of the paved highway between Bogotá and Villavicencio, a new wave of migrants, lured by the possibility of growing dry rice on five- to ten-hectare plots between the Guatiquía and Guayuriba rivers, began the journey down the Eastern Cordillera.[13] They arrived from Tolima, Huila, Antioquia, Boyacá, Cundinamarca, the Santanders, and Valle, bringing with them their culture, their regional foods, and their traditions. Moreover, once the highway reached Puerto López in 1938, many of them continued their journey farther out in the Llanos.[14]

HEALTH

Rueda Vargas believed that improving health conditions was essential to attract more colonos to the intendancy. When López Pumarejo became president in 1934, Meta was still plagued by malaria and yellow fever. Syphilis, tuberculosis, dysentery, and tropical anemia occurred in alarming proportions, and diseases of the liver and spleen were common. In 1925 the Sanitary Commission sponsored by the Rockefeller Foundation arrived in Villavicencio and began treating people afflicted with tropical anemia, but lack of construction materials delayed the commissioners' plans to build sewers and latrines that would greatly contribute to the effort to stop the spread of infections. In 1931 the National Department of Hygiene opened a branch office in Villavicencio directed by Dr. Gustavo Ruiz Mora. As chief médico oficial of the territory, Ruiz Mora improved sanitation in the slaughterhouse, vaccinated children for smallpox, and expanded the Hospital Montfort, which each year treated some two hundred inpatients and eight hundred outpatients. In 1932 private citizens in Villavicencio founded the Junta de Beneficencia Pública del Meta modeled on the guidelines of the national Red Cross. There still was little progress in building latrines, and Ruiz Mora reported an alarming advance of malaria and tropical anemia. He urged that money be made available to combat these diseases and to improve sanitation in Villavicencio.[15]

In 1935 the national budget included COL$5,637 to aid the Hospital Montfort and to purchase drugs, and in 1944 a new wing was added to the facility. By 1937 sewer construction in Villavicencio was nearly complete, and studies were underway for an aqueduct to serve the city. The intendancy was centralizing and regulating public assistance, and the National Department of Hygiene sent two new sanitary commissions to fight malaria, tropical anemia, tuberculosis, venereal disease, and leprosy. From their bases in Villavicencio and Restrepo, the commissioners began informational campaigns to instruct the public about basic health measures that should be taken to avoid these illnesses, and Dieres Monplaisir supported their efforts by publishing articles on disease prevention in the *Eco de Oriente*.[16]

In August 1934 Padre Francisco Savary reported an outbreak of yellow fever in his parish of Restrepo. The cases were unusual, because it was apparent that they had not been transmitted by the *aedes aegypti* mosquito, which until then had been regarded as the principal vector of the disease.[17] Responding to a request from the National Department of Hygiene, the Rockefeller Foundation sent Dr. Elmer Rickard to Restrepo to investigate. By the time he arrived, Colombian technicians had fitted out a laboratory in a dilapidated house and were collecting and inspecting monkeys to test the theory that they might be the virus carriers.

After an examination of liver samples of the fatal cases sent to Rockefeller laboratories in Rio de Janeiro confirmed that the cause of death was a new strain of yellow fever, the foundation appointed Dr. Boshell Manrique to investigate the disease in Restrepo. Manrique conducted topographic studies, made a census of the region, and carried out immunological research in humans and animals. Eventually he discovered that the carriers of the disease were *haemagogus janthinomys* mosquitoes, which inhabited the canopies of the trees in the jungle. He also determined which primates carried the virus and made the first isolation of the virus for inoculation in Acacías in 1935. Based on his findings, the Rockefeller scientists in New York and Rio de Janeiro developed a vaccine, which was used for the first time in Colombia in 1937.[18]

Manrique's investigations were continued by an American biologist, Marston Bates, who arrived in Villavicencio in 1941 with his wife, Nancy, to work in the laboratory originally begun by Manrique but which had been renovated by the Rockefeller Foundation and the Colombian government in 1938. With his associate, Dr. Manuel Roca, Bates continued to investigate the transmission of the yellow fever virus by studying colonies of mosquitoes and experimenting on mice, monkeys, and other tropical animals. After collecting and examining more than two thousand wild animals, he concluded that capybaras, anteaters, and opossums, as well as certain kinds of monkeys, could carry the virus in their blood. Bates and Roca also conducted investigations in parasitology and malaria, and they offered free vaccinations against yellow fever every week to people who came from all parts of the intendancy.[19]

EDUCATION

The López Pumarejo government was eager to promote the development of official schools to complement those run by the Montfort Fathers. Between 1935 and 1937 Rueda Vargas increased the share of the budget earmarked for education from COL$3,850 to COL$10,690. Throughout the intendancy there were twenty-two official schools enrolling 585 boys and 385 girls and twenty Montfort schools with 505 boys and 834 girls. An appropriation of COL$10,000 from the Ministry of Education supported sixteen school restaurants.[20]

Writing in 1942, Dieres Monplaisir reported that in Villavicencio proper there were seven schools for boys with 605 students and five schools for girls with 588 students. In addition, there was *"una escuela complementaria"* for women, a private colegio for boys and two colegios for young women, while in the outlying districts of the town there were five rural schools. Although attempts to begin evening schools had failed on three occasions, Villavicencio finally had a functioning night school called "Olaya Herrera" attended by teachers of the primary schools. Nevertheless, despite efforts being made by the national government and private individuals to promote education, he added, there were still many adults and children who did not have access to schools.[21]

ECONOMY

During the Liberal Republic, economic initiatives in Meta focused on expanding ranching, developing agriculture, and promoting petroleum exploration. With regard to ranching, the government tried to improve beef quality by banning the slaughter of female cows less than ten years of age and increasing the availability of salt collected from the mines at Cumaral and Upín in the foothills of the cordillera. Ever since colonial times, salt, deemed essential for human and animal consumption, had remained a state monopoly. At Cumaral and Upín the government contracted with private entrepreneurs who hired peons to blast the salt out of the mines during the four-month dry season and prepare it for sale in the official store. Primitive extraction methods and lack of roads leading to the mines limited the amount of salt that could be produced and ensured that its cost would be high. In 1938 the mines yielded 924,020 kilograms valued at COL$25,062.[22]

The number of cattle born and raised in the intendancy expanded rapidly when Meta ganaderos began to make wider use of the improved pasture and crossbreeding—practices introduced in the late nineteenth century. By the 1930s Brahman and creole cattle were commonly crossbred to produce animals that were more resistant to local diseases and climatic stress.[23] In 1938 there were forty-two thousand cattle located in Villavicencio and the Meta Intendancy—an amount that increased to three hundred thousand by 1950 before the Violencia wiped out much of the gain.[24]

Every year thirty thousand cattle were driven up the cordillera to market in Bogotá.[25] Many of these animals had originally been raised in Casanare, Arauca, or even Venezuela, and only arrived in Meta after an arduous trek that required up to sixty days on the trail. Once they reached Villavicencio, they were fattened in pastures with improved grasses for three or four months to regain weight lost on the trail. Then they set out again for Bogotá, "plodding along in woven straw boots to protect their hooves" and losing on the six-day journey much of the weight they had recently gained.[26] After the highway opened, ranchers hoped to limit these losses by transporting their steers in trucks to the highlands, but they soon discovered that the narrow curves in the highway made this option unfeasible.

It was now clear that for Meta beef to be competitive, it would be necessary to build in Villavicencio a modern refrigerated slaughterhouse, so that meat could be processed and taken to the capital in refrigerated trucks. In 1941, the ministry of government approved a proposal to get a loan to build a *matadero* (slaughterhouse) capable of processing ten thousand cattle a year, and equipped with a freezing plant and transport trucks. Congress approved another fifty thousand Colombian pesos for it in the centennial grant of 1942, but subsequent freezing of those funds put the plans on hold. At last in 1948 a corporation to build the facility was formed when congress passed Law 28 authorizing the Instituto de Fomento Industrial to purchase 30,000 ten-peso stock shares; the Intendancy took two hundred thousand Colombian pesos worth of stock, and private investors, many of whom belonged to the Sociedad de Ganaderos del Llano, took the rest. Refrigerating equipment was ordered from Sweden at a cost of one hundred forty thousand Colombian pesos. Weighing eighty-five tons, it was shipped via the Orinoco and Meta rivers at an additional expense of twenty-eight thousand Venezuelan bolívars and was assembled in Villavicencio under the direction of an Argentine engineer.[27]

Once the slaughterhouse finally went into operation in 1950, it could process 100 to 150 animals a day plus another 25 for local consumption. Nevertheless, its overall impact was disappointing. Ganaderos, who had hoped to save the millions of pesos lost each year because of weight dropped by the cattle on the drive up the cordillera, saw their hopes dashed when experience revealed, first, that the refrigerated trucks could not negotiate the highway's hairpin turns; second, that it was not cost effective to ship the meat in refrigerated airplanes; and finally, that even when chilled beef did go on sale in the capital, the consumers, who were traditionally "warm meat eaters," refused to buy it.[28]

To encourage agricultural production, the government opened a branch of the Caja de Crédito Agrario in Villavicencio in 1937, and a year later the Ministry of Agriculture began an *internado agricolo* (experimental farm) on land near the town with fifteen scholarship students and an agronomist teacher. Much of the food crop was consumed locally, but by 1938 the intendancy was exporting primarily to Bogotá 55,929 *bultos* of plátanos, 11,326 bultos of corn and 1,649 bultos of yuca with a combined value of COL$142,652.80.[29] In addition, by 1940, seven thousand hectares of land were producing six hundred thousand arrobas of rice—the premier export valued at COL$1.2 million.[30]

A variety of other economic activities were being pursued by this time in Meta. Tropical Oil and Shell International began oil surveys around San Martín, Chafurray, Vorágine, and Chaviva. Tourism was growing thanks to improvements in the Bogotá-Villavicencio road. In 1940, two thousand five hundred visitors came to Villavicencio, prompting Intendant Gonzalo Combariza Martínez to suggest that it was time to build a more comfortable hotel suitable for vacationers.

After the Bavaria Consortium, the largest beer brewery in Colombia, opened a factory in Villavicencio in 1940, alcohol became a growth industry. In the fiscal year 1943–1944, taxes placed on the sale and consumption of foreign and national liquors and fermented beverages raised COL$330,491 or a little over 60 percent of the intendancy's budget of COL$545,053.[31] Bavaria beer proved to be extremely popular, and according to Nancy Bell Bates, who lived in Villavicencio between 1941 and 1947, everyone in town was a beer drinker:

> *Chicha* and *guarapo*, fermentations of corn and cane sugar, have fallen into disrepute, but beer flows on forever. The actual population of Villavicencio is unknown, but I asked a lawyer, a government official, and a leading businessman, and their guess was roughly about 12,000. The statistics on beer consumption are more definite; Don Julio Alvarez, agent for the largest of the beer companies,

Illustration 6.1.   Llanero Musical Group: Harp, Maracas, and Four-String Guitar
Source: Watercolor by Eloy Palacios, a Venezuelan artist, published in Caracas in 1912.

states that in Villavicencio alone there are 12,000 bottles of beer opened daily. "That means," said he, "one bottle of beer a day for every man, woman and child well or ill." "Or even dying," added a bystander with almost a note of pride.[32]

In the mid-1940s the economy continued to grow even without assistance from the national government. By 1947 there were fifty cattle haciendas within the jurisdiction of Villavicencio; twenty-four around Restrepo, twenty in San Martín, two in El Calvario, (one of which belonged to the Montfort Fathers), plus numerous hatos and fundaciones that had "an appreciable number of cattle," and Meta was sending forty-eight thousand steers to Bogotá for slaughter each year.[33] Between 1941 and 1946, 133 titles were registered for 18,667 hectares of land in the intendancy. In 1948, 11,644,050 kilos of rice worth COL$5,589,200 were produced on 10,350 hectares of land, placing the intendancy fourth in Colombian rice production after the departments of Bolívar, Tolima, and Valle. In 1951 Meta exported to Bogotá 561,000 bultos of plátanos, 166,500 bultos of corn, 300,000 bultos of yuca, and one hundred seventy-eight thousand animal skins.[34]

VILLAVICENCIO: A CLASSIC BOOM TOWN

The hub of this vibrant development in the intendancy was Villavicencio, which exhibited all the characteristics of a classic boomtown. In an article published in *Eco de Oriente* on July 27, 1941, Dieres Monplaisir extolled the attractions of the city, which seemed to him all the more impressive since shortages caused by World War II were weighing heavily on towns in the Colombian interior. He wrote that on the eve of its one hundredth anniversary, Villavicencio was

> a city of 8,000 people who have at their service twenty-nine *almacenes* selling hardware, drugs, books, food, clothes, dry goods, automobiles, construction materials, etc.; ninety-three grain and food *tiendas*; three butcher shops, six drugstores; eleven cafés, and twenty cantinas; eight tailor shops not counting Singer and Pfaff machines . . . thirty-five hotels and pensions . . . and the rice and cattle that are exported, the beer that is sold, and the cigarettes that are smoked, even in this time that they call a crisis. These are not the signs of a stagnant town.[35]

In 1942 to mark Villavicencio's centennial, Padre Mauricio published a book entitled, *Lo que nos contó el abuelito: El centenario de Villavicencio, 1842–1942*, which combined a history of the city from its founding with a detailed enumeration of its contemporary attributes.[36] The town's five-day centenary celebration itself was a joyous affair, which climaxed on December 22, 1942, when ten thousand spectators witnessed the crowning of the centennial queen, Margola Burgos, and applauded a "beautiful oration" by the Metense poet, Eduardo Carranza.[37]

Visitors also noted Villavicencio's vitality. Nancy Bell Bates wrote that it was not a "typical" Colombian town, nor even a typical Llanero town, for since the opening of the road and the arrival of airplanes, "people and things from almost everywhere have poured in":

> The planes have been by far the most important factor in opening up the Llanos for they have made accessible in a few hours the remote towns that used to lie thirty or more days away by horse. The possibility of oil too has had a lot to do with the increased activity, for the great companies are centers of employment and stimulators of business wherever they go. Meantime, the rising demand for meat and rice keeps the old industries going too . . .
>
> We have often sat at the top of a rise gazing over the windswept grass and dreamed great dreams of the future of this land. So it is no wonder that Villavicencio reminds us a lot of the boomtowns one reads about in the old Western stories. Building is going on at a great rate but not fast enough to supply the demand; horses and cattle fill the streets at fair time, and bars do about the best business of all. As the main gateway to the vast and as yet undeveloped regions of the Llanos, Villavicencio also has perhaps a great future ahead of it.[38]

For Nancy Bell Bates, Villavicencio was a "gateway," but for Liberal journalist Antonio Bruges Carmona, it resembled the port city of a foreign country, for on its streets *serranos*, or people from the highlands, mingled with those coming from the Llanos. In an editorial published in *El Tiempo* on April 16, 1947, he explained:

> Like a port on the Mediterranean, Villavicencio gives shelter to thousands of people who arrive from all parts and go out [to the Llanos] to look for the fabled Golden Fleece. [The city is] a place of commercial transactions where negotiations are carried on about cattle and salt, rice and rubber, cord and fish, land and pasture, coffee and panela—there are entire blocks packed with bars and cafés filled with the noise of *electrolas* that drown out the sound of dice on metallic tables. At every hour through the streets moves a torrent of humanity who travels on roads made by the oil companies also going out toward the Llanos in search of the Golden Fleece that is black in color and liquid in form. Nobody comes back because all are trapped by the magic of the Llanos with its great rivers and its complete liberty . . . Villavicencio is end and beginning; it is everything of today and nothing of yesterday, and a little of tomorrow. It is definitely a true port.[39]

SUMMARY

Sixteen years of Liberal rule produced striking changes within the Intendancy of Meta and its capital, Villavicencio. The highway connecting Bogotá with Villavicencio was a busy artery for commerce, travelers, tourists, and migrants. New towns had been founded at Puerto López and Puerto Carreño. The number of cattle grazing on Meta pastures had multiplied thanks to improved ranching techniques. Some 354 people, many of them colonos, had successfully acquired legal title to 49,296 hectares of land, and in addition to beef cattle, Meta was now supplying the highlands with large shipments of rice, plátanos, yuca, and corn. Liquor factories in Villavicencio were generating a new source of revenue while international oil companies were searching for exploitable petroleum deposits. Regularly scheduled air flights and wireless telegraph linked the Llanos with the interior. The development of a yellow fever vaccine promised some control over the new strain of the disease that had surfaced in Meta in 1934. Sewers and aqueducts had been built in Villavicencio; the hospital had been expanded and more schools were functioning. A flood of immigrants transformed Villavicencio into the largest city in the Llanos, and population growth in Meta was second only to that in Chocó among the ten national territories.

In 1947 Villavicencio seemed poised to lead the Llanos into fulfilling their destiny as "the Future of Colombia." Unfortunately, after the assassination of Jorge Eliécer Gaitán on April 9, 1948, an undeclared civil war known as "La Violencia" engulfed the plains, threatening to destroy the social and economic progress that the city had so painstakingly achieved.

NOTES

1. Jorge P. Osterling, *Democracy in Colombia: Clientelist Politics and Guerrilla Warfare* (New Brunswick, N.J.: Transaction, 1989), 82.

2. *Memoria del Ministerio de Hacienda y Fomento*, 1869–70, 53.

3. Eduardo Zuleta Angel, *El president López* (Medellín: Ediciones Albon, 1966), 153. López Pumarejo eventually bought a ranch in Meta and built a large house on it, which he called Potosí, where he liked to entertain friends. His son Pedro managed the estate, but the profits were not large, and in the end, because it could only be reached conveniently by airplane, the President did not spend much time there. Nevertheless, his attachment to Meta was genuine, and as the region flourished under his special protection, he became a kind of semi-god to the inhabitants, who bestowed on him the title "Redescubridor del Llano" (Rediscoverer of the Llanos.) See Flórez, *Conozcamos*, 2: 128.

4. *El Tiempo*, November 23, 1936; *Eco de Oriente*, November 29, 1936.

5. *El Tiempo*, August 13,14, 1937; *Eco de Oriente*, August 15, 1937.

6. *Eco de Oriente*, February 23, 1936.

7. *El Tiempo*, February 25, 1936.

8. Baquero, *Departamento del Meta*, 93.

9. *Informe*, Departamento de Intendencias y Comisarías (hereafter cited as DIC) in MMG, 1933, 30; *Informe*, DIC in MMG, 1937, 52.

10. Joelle Diot, "Baldíos, 1931–1971: Legislación y adjudicaciones," *Boletín Mensual de Estadística* (DANE), No. 296 (March 1976), 104; Reinaldo Barbosa Estera, "Llanero conflicto y sabana: historias presentes," in *Los Llanos: Una historia sin fronteras* (Bogotá: Academia de Historia del Meta, 1988), 354–55.

11. Espinel Riveros, *Villavicencio*, 128.

12. *Informe*, DIC, in MMG, 1935; *Eco de Oriente*, February 6, 1938.

13. Raymond Crist and Charles M. Nissly, *East from the Andes* (Gainesville: University of Florida Press, 1973), 45.

14. Ojeda Ojeda, *Villavicencio*, 238.

15. *Informe*, Intendant of Meta, in MMG, 1932, Anexos 2: 115; *Informe*, Intendant of Meta in MMG, 1933; *Anexos*, 2: 99.

16. *Informe*, DIC, in MMG, 1935, 31; *Informe*, Intendant of Meta in MMG, 1937, 49; *Eco de Oriente*, April 24, 1938.

17. Health officials had been aware of the role of the *Aedes* mosquito since the turn of the century. It was essentially a domestic insect that appeared around human habitations, and they sought to control it by destroying its larvae, which developed in pools of standing water.

18. Augusto Gast Galvis, *Historia de la fiebre amarilla en Colombia* (Bogotá: Ministerio de Salud, 1982), 56–57; *Semana* 12, no. 281 (March 8, 1952); 25; Kathleen Romoli, *Colombia: Gateway to South America* (Garden City, N.Y.: Doubleday, Doran, 1941), 167.

19. Nancy Bell Bates, *East of the Andes and West of Nowhere* (New York: Charles Scribner's Sons, 1947), 99–111.

20. *Informe*, DIC, in MMG, 1938.

21. Dieres Monplaisir, *Lo que nos contó el abuelito*, 42–43.

22. *Informe*, DIC, in MMG, 1939, 301.

23. José Bonnet brought the first purebred Brahman cattle into Meta in the 1890s, transporting them down the Orinoco from the island of Trinidad in his steamboat, *El Libertador*; Flórez, *Conozcamos*, 1: 48.

24. *Informe*, DIC, in MMG, 1938, 127; Dieter Brunnschweiler, *The Llanos Frontier in Colombia: Environment and Changing Land Use in Meta* (East Lansing: Michigan State University, 1972), 44.

25. In 1938, for example, the intendancy exported 30,415 cattle valued at 1,9992,965 pesos and 1,580 hides valued at COL$44,470.50. See *Informe*, Departament de Territorios Nacionales (hereafter cited as DTN), in MMG, 1939, 300.

26. Romoli, *Colombia*, 166. It was estimated that an animal weighting 400 kilos lost as much as 189 kilos during the drive up the mountain. See *Semana* 5, no. 93 (July 31, 1948): 2.

27. *Semana* 5, no. 111 (December 4, 1948): 12.

28. Brunnschweiler, *The Llanos Frontier*, 51.

29. *Informe*, DTN, in MMG, 1939, 300.

30. Ossa Varela, *Geografía*, 101; *Informe*, DTN, in MMG, 1940, 128.

31. *Informe*, DTN, in MMG, 1944, 257, 290–91. The Intendancy also received a subsidy of COL$222,540 from the national government, increasing the total funding for that year to COL$767,593.

32. Bates, *East of the Andes*, 183.

33. Ernesto Camacho Leyva, *La policía en los territorios nacionales* (Bogotá: Editorial ABC, 1947), 243.

34. Diot, "Baldios," 104; *El Liberal*, May 12, 1949; *Anales de Congreso*, no. 19 (Nov. 26, 1951).

35. *Eco de Oriente*, July 27, 1941, 4.

36. Dieres Monplaisir included many amusing anecdotes in *Lo que nos contó*. For example, he wrote that in 1931 the first automobile arrived in Villavicencio, having been disassembled in Bogotá and carried over the Cordillera in pieces on mule back. Just outside the town at a place called La Grama, mechanics reassembled the car and drove it the last mile or so into the central plaza, where the locals greeted its appearance with shouts and music. Each paid a fee of five centavos for the chance to drive the car around the plaza, and they took turns driving it in this fashion until they had exhausted its supply of gasoline (98). Dieres Monplaisir, whose life spanned nearly half a century of Villavicencio's history, died of a long disease in September 1947 and was buried in Villavicencio's Central Cemetery. As Garavito Jimenez writes, "The Lord saved him from knowing and suffering the terrible years of the Violencia (1948–1954)." See his *Historia de la Iglesia*, 30.

37. *El Tiempo*, December 24, 1942.

38. Bates, *East of the Andes*, 179–80.

39. *El Tiempo*, April 16, 1947.

7

La Violencia and Its Impact on Villavicencio, 1947–1953

There is general agreement among scholars that the era of La Violencia—the undeclared civil war that lasted from 1946 to 1964—was a major turning point in Colombian history.[1] Because a large part of the early phases of the fighting took place in the Llanos, the conflict had perhaps an even greater impact on the development of Villavicencio than the rest of the country. With the assassination of Jorge Eliécer Gaitán on April 9, 1948, the town was plunged into a bloody struggle that would traumatize its inhabitants for five years or until July 1953 when the principal Liberal guerrilla chieftains accepted an amnesty offered by General Gustavo Rojas Pinilla and turned in their weapons.

Before 1946 Villavicencio was a small, rural town largely inhabited by a mixture of colonos who had come from the interior of the country and people born in the plains. After 1953 it became a magnet for displaced immigrants from nearly every department in Colombia, and with the founding of new commercial and industrial companies, it experienced economic, social, and cultural growth that transformed the "Llano into a true emporium of wealth."[2] After a brief review of the key phases of the Violencia at the national level, this chapter will investigate the specific causes of the struggle in Villavicencio, the key events that affected the town, and the result of the Rojas Pinilla pacification. It concludes with an assessment of the overall impact of the era.

KEY PHASES OF LA VIOLENCIA

Historians usually associate the beginning of La Violencia, which began as a bitter struggle between the Liberal and Conservative parties, with the election to the presidency of Conservative Mariano Ospina Pérez, an event which ended sixteen years of Liberal rule at the national level. Although Ospina Pérez invited six Liberals into his cabinet, violence broke out in several departments as Conservatives, urged on by the supreme chief of the party, Laureano Gómez, and the Catholic Church, attempted to regain political control by attacking and persecuting Liberals. To restore order Ospina Pérez organized a new security force, known as the *chulavitas*, which soon became an extension of the Conservative party and an added instrument of terror against the Liberals. The assassination of populist Liberal leader Gaitán on the streets of Bogotá on April 9, 1948, precipitated unprecedented mob violence in the capital (known as the Bogotazo) and in other cities throughout the country. After the urban violence was over, the "rural aspect of this nightmare of twentieth-century Colombian history continued."[3] Tension heightened on November 9, 1949, when Ospina Pérez closed congress, decreed a state of siege, limited civil liberties, and assumed discretionary powers. This unprecedented move was followed in 1950 by the election of Gómez in a contest boycotted by the Liberals.

During the next three years, Gómez and his surrogate, Roberto Urdaneta Arbeláez, unsuccessfully attempted to turn back the clock on the Liberal reforms and "restore order through the principle of centralized, vertical and hierarchical authority."[4] Although the national economy steadily improved, wages lagged behind prices; the government forcibly broke up strikes, and for laborers it was the worst of times. In rural areas, the Violencia gained in intensity. Expanding into new regions (eventually all of Colombia except the Caribbean area was affected), it increasingly assumed the nature of a class struggle as peasants resisted the efforts of landowners and their hired thugs to eject them from their parcels, and Communist Party activists began organizing strongholds of self-defense among uprooted peasants. The period between 1949 and 1953 saw a rise of resistance in guerrilla zones inhabited by peasants and other fugitives from regions marked by anarchy or terror, many of which were based in the Llanos. As Robert Dix points out, "On the whole, the guerrilla bands were spontaneous in origin, restricted in their range of operation, and limited in their goals—which were often those of self-defense or revenge against local political enemies or local officials."[5]

The inability of the Gómez-Urdaneta dictatorship to defeat the guerrilla movements and restore peace contributed to the weakening of its authority. On June 13, 1953, General Rojas Pinilla seized the presidency supported by the armed forces and representatives of both parties. Rojas Pinilla moved quickly to proclaim an unconditional amnesty to all guerrillas who would agree to return to civilian life. Several thousands accepted this peace initiative. They surrendered their weapons and went back to their old homes, but a few refused to give up, continuing sporadic resistance into the mid-1960s.

Rojas Pinilla's failure to eliminate the violence completely contributed to his overthrow in May 1957 when the leaders of the Conservative and Liberal parties resolved to work together to scuttle the dictatorship and to share power peacefully thereafter in an arrangement that came to be known as the National Front.[6] Although violence would continue, the era between 1946 and 1953 affected the nation in many ways, most obviously by the deaths of two hundred thousand people, the sharp increase in urban populations as peasants fled either willingly or involuntarily to the cities to seek security, and the continued willingness by some guerrilla leaders to resort to violence to challenge rule by the National Front.

CAUSES OF THE VIOLENCIA IN VILLAVICENCIO AND META

There are several reasons that help to explain why an important theater of La Violencia was centered in the Llanos. First, one must point to the inadequacies of the Revolución en Marcha that under Alfonso López Pumarejo had promised so much for the plains people but by the 1940s appeared to have achieved little fundamental change. There is no question that the opening of the Bogotá-Villavicencio highway had improved trade and the general economy or that there were more schools, hospitals, and better communication with the interior. Nevertheless, despite the reforms of 1936, few colonos had been able to gain title to their lands. The vast majority of the vaqueros and peons remained at the mercy of absentee landlords and unscrupulous mayordomos. Cattle rustling and banditry continued to be persistent problems. The annual winter rains that precipitated landslides along the cordillera regularly shut down electricity and telephone service in Villavicencio, San Martín, and Acacías, but outside these towns, such amenities were unavailable at any time. Government services simply did not penetrate into the more remote rural areas. As Mariano Enciso A. of San Martín complained to *El Tiempo* on November 3, 1946, "We are alone and very abandoned: our only hope lies in our repeated petitions to the national government asking for roads, bridges, schools, teachers, Caja Agraria, social assistance, and cheap credit, and this is just, since progress does not come from the Llanos to Bogotá, but from Bogotá to the Llanos."[7]

Second, during the 1940s the cost of living skyrocketed in Villavicencio. Speculation raised prices of even such locally grown food as plátanos to unacceptably high levels, and food shortages were common when landslides interrupted traffic on the highway to Bogotá. On August 24, 1947, Meta authorities vowed that "the Llano and municipios of eastern Cundinamarca will not cease their campaign until the government definitely begins to pave the highway and build bridges over the caños in the Llanos," but their demands that the national government improve the road to protect commerce along the most vital artery to the eastern frontier brought no response.[8]

Third, because of their proximity to Bogotá, the elite in Villavicencio were much more attuned to national developments than were their counterparts in the more distant Llanos intendancies of Casanare, Arauca, or the comisaría of Vichada. Settled primarily by immigrants coming from the Cundinamarcan highlands, the population of Meta by the 1940s was more or less equally divided between the Conservative and Liberal parties. For example, in the presidential elections of May 5, 1946, Ospina Pérez won the intendancy with 4,246 votes based on a majority in the towns of Villavicencio, Restrepo, Acacías, and El Calvario, while Gabriel Turbay triumphed in San Martín, Cumaral, and Uribe; but Ospina Pérez's victory would have been less definitive if Liberals in Villavicencio had not split their votes between two candidates—casting 808 votes for Turbay and 1,504 votes for Gaitán. In fact, the combined votes for the two Liberal candidates in all the Llanos towns was 3,835, revealing that at best Ospina Pérez's victory was marginal.[9]

The congressional vote on March 18, 1947, showed a similar division of party affiliations. In the intendancy as a whole the Conservative slate received 4,222 votes while Liberals split their votes between representatives supporting Eduardo Santos (1,565) and those supporting Gaitán (2,294), for a combined Liberal vote of 3,859. Conservatives predominated once again in Villavicencio, gaining 2,025 votes, but the Liberals were closely behind with 638 votes for the Santistas and 1,299 for the Gaitanistas for a total of 1,937.[10]

As Tomás Ojeda Ojeda points out, "Villavicencio was characterized by a local government controlled by a small directing class."[11] The fact that neither Liberals nor Conservatives held a commanding majority heightened tensions among this elite, especially in 1946 when President Ospina Pérez chose a Conservative lawyer from Boyacá to head the intendancy. From the moment of his arrival in Villavicencio on September 16, 1946, Lisimaco Cárdenas Ojeda was resented as an outsider, and his attempt to rally support from other *boycense* residents alienated the local Conservative leader, Dr. Jorge Sabogal, as well as the Liberals, who had a majority on the municipal council. Widespread criticism of Cárdenas Ojeda convinced Ospina Pérez to replace him with another Conservative, Manuel Castellanos, who held the post until November 1947 when he too was succeeded by a local Conservative, Ricardo Julio Rengifo.

Castellanos was more popular than his predecessor, but his appointment failed to defuse the tension caused by Cárdenas Ojeda's systematic removal of Liberal officeholders during his five-month tenure. In December he fired the Liberal collector of intendancy taxes, Tobías García Espinel, and appointed in his place Daniel Rojas, the publisher of *Eco de Oriente*—the voice of the Catholic Church and of dissident Conservatives. Two Liberal teachers also lost their positions thanks to Cárdenas Ojeda, and a few weeks later he "practically liquidated Liberalism" in Restrepo by appointing Conservatives Eduardo Cediel and Baldomero García as territorial judge and municipal collector of taxes, respectively.[12] Cárdenas Ojeda's actions mirrored those of Conservative officials in Boyacá, Cundinamarca, and Tolima, who were determined to create a strong base for their party, and as in those departments, they stirred up Liberal animosities and created a climate of insecurity.

Although congressional elections were conducted peacefully in March 1946, the balloting for municipal offices in the intendancy on October 5 was a different story. The announced results gave 4,046 votes to the Liberals and 3,702 to the Conservatives. Liberals won in Villavicencio, casting 2,846 votes for their candidates as opposed to the 2,029 garnered by the Conservatives. Once the ballots had been counted, the authorities permitted bars to reopen, and the Liberals began to celebrate their victory. Claiming electoral fraud, the Conservatives started a countermanifestation, and the ensuing melee left four Liberals and two Conservatives wounded; one of whom later died. Intendant Castellanos reported that he had the situation under control within fifteen minutes, but the Conservatives viewed the incident in a different light.[13] They claimed that Liberal mobs had brutally attacked them on election day, and in a telegram to the national party director in Bogotá, Jorge Sabogal declared that they had lost the election because of interference by the intendant and because the army and police had prevented people from freely exercising their votes.[14]

A final factor contributing to unrest in Villavicencio was the politicization of the police. On September 16, 1947, one month before the army opened La Vanguardia airfield at Apiay, the Conservative mayor of Villavicencio, Eliécer Calderón Pardo, fired the Liberal police inspector, claiming that he was revalidating Liberal *cédulas*. The next day Commandant Quintana of the national police discovered one of his officers, Guillermo Lombana, drinking beer at a Liberal bazaar and arrested him for fraternizing with Liberals. Then on September 18 as Lombana was preparing to make a statement to the municipal police inspector about the incident, Quintana murdered him by shooting him five times in the back. A correspondent to *El Tiempo* reported that Intendant Castellanos immediately declared Quintana *incommunicado* and that other Liberal policemen were saying publicly that they "would kill their Conservative officers, if the fact of being a Liberal was sufficient motive to place their lives in danger."[15]

The Liberals do not seem to have raised serious objections to the appointment of Rengifo as intendant after Castellanos resigned the following month. Rengifo was a prominent local Conservative who had lived in Meta for many years and had worked for one of the petroleum companies. President Ospina Pérez accompanied him when he traveled from Bogotá to Villavicencio on January 10, 1948, to take up his official duties, but three months later, the uneasy peace that reigned in the city was irrevocably broken.[16]

VILLAVICENCIO AND LA VIOLENCIA: THE ASSASSINATION OF GAITÁN

The unfulfilled promises of La Revolución en Marcha, widespread, uncontrolled banditry on the plains, the high cost of living, and the sometimes violent political squabbling between the nearly evenly divided Liberals and Conservatives in Villavicencio created a fertile seedbed for the upcoming Violencia, but probably no one could have predicted the ferocity of the riot that occurred on April 9, 1948, when news reached the town that Gaitán had been assassinated. When radio stations began reporting the event about 1:30 PM, the situation in Villavicencio became explosive. Conservatives rejoiced, as Liberals were filled with indignation, hatred, and sadness. To avoid a confrontation, the authorities turned off the electric current, but this action only inflamed the Gaitanistas. They joined a large, armed crowd outside the electrical generator and forced the restoration of power while shouting, "*Viva el partido liberal y abajo los godos.*" (Viva the Liberal Party and down with the Conservatives).[17] Despite calls for calm from the Liberal director, Dr. Jesús Arango, the mob then surrounded the municipal building demanding the resignation of the mayor. When the mayor appeared on the balcony, he tried to shoot his gun over the heads of the people but somehow managed to kill a Liberal named Marco Pardo. The mob, now thoroughly enraged, wanted to set fire to the building, but their leaders dissuaded them, so they stormed instead the offices of *Eco de Oriente*. Smashing the doors open, they seized copies of the latest issue of the paper and burned them in the plaza. The crowd also demanded the resignation of Rengifo, but he held firm. Those not involved in the riot shuttered their businesses and took refuge in their homes. By the end of the day, the city was calm, but three people had died—Pardo and two policemen.[18] Throughout the night, the Villavicences were filled with a fear that grew as they learned more about the chaos occurring in Bogotá.

The following day, clothing, watches, hardware, and other articles looted from stores destroyed by the mob on Carrera 7 in Bogotá and transported down the highway between the two cities, were on sale in Villavicencio at bargain prices.[19] City authorities used the police to maintain order and to stamp out any Liberal uprising. Terror reigned over the inhabitants, as the officials launched an implacable persecution against the Liberals (derisively known as *cachiporros*) whose houses were marked at night as a sign of a death sentence. "Many died of crimes that occurred in their own homes; others were killed in the streets, which were bathed in blood; others by night were obliged to climb into buses that took them to the Guatiquía or Guayuriba River. There the assailants murdered them and threw their bodies into the river."[20]

The reaction in Puerto López was even more violent and perhaps more significant. On learning of Gaitán's death, Eliseo Velásquez led a group of Liberal guerrillas into the town, where they staged a mini-coup, shooting ten policemen and forcing a change in municipal authorities. A native of Líbano, Tolima, Velásquez was a member of a staunchly Liberal family who operated a small sawmill. After Conservatives killed his father in 1946, Velásquez joined the national police and rose to the rank of sergeant. He was taken into custody after he avenged the death of his father by murdering three Conservatives whom he believed to be the killers, but with the aid of Jorge Gaitán, he managed to mount a successful legal defense and recover his freedom.

Velásquez went out to the Llanos in early 1948 and soon emerged as a leader of the disaffected Liberals. The April 9 attack on Puerto López proved to be a turning point in his career. Unprepared to hold the city, he withdrew with his men, but in the words of Russell Ramsey, he had "crossed over the line of no return. Velásquez was now the hard-core revolutionary who could kill and torture, and also inspire romantic legends among the country folk."[21] News of his attack heartened Liberals fleeing towns in Tolima, Cundinamarca, and Boyacá.[22] Regarding Velásquez as the chief of the nascent guerrilla movement, they took the roads to Meta and Casanare to join him, setting the stage for the Liberal insurgency that within a few months would engulf the Llanos.

On March 17, 1949, Ospina Pérez assigned an army company to Villavicencio where persecution of Liberals had continued unabated. The troops found the town in ruins and forty people dead. Four days later Velasquez's guerrillas attacked from the south and on April 29 they went on to attack Nunchía in Casanare. These surprise attacks were mounted, with the tacit approval of the Liberals in Bogotá, to show the power of the guerrillas and to get new weapons. As the tenacity and cruelty of Velásquez increased the fame of the guerrillas, some Liberals considered them authentic heroes of the party while Conservatives dismissed them as *bandoleros*, *chusma*, and *pistoleros* contracted by their rivals.[23]

At the same time the army fought back, forcing many citizens of Villavicencio to flee their homes to avoid getting killed. The townspeople were helpless victims. When they asked the army officers for safe conduct to leave the town, their requests were denied on the basis that they were bandits, and if they fled without such a document, they were certain to lose their cattle, crops, and land. The guerrillas also intimidated them, warning individuals believed to support the government that they would be killed if they did not leave the city.

OSPINA PÉREZ'S COUP

Throughout 1949 national events continued to have a direct impact on Villavicencio. In Bogotá Liberal congressmen blamed President Mariano Ospina Pérez for the continuing partisan civil warfare. During the regular legislative session, they tried to strip him of much of his power and voted to advance the upcoming presidential election from June 1950 to November 27, 1949. The Conservative candidate apparent, Laureano Gómez, returned to Colombia in July after a thirteen-month stay in Spain and immediately rallied far-right Conservatives with inflammatory speeches stressing that Colombia was being subverted by international communism with Liberal support. Fearing that a victory by the fanatical Gómez on November 27 would fan the already atrocious violence occurring throughout the country, the National Liberal Directorate called for a boycott of the election and began formulating a scheme to impeach Ospina Pérez. Before they could act, however, the president closed congress on November 9 and placed the nation under a state of siege.[24] The Liberal Directorate countered by deciding to support a military coup d'etat that would coincide with the Conservative Party's unilateral election of Gómez as president. Informed of the decision by Hernán Durán Dusan, who served as a Liberal liaison with the guerrillas, Captain Alfredo Silva, a Liberal sympathizer, seized control of the small airbase in Apiay southeast of Villavicencio, and on November 25 marched into the city, unaware that the Liberal Directorate had already scrapped their coup plot in favor of promoting a general strike.[25]

Silva, assisted by two young lieutenants in command of rebel forces, seized control of the commercial center of Villavicencio by shooting three policemen but without committing any other act of violence. On the same night Velásquez led a guerrilla band to Puerto López, but found the town too well guarded to risk an attack. Marcelino Beltrán, a colleague of Captain Silva, took the town of Cumaral northeast of Villavicencio, leaving three policemen and a Conservative dead. On November 16 Captain Silva traveled to Cumaral, where rebels continued fighting Conservatives, and attempted to burn voter registration rolls. Because the nearly simultaneous seizure of these three towns created the impression that there was an organized revolt in the Llanos based in Villavicencio, the government quickly dispatched more soldiers and police to put it down. Warned that an army battalion commanded by Colonel Ezequiel Palacios had arrived in Villavicencio and had occupied the city without a shot, Captain Silva returned to Apiay where he was arrested by the army, while many of his associates fled to the east to organize new guerrilla bands.[26]

GÓMEZ-URDANETA PRESIDENCY, 1949–1953

News of the election of Gómez to the presidency on November 27, 1949, was received in Villavicencio and the surrounding Llanos with heightened fear and scorn. In response, additional armed guerrilla groups organized to develop a more effective resistance to the national government. According to sociologists Germán Gúzman Campos, Orlando Fals Borda, and Eduardo Umana Luna, who compiled one of the first books that analyzed La Violencia, there were nineteen such groups in the Llanos who worked within well-defined regions. It is interesting to note that most of the leaders were from the middle class, and only one of them, Guadalupe Salcedo, was native to the Llanos. By contrast, their followers were vaqueros and dispossessed colonos—campesinos pressured by the guerrillas to join in the resistance.

Six of the guerrilla chiefs were especially influential: the aforementioned Velásquez, who, assisted by Marco Tulio Rey, continued to control the region between Guanapalo and Ariporo; Eduardo Franco Isaza, born in Sogamoso into a landowning family, who made his headquarters in Yopal, Casanare; Tulio Bautista, originally from Agua Clara, Boyacá, who headed up a band of four brothers (Pablo, Manuel, Roberto, and Rubén) that dominated the region between the Cordillera and the Cusiana and Upía rivers; Dumar Aljure, born in Giradot, who deserted the army to join the guerrillas in Casanare in 1950; and Guadalupe Salcedo, who was born in Tame, Arauca, and controlled the region between Puerto López and Arauca. These leaders adopted contrasting strategies. At one extreme were Velásquez and Rey who unleashed brutal operations to do as much damage as possible. At the other, was Eduardo Franco, who did not reject violence, but worked with other leaders for a positive program of social action.[27]

By the beginning of 1950, organized guerrilla bands in the Llanos included some two thousand five hundred combatants who had many sympathizers living in Villavicencio and the surrounding region. They operated a radio transmitter and broadcast messages that called for the defeat of the government from a station known as "The Voice of Liberty, Free Radio of Colombia." They had the backing as well of the National Liberal Directorate, men who did not sanction the formation of the guerrillas, but reasoned that as the bands existed, they could be used either to pressure the government or create conditions for a favorable military coup. According to Paul Oquist, the guerrillas at times accepted the National Liberal Directorate as their supreme mentor. On other occasions they considered the group to be made up of hypocrites "content with newspaper polemics while peasants were slaughtered by the police and the army."[28]

In March 1950 Minister of War Urdaneta Arbeláez, fearing that the guerrillas might be strong enough to seize Villavicencio, decided to station the Vargas Battalion in Apiay. The head of the battalion, Major Eduardo Roman Bazurto encouraged self-defense by local militias against the guerrillas and began a punitive campaign with the object of controlling all the towns or haciendas used by the rebels to get cattle, money, and recruits. War planes taking off from airports in Bogotá and Apiay indiscriminately bombed houses and ranches, often killing civilians and Indians who had no connection with the guerrillas, while partisan fighting raged on within Villavicencio. According to eyewitnesses, the most horrible vendettas occurred in the plaza Villa Julia where campesinos who came to the plaza to sell their goods were often shot on sight. Many of them disappeared or were thrown in jail, later to be decapitated and their bodies thrown in the rivers. Such atrocities turned friends against one another, their political loyalties and sensibilities whipped to a frenzy by party leaders.[29]

This untenable situation forced many to flee. Even before 1950 more than five thousand people, who had colonized land or worked in Villavicencio, had left their homes to seek safety in Bogotá, abandoning property that could never be recovered because of their lack of formal deeds.[30] To try to reduce the interparty rivalry in Villavicencio, the jefe civil y militar of Meta decided to resettle Liberal refugees in the Ariari River Valley and the Conservatives along the banks of Cubarral, giving each group safe conduct passes so they could move freely to those destinations. In La Vega and in the Alto Ariari, Liberals had organized themselves into small armed groups. They were soon joined by Héctor Morales who became the leader of the guerrilla forces there. Other guerrilla leaders who infiltrated the Ariari Region at this time included Plinio Murillo Varón (better known as Sargento Veneno) and Dumar Aljure, while Bernardo Giraldo ("El Tuerto") staked out his domain in Nunchía. Most of the later refugees who arrived in Alto Ariari were from Tolima, fleeing official repression in the town of Villarica. In the majority, members of the Liberal Party, they accepted the organization in place there. Likewise in La Vega del Ariari, a Liberal majority was consolidated under Dumar Aljure.[31]

An uneasy peace developed between the Liberals and Conservatives in the Ariari region. Geographer Raymond Crist, who visited the area in 1956, wrote that the Ariari River formed a boundary line between the two parties "who have a fierce and deadly hatred of each other." The Conservatives on the left bank of the river controlled the road, but the Liberals on the other side had the best land. These enemies, Crist observed, "are trying to cooperate enough to put a cable across the river which can be used by both factions . . . the serious workers do want peace and work, rather than fighting

and revolutionary activity. Everyone was happy that the June 1953 coup d'e-
tat of President Rojas Pinilla put an end temporarily to fratricidal strife and
opened the way for production effort again."[32]

Heavy fighting continued throughout the Llanos until the middle of 1951
when José Gnecco Mozo, a Conservative lawyer, convinced Urdaneta Arbeláez that the government would achieve more by negotiating with the
guerrillas rather than trying to crush them. Accordingly, he went to a finca
north of Villavicencio to confer with the guerrilla band of Luis Alberto Parra.
Negotiations were also made with the Bautista brothers and Franco Isaza
who gave Gnecco Mozo a list of demands. The guerrillas stipulated that
Gnecco Mozo be named governor of the Llanos "because he is the only one
in whom we may trust," that troops be withdrawn to their pre-1949 positions, and that the government begin plans to create rural credit, build roads,
and organize free public schools. Urdaneta refused to accept these demands.
"Gnecco Mozo was discredited, vilified, and even detained for a short period," and the government intensified attacks on the guerrilla units.[33]

At the end of 1951 Urdaneta once again decided to try negotiations. This
time he asked ex-President López Pumarejo to carry out discussions with
the guerrilla leaders. López Pumarejo visited the guerrillas during a general
cease-fire, but the talks were unproductive because the rebels were convinced that the government did not truly desire peace. This conclusion was
borne out when in June 1952 Urdaneta proceeded to launch the largest military operation against them.[34] Other battalions joined the brigade stationed in Villavicencio, and riverboats manned by the navy as well as airplanes to transport soldiers were added. The army was ordered to burn
hundreds of homes, villages, cemeteries, pastures, and to kill anyone who
might approach them on the road. Two columns of soldiers marched toward Villavicencio and Sogamoso, leaving in their wake lines of burning villages and waves of refugees on the road. Airplanes from Apiay bombed and
burned Puerto López, el Turpial, las Delicias, el Frío, and San Pedro de Arimena leaving their inhabitants dead or homeless. The guerrillas fought back
with equal force, and on July 12 Guadalupe Salcedo and Alberto Hoyos ambushed a ninety-six-man rifle company near Puerto López, "an action sig-
naling sharply renewed conflict throughout the region. The Puerto López
massacre intensified the debate over the role of Liberal leaders in encouraging armed resistance in the Llanos."[35]

On July 20, 1952, the guerrilla leaders met at the Hato San Jorje to discuss new strategies and ways to acquire additional weapons. Among their
decisions were resolutions to attack the Conservative post of Sevilla and to
urge the National Liberal Directory to take new action in supporting the effort for peace. To this end, they sent a letter to López Pumarejo that contained their position and petitions. López Pumarejo responded by writing
an extensive letter to ex-President Ospina Pérez that was published in *El*

Tiempo and *El Espectador* on September 4, 1952. López Pumarejo rejected the arguments for continued fighting but recognized the underlying causes for rebel actions.[36] In September, Conservative mobs went on a rampage in Bogotá, destroying the offices of Liberal newspapers, *El Tiempo* and *El Espectador*, as well as the homes of Carlos Lleras Restrepo and López Pumarejo. Greatly dispirited, the two men went into foreign exile, leaving behind a "shattered, dispirited, and leaderless Liberal Party."[37]

After this setback, the fighting in the Llanos escalated with greater intensity on both sides. The army began to shoot guerrilla prisoners and sometimes those who were merely suspects. One of the early casualties was Velásquez whom Venezuelan authorities had imprisoned at the end of 1950. On September 3, 1952, they released him from prison. He immediately rejoined the rebels only to be killed on September 9. Two days later Isaza met with the remaining guerrilla leaders and issued the "First Law of the Llanos." The text of the document, signed by Isaza as Jefe del Estado Mayor and Salcedo as Jefe Supremo, consisted of eighty articles and was the first attempt by the rebels to organize a government over the land they controlled.[38] The killing of the five Bautista brothers in skirmishes with the army in November and December of 1952 further consolidated Isaza and Salcedo's leadership of the guerrillas.

By the beginning of 1953 the rebels controlled approximately 90 percent of the Llanos. Part of the reason for their success was that the attention of the army had been diverted to rebels in other parts of the country, including those occupying the mountain passes in Chita and El Cocuy in the high Andes. But even more important, as Army Colonel Gustavo Sierra Ochoa asserted, was that the resistance movement enjoyed "the sympathy and complicity of the greatest number of the inhabitants of the region."[39] As the official government presence diminished in the Llanos, the guerrillas were able to consolidate the nature of their domination. Guerrilla legal codes, courts, and taxes replaced those of the national government, and by June 1953 when the guerrillas issued the "Second Law of the Llanos," the scope and quality of their control indicated that a protracted stalemate had been created on the Plains."[40]

VILLAVICENCIO, 1949–1953

As the largest city in the Llanos, Villavicencio suffered disproportionately from the partisan violence and the unstable conditions that caused some five thousand colonos to flee from the territory. Conservative Pedro Pablo Carmargo, who visited the city in April 1953, reported that in "Villavicencio, everyone thinks of war; the horrible murders by the bandits, the alarmist stories in the press, the rumors and gossip that circulate daily have created a curtain of smoke over everything. The National Army struggles implacably against the rebels who have extinguished that picturesque life filled with romanticism of the Llanos."[41] To make matters worse, Villavicencio continued to be vulnerable to fires. In 1951 alone, there were four fires: The last one that occurred on December 28 destroyed eleven houses and caused damage estimated at two hundred fifty thousand Colombian pesos.[42]

Other developments during the period between 1949 and 1953 were not necessarily so negative. In August 1951, for example, when the Jefe of the National Territories, Dr. Horacio Rosero Caicedo, submitted his annual report to Minister of Government Domingo Sarasty M., he reported that during the previous year, the government had established in Villavicencio a vocational school, an experimental farm, and a basketball stadium "which is one of the best in the republic." Work was continuing on the refrigeration plant whose existence would solve the problem of sanitizing meat eaten locally.[43] The Cristo Rey monument had been installed. Villavicencio had air and land communications as well as radio telephones. Rosero conceded that much of the budget of COL$2,107,789 had been spent on public order, and that the violence had greatly diminished the economic life of the intendancy. In addition, more money was needed for the anti-tuberculosis hospital and to reorganize the liquor factory. Nevertheless, he concluded that the city had remained a true social, cultural, and commercial center that continued to grow despite la Violencia.[44]

From a political standpoint, sixteen men held the post of Villavicencio's mayor between 1949 and 1953, six of whom were military officers. In 1949 the mayor's office changed hands five times, but the average for each of the other years was three incumbents.[45] The chief authority for the city and the region, however, was the jefe civil y militar, a position created on October 23, 1951. This officer's jurisdiction included Meta, Arauca, Casanare, Vichada, and Vaupés, and he was responsible for the maintenance of order, reconstruction, and the promotion of agriculture and cattle. To assist him in the latter endeavors, the government pledged one million Colombian pesos from the national treasury for reconstruction, improvement of roads, and to help build houses for those who had lost their homes unjustly.[46] The president appointed Colonel Carlos Bejarano to this position, who held the post until July 11, 1952, when he was replaced by Colonel Pedro A. Muñoz.[47]

Bejarano immediately announced that he would begin his duties on November 7. One of his first actions was to organize a committee made up of representatives of the ranchers and farmers in the Llanos charged with developing a regional plan to make optimal use of the million-peso subsidy.[48] The selection of Colonel Bejarano as jefe civil y militar brought the following warning from the news magazine *Semana*:

Simple good will is not enough. Words count for little when one tries to complete a very difficult task . . . (Bejarano) is going to have to bring about the economic and social recovery of those zones in which political violence has wrought great evils.[49]

Another important political development occurred on November 21, 1951, when Enrique González Reyes introduced in the Cámara de Representantes in Bogotá a bill to erect the National Intendancy of Meta into a department, notwithstanding the fact that it lacked the 200,000 inhabitants required by the constitution. Noting that Congress had already established a precedent in 1947 by elevating Chocó to departmental status without the necessary number of inhabitants, González pointed out that the intendancy produced more than COL$2 million of annual income. In addition, in 1950 it sent to Bogotá 561,000 bultos of plátano, 300,000 bultos of yuca, 500,000 bultos of rice, 166,500 bultos of corn, 178 hides, 40,000 head of cattle, and 10,000 pigs. He also pointed out that the possibilities of discovering petroleum in Meta were high. González closed his argument by emphasizing the need for basic government institutions in the Llanos such as Crédito Agrario, Fomento Industrial, and Crédito Territorial. With all the banditry that currently existed, the Llanos could not be tamed just by money but by good administrative organization. Regretfully, congress failed to act on this bill which was not taken up again until the creation of the National Front in 1958.[50]

González Reyes's bill suggests that despite the Violencia, Meta continued to supply cattle and agricultural products to Bogotá channeled through Villavicencio. Cattle, of course, was the main economic product of the region, and at the beginning of the rebellion, the most prosperous Liberal cattlemen were instrumental in organizing and financing the guerrillas, because they felt threatened by the arbitrary Conservative authorities. Their attitude changed, however, when the guerrillas started to encourage their workers to ask for social improvements and to demand "voluntary" contributions of cattle to support their struggle. As the government began to systematically repress people in the areas who had supported the guerrillas, the majority of Liberal cattlemen switched allegiances and began regarding the rebels as bandits. An important reason for this change was the guerrillas' decision to impose a tax on cattle leaving the plains (10 percent for Liberal cattle and 20 percent for Conservative), and the army's decisions to prohibit the sale of cattle belonging to insurgents and to impede their receipt of supplies by means of an economic blockade of the region. Throughout the conflict, the army demanded safe conduct passes for cattle leaving the area. Thus, Conservative cattle were free to pass. Liberal cattle had to be proven to belong to government collaborators, while insurgent Liberal cattle were theoretically vetoed. "In practice, the latter were bought by Conservative businessmen or by army officers at discount prices. . . . Numerous large fortunes were made by these means, including the initial wealth of some of the richest families in contemporary Villavicencio."[51] In order that the cattle could be removed from the grasslands and shipped to market, the two sides agreed to what Oquist calls a "cattle truce," but once the cattle had been taken out of the area, the army promptly renewed hostilities.

In January 1952 *Semana* reported that to stop the loss of cattle to the guerrillas, the military command was urging ranchers in Casanare and Arauca to use airplanes to fly their steers to Villavicencio rather than trying to drive them there on foot in the traditional manner. The advantages of this scheme were that the animals would lose less weight on the brief flight and would not have to spend so much time in Villavicencio recovering. On the other hand, *Semana* pointed out that the cost of transport for eight head of cattle would be one thousand one hundred Colombian pesos while the cost of driving cattle to Villavicencio from the most distant points in Casanare was approximately thirty Colombian pesos a head. Moreover, most of the brokers in Villavicencio preferred to buy reduced weight cattle and allow them to graze in local pastures to become fat enough for the trip up the mountain to Bogotá. In short, the report concluded that for cattle transport, the land system offered more advantages than air travel.[52]

The practice of issuing safe conduct passes also applied to rice farmers. In June 1952 Colonel Bejarano met with the head of the Federación Nacional de Arroceros who informed him that there could be no rice harvest unless the growers were guaranteed safety for their workers to gather the crop and the right to transport their products. Bejarano agreed that rice farmers should come to the central headquarters to get the safe conduct passes that would grant them free entrance and transit in the different areas, which until then the authorities, for reason of public order, had suspended free access to private citizens.[53]

From a social standpoint, one of the most interesting developments was that despite the fact that many people fled from Villavicencio fearing for their lives, scores of migrants, displaced from equally troubled areas in other parts of the country, began arriving in search of a better future. A census reported on May 9, 1951, set the population of the city at 17,194, down from the 24,315 recorded in 1938.[54] Ojeda Ojeda reports that between 1949 and 1951, approximately 6,000 people abandoned Villavicencio and Meta, ranking it sixth among departments with the highest rate of out migration to other places. Another 9,000 people were killed, placing Meta fifth among departments in this category. On the other hand, according to DANE (Departamento Administrativo Nacional de Estadística), between 1948 and 1965, 16,000 migrated to the city and the territory, although the majority of this influx occurred after the guerrillas laid down their arms in 1953. The new arrivals, who came from Tolima, Santander, Boyacá, Cundinamarca, Huila, Caldas, Antioquia, and El Valle, were also fleeing la Violencia, and they arrived with the hope of colonizing public lands to begin a new life for their families.[55] This influx would become only the first wave of the enormous number of people who would swell the population of Meta to 219,976 in 1993.

NOTES

1. The literature on La Violencia is immense and constantly expanding.
2. Espinel Riveros, *Villavicencio*, 200.
3. Harvey F. Kline, *Colombia: Portrait of Unity and Diversity* (Boulder, CO: Westview Press, 1983, 49.
4. Osterling, *Democracy in Colombia*, 91. After Gómez suffered a life-threatening heart attack, in October 1951, he appointed Roberto Urdaneta Arbeláez as acting president, but Gómez continued to control the government from his sickbed. See James D. Henderson, *Modernization in Colombia: The Laureano Gómez Years, 1889–1965* (Gainesville: University Press of Florida, 2001), 352.
5. Robert H. Dix, *Colombia: The Political Dimensions of Change* (New Haven: Yale University Press, 1966), 370.
6. Bushnell, *Colombia*, 222.
7. *El Tiempo*, November 3, 1946.
8. *El Tiempo*, August 24, 1947.
9. *Informe*, Jefe de la Sección Primiera (Negocios Generales), June 10, 1946 in MMG, 1946, 86–87.
10. *El Tiempo*, March 21, 1947.
11. Ojeda Ojeda, *Villavicencio*, 205.
12. *El Tiempo*, December 21, 1946.
13. *El Tiempo*, October 8, 1947.
14. *El Siglo*, October. 8, 1947; *El Tiempo*, October 9, 1947.
15. *El Tiempo*, September 16, 1947; *El Tiempo*, September 18, 1947.
16. *Semana*, 4, no. 64 (January 10, 1948), 8.
17. Ojeda Ojeda, *Villavicencio*, 182.
18. *El Liberal*, April 18, 1948; *El Liberal*, April 19, 1948.
19. Ojeda Ojeda, *Villavicencio*, 182.
20. Ojeda Ojeda, *Villavicencio*, 182. There is no good English equivalent for the derogatory term *cachiporo*, but the best my Colombian colleagues could come up with is blackjack-wielders.
21. Russell Ramsey, "The Modern Violence in Colombia, 1946–1965," (Ph.D. diss., Gainesville: University of Florida, 1970), 195. See also Germán Guzmán Campos, et al., *La Violencia en Colombia*, 2nd ed., 2 vols. (Bogotá: Tercer Mundo, 1962–1964) 1: 174–77.
22. Justo Casas Aguilar, *La Violencia en los Llanos Orientales* (Bogotá: ECOE Ediciones, 1986), 17.
23. Ojeda Ojeda, *Villavicencio*, 185.
24. Henderson, *Modernization*, 319–21.
25. Paul Oquist, *Violence, Conflict, and Politics in Colombia* (New York: Academic Press, 1980), 201.

26. Ojeda Ojeda, *Villavicencio*, 189. Silva was tried on two occasions for his actions and sentenced to five years in prison. In May 1951 he was permitted to go into exile in Guatemala. *El Siglo*, May 15, 1951.

27. Guzmán Campos, et al., *La Violencia*, 1: 62.

28. Oquist, *Violence*, 202.

29. Ojeda Ojeda, *Villavicencio*, 187.

30. Ojeda Ojeda, *Villavicencio*, 190.

31. Oscar Gonzalo Londoño D., "Aproximación a la Historia Regional del Ariari (1950–1970)," in *Los Llanos: Una historia sin fronteras* (Villavicencio: Academia de Historia del Meta, 1988), 393–95.

32. Raymond E. Crist and Ernesto Guhl, "Pioneer Settlement in Eastern Colombia," in *Annual Report of the Smithsonian* Institution (Washington, D.C.: Smithsonian, 1956), 398.

33. Oquist, *Violence*, 206.

34. Oquist, *Violence*, 206.

35. Henderson, *Modernization*, 356–67.

36. Eduardo Franco Isaza, *Los guerrillas del llanos* (Bogotá: Librería Mundial, 1959), 296–97.

37. Henderson, *Modernization*, 357.

38. For the complete text of this law see Casas Aguilar, *La Violencia*, 85–88.

39. Oquist, *Violence*, 209.

40. Oquist, *Violence*, 210; for the complete text of the Second Law of the Llanos see Casas Aquilar, *La Violencia*, 89–98.

41. *El Siglo*, April 22, 1953.

42. *El Siglo*, December 28, 1951.

43. Brunnschweiler writes that a "relatively well-equipped freezing plant [*frigorífico*] went into operation in Villavicencio in 1950, concentrating on freezing carcasses. It failed because the refrigeration trucks could not negotiate the miserable conditions of the Bogotá-Villavicencio highway and the distaste in Bogotá for chilled meat," Brunnschweiler, *The Llanos Frontier*, 51.

44. *Informe* del Jefe de TN, August 16, 1951, in *Colombia: Un año de gobierno, 1950–51* (Bogotá, 1951) 2: 368–373.

45. Espinel Riveros, *Villavicencio*, 226.

46. *El Siglo*, October 21, 1951.

47. *El Siglo*, July 11, 1952.

48. *El Siglo*, November 3, 1951; *El Siglo*, November 4, 1951.

49. *Semana*, October 27, 1951.

50. Flórez, *Conozcamos*, 1: 73–76.

51. Oquist, *Violence*, 205.

52. *Semana* XII: 272 (January 5, 1952).

53. *El Siglo*, July 1, 1952.

54. *El Siglo*, May 12, 1951; Espinel Riveros, *Villavicencio*, 191.

55. Ojeda Ojeda, *Villavicencio*, 205.

8

The Rojas Pinilla Dictatorship and the Pacification of the Llanos, 1953–1958

On June 13, 1953, Army Commander Lt. General Gustavo Rojas Pinilla, with the support of all political groups in the country except the Laureanista wing of the Conservatives, staged a military coup that ended the presidency of Laureano Gómez. Born in Tunja in 1900, Rojas Pinilla had studied engineering before entering the Colombian Military Academy. He received his commission in 1920. After an extended period of inactive duty, he advanced through army ranks, culminating his career in 1950 with his appointment as commander of the nation's military forces. Gómez had approved Rojas Pinillas's promotion but feared the general's potential power and saw that he was assigned to a variety of posts abroad. Distressed by policies adopted by his acting president, Roberto Urdaneta, Gómez resumed power on June 12, 1953, determined to remove Rojas Pinilla from his post. When he attempted to carry out this threat on June 13, however, the general announced that the armed forces had seized power. Two hours later, Rojas Pinilla, in a radio address to the nation, called for peace with the following words:

> No more blood, no more depredations in the name of any political party, no more rancors between sons of the same immortal Colombia. Peace, law, and justice for all, without distinction, but with special consideration for those less favored by fortune—for the workers, for the poor. The patria cannot live in peace while its children are hungry and naked.[1]

Rojas Pinilla immediately made good on his initiative. On June 19, he declared a general amnesty for all those involved in the violence except military deserters. "Those engaged in insurrectional activities, or other forms of violence, had merely to surrender their arms in order to return to civilian normality."[2] To publicize this policy, Rojas Pinilla sent air force planes over guerrilla strongholds in the Llanos, Antioquia, and Tolima to drop leaflets, signed by his new Minister of War General Alfredo Duarte Blum, announcing that Gómez had fallen and that the government would extend guarantees to all who wished to lay down their weapons. Many guerrilla leaders rushed to accept the amnesty. Following preliminary discussions that hammered out agreements on the terms of surrender, a flurry of meetings took place between army units and rebels during which ex-combatants relinquished their arms. "Between July and September 1953, over ten thousand guerrillas accepted the government's terms, and at year's end resettlement workers had helped nearly five thousand people displaced by the Violencia return to their homes and had aided more than thirty thousand others who had fled to Bogotá and other towns and cities."[3]

At the national level, the impact of Rojas Pinilla's dictatorship is controversial. On the one hand, given the protracted partisan fighting, members of the elite factions of both parties welcomed his military coup. In the first six months he was able to staunch the Violencia, relax press censorship, and release political prisoners. Underwritten by high prices for coffee on the international market, his government began an extensive series of public works projects and improved the system of credits for small farmers.

On the other hand, as time passed, the regime took on the character of a classic military dictatorship. The creation of the National Secretariat of Social Assistance (SENDAS) headed by Rojas Pinilla's daughter, Maria Eugenia, appeared to be patterned after the policies of Juan Perón, as did the general's talk of creating a "third force" and his call for a national convention to draft a new constitution. The lull in the Violencia proved only temporary, with renewed fighting in some parts of the country along the same lines as before, and as years passed, Rojas Pinilla appeared to be taking steps toward the establishment of a personal dictatorship with populist features. Press censorship returned, and the partisan elite became increasingly uneasy. By early 1957, the regime had alienated most organized groups in Colombia, including the Catholic Church, labor unions, and the two political parties. After a general strike, on May 10, 1957, top military officers forced Rojas Pinilla to leave the country. With the dictator's departure, those same leaders formed a caretaker military junta, which governed until civilians took over on August 7, 1958.

In the case of the Llanos in general and Villavicencio in particular, the impact of Rojas Pinilla's rule, while still controversial, reveals some genuinely positive accomplishments. As this chapter will show, for the first time since the Alfonso López Pumarejo administration of 1934–1938, the central government made the Llanos Orientales a national priority. The policies that the general undertook may not have solved the problems of the Llanos, but they won for him the region's gratitude, and they ignited the economic and social boom that would make Meta and the city of Villavicencio among the fastest growing regions in the country.

RESTORING PEACE IN THE LLANOS

Rojas Pinilla had a special interest in restoring peace to the Llanos Orientales, which he had first visited as a young engineer in 1928. As a Boyacense, he had a better understanding of the mindset of the ranchers and the Llaneros than did many other government leaders in Bogotá. While taking part in the conflict over Leticia in 1933, he studied the best routes for communication and air networks between the eastern territories and Bogotá. Returning to Colombia in September 1952, after serving a stint in Washington, D.C., Rojas was acutely aware that the conduct of the armed forces and police in fighting the Violencia was badly organized, and that the Llanos was the region most affected by the guerrillas.

In November 1952 as Commander of the Armed Forces, Rojas Pinilla traveled to Villavicencio, Arauca, and Yopal, receiving an enthusiastic reception in each town. When *El Siglo* interviewed him on his return to Bogotá, Rojas Pinilla emphasized that the ranching and agricultural industries of the region had immense potential, but by limiting the number of cattle to be exported, the policies of the jefe civil y militar were causing great anxiety among the ranchers. Moreover, the lack of roads throughout the plains only aggravated the collapse of public order. Rojas Pinilla concluded that the "antisocial movement," which began in the Llanos, had brought some positive consequences. "The Intendancy of Meta is being pushed into becoming a department. With the *bandolerismo*, its potential is stagnated, but as soon as normality is reestablished, it will resume its surprising growth."[4] As this interview reveals, Rojas Pinilla deviated from the position of former acting President Urdaneta Arbaláez by regarding the guerrillas not simply as bandoleros but as victims of government neglect and party hatreds.

It is ironic that on June 18, five days after Rojas Pinilla seized control of the country, the guerrillas in the Llanos issued a document called "The Second Law of the Llano," which recognized Salcedo as head of the guerrilla revolutionaries and Eduardo Franco as his chief of staff. In addition to organizing the rebel government and the armed forces, its 224 articles codified agrarian reform, control of cattle, and council representation, and articulated some of the ideas that were later adopted by the National Front government under Alberto Lleras Camargo.[5] Despite this manifestation of their considerable military and political strength throughout the Llanos, the guerrilleros were eager to lay down their arms. The following week, they sent a letter to President Rojas Pinilla in which they accepted the terms of the *entrega* (handover of weapons) as a basis for negotiations and, as proof of their good intentions, they ordered a cease-fire against the army in ten towns, most of which were in Boyacá and Meta.[6]

Rojas delegated his Minister of War, Duarte Blum to head up the talks with the guerrilla leaders. Once the rebels had received repeated assurances of full economic and social aid to help them return to civil life and guarantees of their personal security, they were quite willing to hand over their weapons. In July Guadalupe Salcedo delivered 6,000 men over a period of several days. Eduardo Fonseca and Eduardo Franco Isaza followed in August. Between September 9 and October 7 Dumar Aljure and nine more leaders with 1,489 men handed over their guns. Thousands of other guerrillas did not wait for the ceremonies but simply laid down their weapons and returned home.[7] The army also collected the guns of the so-called *guerrillas de paz* or irregular forces formed by citizens to help the army fight the guerrillas.[8] These entregas received extensive publicity in the Bogotá newspapers. On one such occasion Rojas Pinilla invited forty-five North American journalists to observe the ceremony, and on another he traveled with his wife, Carola, and his daughter, María Eugenia, to oversee personally the operation.[9] In October a committee headed by Maria Eugenia journeyed to Yopal and San Luis de Palenque bringing provisions, clothes, and medicine where they received a joyous welcome from the inhabitants.[10]

Paul Oquist has noted that the return to "normality" in the Llanos "occurred at an incredibly fast pace." The speed of the transformation supports the theory that the principal reason for the uprising in the Llanos was party hatreds and government repression, and that "the return of guarantees for Liberal citizens ended the basis of the conflict."[11] Although in other regions of Colombia, where there were several successful efforts to revive guerrilla fighting for social revolutionary purposes, in the Llanos the efforts of Castro-inspired Tulio Bayer and "Minuto" Colmenares failed to spark resistance, at least for the first three years. Oquist concludes that in the plains, unlike eastern Tolima or northern Boyacá, the reconstruction of state power and authority proved to be a relatively simple task and was solid.[12]

THE PROBLEMS FACING RECONSTRUCTION IN VILLAVICENCIO AND THE LLANOS

On September 19, 1953, *El Tiempo* published a solemn assessment of the impact that la Violencia had had on the Llanos in general and Villavicencio in particular:

> This four-year war that has ended has left as every war does only death, misery and ruin. Fields abandoned and destroyed by the force of nature; towns lev-

eled; people who wander through the Llanos seeking help, showing in their bodies and souls the tremendous vestiges of the struggle without truce and without hope; epidemics that destroy human beings and thousands of skeletons that testify to borders of hate and desperation.

The article went on to note that before the war, the Llanos and its cities were flourishing. Now, the haciendas were abandoned, the cattle scattered without control throughout the plains, while crops were rotting for lack of care. Public health, however, was the greatest problem. Anemia, tuberculosis, tapeworms, malnutrition, and malaria assaulted the population, most of whom had endured four years without shelter, food, salt, or drugs. In Villavicencio, "It is estimated that beside those who died directly from violence, there are 28,000 deaths due to the following causes: malaria, 12,000; anemia, 4,000; malnutrition, 3,000; tuberculosis, 4,500; amoebas, 3,000; and other, 1,500. This means that more than twenty percent of the population before 1948 was an indirect victim of the war."[13] A final problem that the *El Tiempo* article did not mention but was just as serious, was the waves of migrants who were descending on Villavicencio, a small town still reeling under the impact of four years of war without adequate sanitation, sewers, or housing.

PAZ, JUSTICIA, LIBERTAD Y ORDEN (PEACE, JUSTICE, LIBERTY AND ORDER)

Using the slogan *Paz, Justicia, Libertad y Orden*, the Rojas Pinilla government began to address these issues by establishing special agencies in Villavicencio. In October 1953 the general signed a decree creating a special tribunal known as the Corte Militar de Casación y Revisión. Located under the aegis of the Ministry of War, this court's mandate was to process thousands of criminal and civilian cases, and it was authorized to grant immunity even for men who had deserted from the army to join the guerrillas.[14]

To assist the reentry of former rebels into civilian life, the Oficina de Rehabilitación y Socorro (ORS) was set up on July 2. Headed by Drs. Bernardo Aguilero Camacho and Justiniano Ramírez Melendez, this office distributed clothes, food, and medical treatment. After Minister of Health Dr. Bernardo Henao Mejía toured the Llanos in September, plans were laid out for the opening of eight medical clinics scattered throughout the region; a fleet of three Beaver ambulance planes for the transport of the sick; a three-hundred-bed hospital to be built in Villavicencio; and a fleet of boats on the Meta charged with the job of sanitizing the area bathed by that river.[15]

Without doubt the biggest challenge was the resettlement of thousands of refugees and migrants who came to Villavicencio either to reclaim lands they had abandoned or to colonize tierras baldías. Of the former group, it is estimated that as many eight hundred parcels had been lost during the Violencia due to forced abandonment or panic sales. To provide immediate assistance, the Caja de Crédito Agrario was authorized to make up to COL$5 million available in loans to colonos, and on September 26, the commission received COL$300,000 to begin the process.[16]

In 1948 Ospina Pérez's government had created the Instituto de Parcelaciones, Colonizaciones y Defensa Forestal to support spontaneous colonization, but in 1953 Rojas issued a new decree replacing this entity with the Instituto de Colonización e Immigración. In 1956 the functions of this second institute were assigned to the Caja Agraria which opened a division of colonization and parcelations that was specifically instrumental in promoting planned colonization of the Ariari River Valley in Meta as well as projects in Caquetá, Sarare, Sumapaz, and Lebrija (Santander). The Caja Agraria, with an uncertain knowledge of the agricultural challenges posed by the Llanos, made grave mistakes in planning. It tried to create colonies that it officially organized and controlled by promising to build roads, to supply credit and technical assistance, and to provide schools. Unfortunately, such official colonies covered only small zones of the vast areas deemed tierras baldías, and because the wave of spontaneous colonization continued unabated, conflicts ensued, causing the failure of the official efforts.[17] Despite its announcement of plans for new colonies in the press and the radio, the government was unable to carry them out. As a result the refugees struck out on their own, claiming uncultivated land that they believed was tierra baldía. Conflicts occurred when hacendados continued the practice of usurping land staked out by new arrivals. As in the past, the state was too weak to enforce laws that would protect the newcomers from losing their claims.[18]

In the Ariari region under the leadership of Polinio Murillo, Liberals aided by some Communists had formed self-defense bands and agrarian syndicates to resist Conservative incursions. Although there were occasional violent encounters, the two groups managed to get along until the end of 1958. In La Vega del Ariari where some one thousand five hundred families had settled, Bernardo Giraldo challenged the leadership of Dumar Aljure, and at the end of 1956 a decision was made to divide the region into two zones. Both men followed the orders of the official Liberal Directorate. In that same year, Boca de Monte, a former military post, was converted into the municipio of Granada, which would soon become the dominant settlement, the "epicenter of all economic and political activities of the region."[19]

Colonel Luis Carlos Turriago, jefe civil y militar of Meta, estimated in 1955 that an average of one hundred families or three hundred people were arriving every month in Villavicencio. He confessed that apart from the aid provided by the intendancy to build roads and schools, there had been no official help extended to these migrants to enable them to begin new colonies.[20] Moreover, because Villavicencio was a small town, it was in no position to attend to the fundamental needs of the newcomers. Aqueducts inadequate to supply water, deficient electricity, and lack of housing were only some of the problems made worse by the city's tiny budget. Institutions such as the Banco Central Hipotecario and the Instituto de Crédito Territorial gave money for housing for the wealthy, but the popular classes remained without adequate shelter. As Tomás Ojeda Ojeda explains, highland refugees from the violence who arrived in Villavicencio "traumatized by nightmares of terror and the tragedy that accompanied even their dreams, really did not know what to do next, and neither did the government entities that were supposed to supply aid. Neither the government nor the Red Cross nor the city could find solutions to these problems."[21]

In September 1954 Rojas Pinilla embarked on a bold and controversial plan to help the thousands of uprooted, homeless, and penniless campesinos who had flocked to cities throughout Colombia by establishing a National Secretariat of Social Assistance (SENDAS), with his daughter, María Eugenia Rojas de Moreno, as head of the organization. Acting through SENDAS, the government as of January 1955 granted COL$9,000 in loans to peasants and small farmers in the Llanos, and COL$16.6 million to 11,700 people in other areas of the nation; 18,500 people were given assistance to incorporate themselves into the life of Bogotá; 500 people were repatriated after having fled to Panama, and 1,000 similarly assisted who had crossed into Venezuela. Subsidies of COL$173,000 were given to children left orphaned by the fighting; and 26,000 petitions for restoration of property lost through sale or illegal occupation were acted on.[22]

Under the aegis of SENDAS, social security was extended to peasants. There were plans to establish nursing homes for infants, and kindergartens and social welfare centers in all principal cities. After one year of service, *Semana* conceded that SENDAS "has given evident public services, with the establishment of councils in five hundred municipalities of the country, with direct aid to private beneficent organizations, with the establishment of child and infant centers, and in the reorganization of homes and the readaptation of thousands of peasant families."[23] According to María Eugenia Rojas, "SENDAS was a magnificent experience that merited being studied by groups coming from different countries," but the similarities of its organization along with many of the other initiatives begun by Rojas Pinilla, smacked too much of Peronism. Once Rojas Pinilla was overthrown in 1957, SENDAS was disbanded.[24]

The Rojas Pinilla regime was the first since that of López Pumarejo to emphasize the importance of the national territories and especially the Llanos.

On November 13, 1953, the general became the first Colombian president to visit the islands of San Andrés and Providencia. He used the occasion to declare San Andrés a free port and to order the construction of an airport that would tie it closer with the mainland. But Rojas Pinilla's primary concern was with the Llanos. During his trial by the senate in 1959, he explained that before he came to power, "without a doubt, the most convulsed area in the country was the Llanos Orientales":

> I believe that in all the departments, everyone, when he is a child, is taught that Colombia's independence is due in large part to the Llaneros. When I was in school in Boyacá, they told us that the Llanero conducted his business without need of official documents because the word of the Llanero was a public document. Personally I have always had a great respect, a great admiration for those people of the plains, and I wanted to bring peace there after June 13.[25]

In a speech delivered in Villavicencio on January 22, 1955, Rojas set forth a four-point program for the development of the Llanos. First, with Decree 112, he created the Federación Nacional de Ganaderos with the goal of strengthening the cattle industry and elevating it to be equal with coffee, already represented by the Federación Nacional de Cafeteros. Second, he announced a plan to encourage foreigners and foreign investment in the Llanos by offering one or more hectares of land in the region for each head of hybrid cattle a foreign citizen or Colombian might import. Additionally he planned to build a factory, which would use cattle byproducts to make fertilizers and articles for domestic life, and to establish slaughterhouses in the municipios to coordinate the distribution of meat. Third, he promised to develop a series of highways, which would contribute to the conversion of the intendancy of Meta into a department. These highways were from Sarare: Socha to Río Casanare; from Cusiana: Valle de Tenza to the Río Meta, and upgrades to the Bogotá-Villavicencio highway. Finally, he announced that the Ministry of Public Health was developing plans to construct health centers, housing, and facilities to supply potable water to the entire population.[26]

Rojas Pinilla's first eighteen months in office were highly successful, and the inhabitants of Meta, Casanare, and Arauca were grateful to him for bringing peace so quickly to their region. With his daughter Maria Rojas Moreno, he visited the Llanos frequently. To express their appreciation for his support, the ranchers, apparently spontaneously, presented Rojas Pinilla with three thousand head of cattle and three hatos (one each in Meta, Casanare, and Arauca), which according to ex-President López Pumarejo, who was at the ceremony, were worth one million Colombian pesos.[27] Rojas Pinilla, in consultation with his family, decided to give these hatos together with the cattle to SENDAS to benefit refugees in the Llanos and to mark the occasion he declared June 15, 1955, the "Day of the Rancher."[28]

THE DOWNFALL OF ROJAS PINILLA

Despite Rojas Pinilla's initial victories, historian David Bushnell suggests that four basic weaknesses doomed his presidency. The first was the increasingly heavy-handed nature of the regime expressed in the decline of press freedom and the use of strong-armed tactics against the opposition. The second was the hardening of opposition from the traditional political parties. Rojas Pinilla had been able to take power because, while Conservative in his leanings, he had no formal affiliation with either of the two parties. Although he granted women the right to vote, a long overdue measure, he held no elections in which they could exercise this right. His attempts to create a populist-Peronist style government disenchanted Liberals first and then the Conservatives. Third, both groups were uneasy about his socioeconomic policies and especially "his frank attempt to build up organized labor as one of the two main props of his regime, alongside the armed forces."[29]

Finally, his biggest problem turned out to be the resurgence of the Violencia, first in eastern Tolima and the Sumapaz region of Cundinamarca and later once again in the Llanos. Even in 1953 there had been guerrilla chiefs who had refused to surrender. By 1954, Rojas Pinilla, believing the Tolima resisters to be Communists, permitted the army to carry out a raid near Villarica, resulting in the deaths of several campesinos and the arrest of their leader, Isauro Yosa. The army and the national police began patrolling the region, and when a group of armed men ambushed them in late March 1955, Rojas Pinilla declared eastern Tolima a "Zone of Military Operations."[30]

In the Llanos there were no major outbreaks, but many of the former guerrillas believed that the government had broken its promise to those who had laid down their arms. For example, on June 13, 1954, the government conceded amnesty to all people accused of political crimes committed before January 1, 1954, but this amnesty was not extended to men like Dumar Aljure who had deserted from the army and fought against the armed forces. For that reason, Aljure took up his weapons once again as did Carlos Roa. In 1955 Rojas Pinilla stationed the army's VII Brigade in Villavicencio, and in April airplanes again began dropping bombs on houses and families in the Llanos.[31]

In the words of Justo Casas Aguilar, by 1956, despite government reforms, the majority of people in the Llanos were facing nearly the same problems as before: official persecution; provocation on the part of the Conservatives; lack of resources for work; isolation; lack of schools; and lack of help for small farmers—and it was these problems that provoked armed resistance once again.[32] In November of that year the ex-guerrillas presented a list of demands to Colonel Luis Turriaga that included among other points that the government stop persecuting Roa and Aljure; that it withdraw the civilian Conservative groups and especially the "pajaros"; that it provide absolute freedom for all prisoners jailed by the past regime who were residents of the Llanos; and that it comply with the promises it had made in the first days of June 13, 1953. Turriaga responded that the government was working hard to comply with these demands and denied that it had anything to do with the arrival of the pájaros. He urged the guerrillas to respect the legitimate authorities; dedicate themselves to honest work; collaborate with the armed forces to maintain peace; and reject any foreign intervention that threatened to upset public order.[33]

This dialogue proved to be unproductive. Guzmán Campos observes that January 1957 proved to be a key month for the renewal of the Violencia in the Llanos when ex-guerrillas protested an incident of army violence in El Ariari near San Martín and called for the removal of the lieutenant who was acting as mayor of that town. They also objected to the increase of cattle theft stating that "it is publicly known in Villavicencio that the stealing of cattle is supported by various officials of the army in order to obtain two ends: to get rich . . . and because they know that the increase of robbery will demoralize the revolutionary movement." Finally, on February 28, 1957, the ex-revolutionaries issued a statement expressing their solidarity with the guerrillas then active in Tolima."[34]

Rojas Pinilla's inability to end the Violencia inevitably eroded the support that he had received when he first took power."[35] As he began making preparations for a second term in office, Liberal ex-president Alberto Lleras Camargo and Laureano Gómez signed a pact in Spain to work together to overthrow the dictator and to share power peacefully thereafter. A general strike on May 6–10, 1957, won the support of most major social groups and both political parties, and "when the rest of the military high command suggested to Rojas Pinilla that he quietly withdraw for the good of the country, he made his way to exile."[36]

IMPACT ON VILLAVICENCIO

Throughout the Rojas Pinilla era, the post of jefe civil y militar, the highest administrative office in the intendancy of Meta, continued to be held by military officers. Three men served between September 1953 and November 1957: Manuel A. Iregui, Luis C. Turriago, and Enrique Villavisar. Lieutenant Jaime García Ulloa held the post of alcalde from 1954–1955. Two men served in 1956—Jorge Rincón Osorio who was succeeded by Leonardo Garavito Martínez. They were followed in 1957 by Captain Hernando Cleve and José Antonio Barrera.[37]

Before the Violencia, the intendancy had been divided into three municipios: Villavicenio (created in 1850), Restrepo (1915), and Acacías (1947). Due to the surge in colonization, six more were established between 1953 and 1958. These were, in 1955, Cumaral, Puerto López, and El Calvario; in

1956, Granada and Guamal; and in 1958, San Martín.[38] Nancy Espinel Riveros notes that these new municipios were carved out of what previously had been known as the Territory of San Martín. Because most of the newcomers settled in the Ariari region, Granada became the epicenter of colonization and violence while San Martín continued to be an enclave of traditional customs.[39]

Even after peace had been restored, it was difficult for the inhabitants of Villavicencio to leave the city. To go to another town, they had to acquire safe conduct passes because traveling without one exposed them to arrest by the army.[40] By contrast, as already mentioned, migrants from Tolima, the Santanders, and Viejo Caldas were pouring into the city. Between 1951 and 1964 Villavicencio's population grew from 17,000 to 45,000, a rate of 78.6 percent, making it the fastest growing town in Colombia. The urban area increased from 43.7 blocks in 1937 to 82.5 blocks in 1958 to 332.1 blocks in 1964.[41] Despite this growth, scrubland, forests, and farmers cultivating yuca and plátano on small plots continued to surround the city at least until 1960. Hunters could still find deer, armadillos, *lapas* (a large rodent), *pajuiles* (wild turkeys), *pavas* (pea-hens), and monkeys, although 1955 was the last year the *cajuches* or wild hogs were seen passing through the town on their way from the Guatiquía River to Calvario.[42]

Villavicencio quickly recovered its economic momentum. On June 13, 1955, the jefe civil y militar reported the intendancy's income had grown from COL$1,611.744 in the fiscal year 1952–1953 to COL$5,037,601 for the fiscal year of 1954–1955. The primary sources of revenue were taxes on tobacco, degüello, liquor, and telephone service. He added that this remarkable increase had been obtained without the imposition of new taxes.[43] The colonization of the Ariari region accounted for the increasing harvests of beans, coffee, rice, and corn. Even though the Bogotá-Villavicencio highway was still limited to one-way traffic, Villavicencio remained the main center for distribution of machinery, food, and merchandise from the highlands to the nearby Llanos towns, and it continued to supply Bogotá with agricultural products and cattle. The resumption of the annual arrival of *sacas*, or cattle driven to Villavicencio from Arauca and Casanare, brought as well an influx of the culture of the Llano Adentro. Llanero music, food, and folkways became more prevalent, challenging the Andino aspects that had dominated Villavicencio up to that time.

Industry also grew. The Bavaria Brewing Company, established in 1946, increased its capacity so that by 1961 it was turning out each month three hundred fifty thousand dozens of bottled beer to supply the market in the Llano and eastern Cundinamarca. In 1955 the Torres brothers—Guillermo and Armando—formed a liquor company that six years later produced monthly twenty thousand bottles of "Llanero" and "Ariari" aguardiante.

An article published in *Semana* on March 28, 1955, noted that Villavicencio had progressed "notoriously." The city's inhabitants could see films in four different movie theaters. The newly founded Radio Villavicencio was broadcasting autochthonous music, especially *bambucos* and *galerones*, and publication had begun of a weekly newspaper, *El Llanero*. Recommending Villavicencio as a rewarding tourist destination, the reporter mentioned such amenities as the Hotel Meta, the Hotel Casino of Villa Julia, and the country club, Club Campestre.[44]

With regard to religion, on January 29, 1953, the Gómez-Arbeláez administration had renewed the Convención Sobre Misiones, originally signed with the Vatican in 1902 and slightly modified in 1928. The 1953 agreement specifically outlawed forms of Christian activity other than Roman Catholicism in those regions designated as national territories and reaffirmed the obligation of the church not only to convert Native Americans but also to supervise public and private elementary and secondary schools in the eleven vicariatos apostólicos and seven prefecturas apostólicas already in existence. To support these activities the government pledged to contribute thirty thousand Colombian pesos annually to each of the vicariatos and prefecturas and another three hundred sixty thousand pesos for the needs of the missions.[45]

By this agreement Villavicencio continued as the seat of the Vicariato Apostólica del Meta administered by the Compañía de María. In 1939 Monseñor Francisco José Bruls had replaced José María Guiot as the vicario apostólico. During Monseñor Bruls tenure the Montfort Fathers continued to play a dominant role in the life of the community's twenty-one parishes.[46] After the old cathedral burned down in 1947, they supervised the building of a new church, and in 1955 Bruls inaugurated the Temple de la Virgen del Carmen. Three other churches existed in the city at this time: Perpetuo Socorro, la Santa María Reina, and El Divino Niño. In addition to the official schools, the Hijas de la Sabiduría administered several private ones and the Christian Brothers directed the Colegio de la Salle.[47] To respond to the booming colonization south of the city, the Monseñor Bruls assigned PP. Benedicto Villalba, Gilberto Linares, and Ignacio Días to serve the new town of Granada. By 1960, however, the needs of this large area proved beyond the capabilities of the Montfortians, and the bishop petitioned Pope Paul VI to create a new prefectura apostólica. In 1964 the Pope acceded to this request, establishing the Prefectura del Ariari and assigning its jurisdiction to the Salesians of Don Bosco.[48]

SUMMARY

By ending the guerrilla war in the Llanos, the Rojas Pinilla regime opened a new chapter in the development of Villavicencio and Meta. In his report of 1955, Colonel Turriago wrote:

Today the Intendancy enjoys a climate of prosperity and peace due to military authorities that know how to practice the postulates of Peace, Justice and Liberty. The man of violence has exchanged places with the man of peace, and little by little the bitter memories of the time of barbarity are being erased.[49]

Clearly Villavicencio had begun its dramatic expansion that would continue throughout the rest of the century, but despite Turriago's upbeat assessment, the dictator's solutions to the underlying problems of the Llanos were too little, too late, and unevenly applied. Partisan antagonisms, inadequate support of the new migrants, as well as the army's violation of its own guarantees would remain to haunt the National Front after the overthrow of Rojas Pinilla on May 10, 1957.

NOTES

1. Carlos J. Villar Borda, *Rojas Pinilla: El Presidente Libertador: Biografía* (Bogotá: Editorial Iqueima, 1953), 101.
2. Oquist, *Violence, Conflict and Politics*, 187.
3. Henderson, *Modernization*, 366–67.
4. *El Siglo*, November 14, 1952.
5. Ojeda Ojeda, *Villavicencio,*198; Guzmán Campos, *La Violencia*, II: 79–80. The complete text of this document can be found in Casas Aguilar, *La Violencia*, 89–98.
6. Russell W. Ramsey, *Guerrilleros y soldados*, 2nd ed. (Bogotá: Tercer Mundo, 2000), 223.
7. According to Ramsey, of forces estimated at twenty thousand, less than two thousand guerrillas formally surrendered, and the rest simply returned home. He could find no documents supporting the official army figure of six thousand five hundred men who voluntarily delivered their weapons (227).
8. *El Tiempo*, September 18, 1953.
9. Ramsey, *Guerrilleros*, 226; María Eugenia Rojas de Moreno, *Rojas Pinilla: Mi padre* (Santa Fe de Bogotá: Panamerican Formas e Impresos, 2000), 151–55; *Semana* (September 21, 1953) 15: 361.
10. *El Tiempo*, October 10, 1953.
11. Oquist, *Violence*, 210. A cynic might add that since the government presence had always been low in the Llanos, it was not so difficult to reestablish a semblance of authority.
12. Oquist, *Violence*, 210.
13. *El Tiempo*, September 19, 1953.
14. Ojeda Ojeda, *Villavicencio*, 199; Rojas de Moreno, *Rojas Pinilla*, 151–53.
15. *El Tiempo*, September 19, 1953.
16. *El Tiempo*, September 26, 1953.
17. Myriam Jimeno Santoyo, "Los procesos de colonización. Siglo XX," in *Nueva historia de Colombia*, ed. Alvaro Tirado Mejía, 8 vols. (Bogotá: Planeta, 1989), 2: 385.
18. Ojeda Ojeda, *Villavicencio*, 62.
19. Londono, "Aproximación," 396.

20. *Informe del Jefe Civil y Militar,* June 13, 1955, 486.

21. Ojeda Ojeda, *Villavicencio,* 63.

22. Vernon Fluharty, *Dance of the Millions: Military Rule and Social Revolution in Colombia, 1930–1956* (Pittsburgh: University of Pittsburgh Press, 1957), 250.

23. "Si Podemos," *Semana,* (February 21, 1955), p. 8, cited by Fluharty, *Dance,* 251–52.

24. Rojas de Moreno, *Rojas Pinilla,* 195.

25. Gustavo Rojas Pinilla, "Discurso, February 27, 1959," in *Rojas Pinilla ante el Senado,* ed. Gustavo Rojas Pinilla (Bogotá: Editorial Excelsior, 1959), 581.

26. Rojas Pinilla, "Discurso pronuncido el 22 de 1955 (Villavicencio) in Gustavo Rojas Pinilla, *Mensajes y Discursos* (Bogotá: Empresa Nacional de Publicaciones, 1955), 21–24.

27. Rojas Pinilla, *Rojas Pinilla ante el Senado,* 33–34.

28. Rojas Pinilla, "Palabras de Su Excelencia el 15 de Junio de 1955," in Rojas Pinilla, *Mensajes y Discursos,* 68; Rojas de Moreno, *Rojas Pinilla,* 196–201.

29. Bushnell, *Colombia,* 219.

30. Henderson, *Modernization,* 371.

31. Ojeda Ojeda, *Villavicencio,* 202.

32. Casas Aguilar, *La Violencia,* 128–130.

33. Guzmán Campos, *La Violencia,* 2: 177–79. "Pájaros" was the name given to Conservative paramilitary organizations that proliferated during the resurgence of la Violencia under Rojas Pinilla. "These groups were composed of civilian gunmen who could be called upon to act singly or in groups to help the army and police enforce their rule." See Henderson, *Modernization,* 374–75.

34. Guzmán Campos, *La Violencia,* 2: 202.

35. Bushnell, *Colombia,* 222.

36. Bushnell, *Colombia,* 222.

37. Paredes Cruz, *Departamento del Meta,* 45; Espinel Riveros, *Villavicencio,* 226.

38. Espinel Riveros, *Villavicencio,* 228.

39. Espinel Riveros, *Villavicencio,* 198.

40. Ojeda Ojeda, *Villavicencio,* 242.

41. Gloria Evelyn Martínez Salas, "Crecimiento Urbano Acelerado y Marginalidad Reciente de la Ciudad de Villavicencio," in *Por los caminos del Llano,* 2: 202–4.

42. Ojeda Ojeda, *Villavicencio,* 242–43.

43. Informe del Jefe Civil y Military, June 13, 1955, 489.

44. *Semana,* XVIII: 438 (March 28, 1955), 15.

45. For the full text of the Convención, see *Conferencias Espiscopales de Colombia, 1908–1953,* 2 vols. (Bogotá: Editorial El Catolicismo, 1956), 1: 549–55.

46. Flórez, 1: 104–5; 108.

47. Paredes Cruz, *Departamento del Meta,* 155–57.

48. Martín González Angel, *La Prefecture Apostólica del Ariari (Colombia): Estudio Histórico* (Madrid: Central Catequisita salesiana, 1977), 95.

49. *Informe del Jefe Civil y Militar,* June 1955, 485–506.

9

Villavicencio during the National Front, 1957–1974

The threat posed by Rojas Pinilla's populist leanings and his increasingly independent actions proved to be the final outrage that drove Liberal and Conservative leaders to agree to postpone (at least temporarily) the party strife that had caused so much damage to the social and economic fabric of the country to jointly attempt to oust the dictator. After meeting in Spain on July 26, 1956, Laureano Gómez and Alberto Lleras Camargo announced the Declaration of Benidorm that affirmed the principle of political cooperation. This agreement was followed in 1957 by the Pact of Sitges, which stated that whatever the results of the next four elections, power would be shared equally between the two parties, with the presidency alternating every four years. In addition, all legislative bodies would be divided equally between Liberals and Conservatives; all congressional legislation would require a two-thirds majority to take effect; a minimum of 10 percent of the national budget would be assigned to education; and women were to enjoy equal political rights.

After the forced departure of Rojas Pinilla on May 10, 1957, and a year of rule by an interim military junta, this unique arrangement, known as the Frente Nacional (National Front) took effect when Alberto Lleras Camargo, a Liberal, won the first post-Rojas Pinilla election and took power on August 7, 1958. He was succeeded by Conservative Guillermo León Valencia (1962–1966), Liberal Carlos Lleras Restrepo (1966–1970), and Conservative Misael Pastrana Borrero (1970–1974).

Numerous studies of the Frente Nacional period have concluded that the policies adopted by these four presidents met only mixed success. Certainly, on the one hand, they brought an end to partisan violence. There was significant growth in Colombia's economy, a notable improvement in public education, and some gestures made toward social reform. On the other hand, as David Bushnell points out, there was little change in overall patterns of inequality, and none of the four administrations was able to suppress a new phenomenon—leftist guerrilla insurgency.[1]

As this chapter will show, Villavicencio experienced many striking developments during this twelve-year period. In 1959 the city gained importance when Congress elevated the Intendancy of Meta to the status of a department with Villavicencio as its capital. In 1964 the Vatican established Villavicencio as a diocese and separated from it the apostolic prefecture of Ariari. There were improvements in the Bogotá-Villavicencio highway and other transportation networks. Migrants continued to stream into the territory. They staked out claims and contributed to the growing economy based on agriculture, ranching, and petroleum. With the impulse of modernization, many of the small-town aspects of Villavicencio disappeared, and life in the urban center took on new overtones. Finally, inspired by Castro's successful revolution in Cuba, violence in the Llanos reemerged in the form of Marxist guerrilla bands, while officials in Villavicencio sought to solidify its identity as the "Gateway" not only to the Llanos but also to Llanero culture.

A NEW DEPARTMENT

Efforts to transform the Intendancy of Meta into a department began in the 1940s. They gathered momentum when congress granted the Intendancy of Chocó departmental status in 1947 even though it lacked the 250,000 inhabitants required by the Constitution of 1888. (By the 1938 census, there were only 111,216 people in Chocó.) As noted in chapter 7, in November, 1951, Deputy Enrique González Reyes presented a bill to declare Meta a department, emphasizing that its annual income was four times the minimum stipulated in the constitution and that its economy was far more viable than that of Chocó. The Chamber of Deputies unanimously approved the González Reyes bill and sent it on to the senate for consideration, but it became a dead letter after Rojas Pinilla unseated President Gómez on June 13, 1953, and suspended congress.

By 1959 it was clear that a change in Meta's status was long overdue. Three days after his inauguration, President Alberto Lleras Camargo gave a speech in Villavicencio emphasizing the importance of the region despite its abandonment in the past. "No longer," he stated, "can the llanos be called a reserve for future centuries":

> Experience shows that there is a vast zone of fertile soil and abundant water where Colombians can create in a short time a much richer civilization than that which began to extend on the opposite side of the Cordillera from the

time of the Spanish arrival. Within the next half century this fortunate region will be one of the most prosperous of the Republic.[2]

On September 9, 1959, at the initiative of Representative Hernando Durán Dussán, President Lleras approved Legislative Act No. 2 modifying the constitution to allow Meta to become a department even though it lacked the requisite two hundred fifty thousand inhabitants. Durán Dussan immediately followed this action by presenting a bill on September 15 that, when signed by President Lleras on December 16, became Law 118 of 1959 "that Creates and Organizes the Department of Meta." Ernesto Jara Castro, who had been appointed Intendant of Meta on September 7, 1959, was invited to stay on as head of a transition government until the department could be formally inaugurated.

The Departamento Administrativo Nacional de Estadística (DANE), using the census of 1951, calculated the population of the Meta in 1960 at 80,790 inhabitants. The capital, Villavicencio, was estimated to have 41,910 inhabitants. The other eight municipios, all situated in the northwestern part of the new department were Acacías with 5,680 people; San Martín with 8,000; Puerto López, Granada, Restrepo, Guamal, Cumaral, and El Calvario. By 1970 the department had added nine more municipios to bring the total to eighteen. The newly created towns were Cabuyaro, Cubarral Castilla, Fuente de Oro Puerto Gaitán, Puerto Lleras, San Carlos de Guaroa, San Juan de Arama, and Vistahermosa. By 1972 DANE put the population of Meta at 322,261. Thirty-five percent, or 112,130, of these people resided in Villavicencio, making the town and the department the fastest growing region in Colombia.[3]

The formal inauguration took place on July 1, 1960, in Villavicencio and was attended by President Lleras Camargo; Minister of Government Alberto Zuleta Angel; Minister of Public Health Alfonso Ocampo Londoño as well as other dignitaries. In his speech, Lleras stressed that the department had been created under the most auspicious circumstances because it would be controlled not by one political party but by two. He urged the people of Meta to use this opportunity to move on from civil war to peace. Emphasizing the glorious past history of the Llaneros who had contributed so much to Colombia's independence, he concluded:

> My spirit is filled with faith, and I am certain that not only do we begin a new political form here, but a new existence; that we are incorporating more closely into the patria the economy, morality and political spirit that is represented by the legendary Llanura Oriental.[4]

Initially, the first governor was to be Dr. Marco Antonio Hoyos Vega, a native of Arauca, but he declined the post for personal reasons. A second nominee, Dr. Jorge E. Santos Salinas also withdrew, so that Dr. Jara Castro remained the chief administrator of the department until March 15, 1961, when he surrendered the position to Dr. Camilo Castro Chaquea, a native of San Martín and a prominent figure in cotton exports. Castro Chaquea's regime lasted less than eight months because in November 1961 he was replaced by Carlos Hugo Estrada, a native of Villavicencio and former mayor of the capital. Eight more men served as governors between 1962 and 1974.[5] All of them faced the same key tasks outlined by Hoyos Vega before he declined the governorship: the need to improve transportation, to increase electrification, to build schools, and to maintain peace throughout the territory.[6]

A NEW DIOCESE

Throughout this era the Montfortians continued to exercise considerable moral and political influence over the city. Meta's new status required a reorganization of ecclesiastical authority because as a department it could not remain a missionary territory. On February 11, 1964, the Vatican converted the apostolic vicariate of Villavicencio into the Diocese of Villavicencio and appointed Monseñor Frans Joseph Bruls Canisius of the Compañía de María as its first bishop. Bruls Canisius directed the diocese for five years. On his retirement in 1969 he was replaced by another Montfortian, Monseñor Gregorio Garavito Jiménez, who would serve as bishop until May 3, 1994. By 1976 nine secular priests had joined thirty-seven religious clerics to minister to the estimated two hundred ninety thousand Catholics living within the diocese.[7]

With Villavicencio's elevation as a diocese, the territory surrounding the rapidly expanding municipio of Granada was separated from the bishop's jurisdiction to keep its mission status. On January 16, 1964, the Vatican designated this region as the apostolic Prefectura del Ariari and assigned its rule to the Salesians. Monseñor Jesús María Coronado served as the first apostolic prefect with jurisdiction over approximately one hundred forty thousand people in the parishes of Granada, Fuente de Oro, Bajo Ariari, Vega del Ariari, Alto Ariari, and La Macarena. On September 14, 1973, P. Hector Jaramillo Duque succeeded Coronado and directed the prefecture until 1981.[8]

TRANSPORTATION

In 1960 the department had 780 kilometers of roads, but many of these were impassable during the rainy season or winter. By 1972 there were approximately 1,025 kilometers within the department including the 110-

kilometer highway linking Villavicencio to Bogotá. One of the most important initiatives during the Frente Nacional era was the proposal by the Peruvian President Belaúnde Terry in 1963 to study the feasibility of the so-called Carretera Marginal de la Selva—a 5,596-kilometer highway designed to link Santa Cruz, Bolivia, with Arauca, Colombia, by connecting disparate stretches of existing roads that followed the edge of the Cordillera Oriental. Belaúnde's plan won the support of the ministers of public works of Bolivia, Peru, Ecuador, and Colombia, but little progress was made in the next decade. A more tangible achievement was the completion in May 1964 of a bridge one thousand meters in length over the Ariari River that opened up a major colonization region to year-round motor traffic. President Guillermo Valencia inaugurated the bridge, and in his address to the First Congreso de Territorios Nacionales, he described it as a major step toward restoring tranquility in the Llanos.[9]

The Bogotá-Villavicencio highway, as the sole road linking the Llanos to the highlands, retained its position as the primary factor in the development of Villavicencio and the territory beyond it. In the early 1960s the highway was opened to two-way traffic, and by 1972, 80 percent of it had been paved. Road improvements facilitated the transport of products and materials to Villavicencio and made the huge consumer market in Bogotá even more accessible to products from the Llanos. By the 1970s, large quantities of corn, rice, African palm, cotton, plátano, yuca, and six hundred head of cattle were trucked daily from Villavicencio to Bogotá, amounting to some 20 percent of the capital's supply of these items.[10] Despite this heavy traffic, mud slides and rockfalls during periods of steady rain interrupted the free flow of travel every year. In 1973 Dieter Brunnschweiler pointed out that the "only solution—to secure a safe passage in the hazardous sections among the unconsolidated and extremely steep slopes in the lower Rio Negro valley—is an eventual transfer of the route to the opposite side of its present location." He noted that plans for such a move had been drawn up, "but as long as the road holds up, literally speaking, it would undoubtedly be considered extravagant by the national highway planning commission to build a new road where one and—compared to other trans-Andean highways—a good one, already exists."[11]

In particular, the precarious passage of the road around a ridge known as Quebradablanca was a disaster waiting to happen. After a landslide in early March 1974 had interrupted traffic and left two travelers dead, thirty thousand people staged a demonstration in Villavicencio to protest "the national government's abandonment and to demand a solution of the Quebradablanca problem." This group, which included the organization of transporters and the general citizenry, demanded that the government build a new and safer route between Bogotá and Villavicencio, and they complained that the special air service that President Pastrana Borrero had set up to help to restore communication until the road was repaired was insufficient. At the same time, local rice farmers sent the president a letter stating that approximately fifty thousand tons of cotton and rice were running the risk of rotting if transit on the road was not immediately restored.[12]

On June 15, 1974, a gigantic landslide fell on the road at Quebradablanca, virtually isolating Villavicencio and the Llanos from the Colombian highlands. The government authorized the use of two hundred cases of dynamite to clear the passageway, and the Minister of Public Works, Argelio Durán Quintero, personally supervised the operation.[13] On June 21 the road was blocked again, inspiring an editorial in *El Tiempo* that lamented the situation and pointed out that the Llanos was a region forgotten by the government. "It needs roads that can withstand the cycle of droughts and rains. . . . The Llanos are important not only for cattle but also for agriculture and especially rice. With regard to the road, it is indispensable to look for an alternative route which will avoid the frequent blockage at Quebradablanca and establish easy and permanent communication."[14] That evening heavy rains caused three new landslides to fall on Quebradablanca, interrupting traffic and stranding hundreds of vehicles and travelers waiting for the debris to be cleared. Three days later another landslide knocked out the Quebradablanca bridge and again interrupted traffic until a provisional bridge could be set up.

By this time panic was increasing both in Bogotá and Villavicencio. In the former, the delay was causing a spectacular price increase on products shipped in from the Llanos. For example, a truckload of yuca, which normally cost three hundred Colombian pesos, had risen to one thousand two Colombian pesos, but the distress in Bogotá paled when compared to the situation in Villavicencio. According to *El Tiempo* reporter Humberto Diez, if the Quebradablanca bottleneck were not resolved, "many millions of pesos worth of rice produced on 480,000 hectares would not reach the capital. Also affected would be 15,000 hectares of corn; 20,000 hectares in African palm oil; 13,000 hectares in cotton; 60,000 hectares in plátano; 20,000 hectares in yuca, and more than 600 head of cattle that were shipped daily from Villavicencio to Bogotá." Díaz concluded, "The people of the Llanos can not wait three years for a new road to be built. Because of the present emergency 20 million [Colombian] pesos daily are being lost in food which producers are forced to throw into rivers because they can't get it to the interior."[15]

The long-expected disaster finally occurred at 4:00 PM on June 28. Exacerbated by days of steady rain, an avalanche of earth fell, blocking eight hundred meters of highway at the Quebradablanca site and burying some thirty vehicles including five buses packed with passengers, fifteen trucks, a tanker truck, and a camper. Many of the bodies could not be recovered, but it was estimated that the death toll reached three hundred.[16] To deal with the aftermath of the tragedy, special air flights were scheduled to carry food and necessities into Meta and transport hundreds of people stranded in Villavicencio back to Bogotá. In his defense Minister Durán Quinto explained that in 1974 the office of public works had already spent COL$60 million of a $COL90 million highway budget on the Bogotá-Villavicencio road, but Meta's senators Hernando Durán Dussán and Alfonso Latorre Gómez were unconvinced. They challenged the minister that the government was simply not doing enough to prevent more than a third of the country from being completely isolated due to the hazards of the single road that connected it with the interior.[17]

In addition to reopening the highway as quickly as possible, proposals were made to build new roads, but in the end, the government resolved the situation by constructing a detour around Quebradablanca from San Luis de Gaceno to Villanueva in Casanare, an alternative route that connected with an existing road between the Humea and Upía rivers. It also constructed a tunnel 270 meters in length through Quebradablanca and a bridge 115 meters long over the Quebradablanca canyon to alleviate the immediate problems.[18] Nevertheless, the government could not easily erase the impact of the disaster. Not only was the loss of life horrific, but also the tragedy and its aftermath dramatically underscored the vital role that Meta had come to play in Bogotá's economy. Likewise it revealed the precarious nature of the connection between the two regions, depending as it did on the viability of an extremely dangerous road.

By 1971 there were approximately two thousand seven hundred kilometers of roads (including the Bogotá-Villavicencio highway) in Meta, but traffic on many of them was limited to the dry season. The Meta River, that flows one thousand two hundred kilometers from Puerto López to Puerto Carreño to meet the Orinoco, offered a potential fluvial highway to transport cargo from Villavicencio to the Atlantic. In the 1960s the river was still 92 percent navigable, but its possibilities were largely underutilized during the Frente Nacional. Far more important was air transport as was aptly demonstrated during the interruption of traffic on the Bogotá-Villavicencio highway. Villavicencio had two airports, Vanguardia and Apiay, and nearly every town in the Llanos had some kind of landing strip. Commercial airlines including Avianca, Urraca, Satena, Laica, Tacatá, Tam, and FAC operated routes in the Llanos , but the runway of Vanguardia, the fifth busiest airport in Colombia in terms of cargo and passengers, was still unpaved, and except in emergencies, abandoned by the Aeronáutica Civil. Already in the 1960s there was talk that the Apiay field, used by the Colombian Air Force, might eventually serve as an alternative airport to Bogotá's El Dorado, but no action on this proposal was taken at this time.[19]

POPULATION GROWTH IN VILLAVICENCIO

A breakdown of DANE's census of 1964 revealed that Villavicenio had a population of 58,430, or 35 percent, of the 165,530 people in the department. Of the departmental total, 47 percent were native Llaneros, while 52.5 percent came from Cundinamarca, Tolima, Huila, Boyacá, Valle, Caldas, and the Santanders. With regard to the economically active population, 85.4 percent were men and 14.6 percent women. In terms of their occupations, 37.2 percent were workers, 30 percent employees, 16 percent *patronos*, 16.2 percent independent workers, and 0.6 percent had other occupations. Among this group, 64.5 percent were working in agriculture, forestry, hunting, and fishing; 15.5 percent in service jobs; 6.3 percent in trade; 5.8 percent in industry; 3.5 percent in construction; and 4.4 percent in other activities. Of the towns outside of Villavicencio, the largest in terms of population was Puerto López with 18,054, followed by Acacías with 16,612, and Granada with 10,239.[20]

The impact of Villavicencio's rapid population growth between 1956 and 1965 was readily discernable. As Brunnschweiler observed in 1973, "The cozy, small-town atmosphere around the plaza is rapidly disappearing in the process of the transformation of the old core into the main commercial center of the city."[21] Besides Villavicencio's physical expansion from a few blocks to a sprawling urban complex of eighteen densely populated *barrios*, there were unmistakable signs that it was assuming functions that elevated it into the order of major regional centers in the hierarchy of Colombian cities. On some streets, all the shops continued to be dedicated to a single handicraft, such as tanners and saddlers, blacksmiths and hardware, or clothiers and tailors, but high-rise buildings were beginning to loom over the tin-sheeted roofs of the old town. These new structures provided office and residential space in the upper stories, while the older stores housed workshops and sales rooms. Below the covered market was the wholesale district with a concentration of warehouses and transport-oriented establishments. This section also included several blocks of restaurants, bars, and inns that composed what was known as the *zona de tolerancia* (red light district).

Around the periphery of the city there was an explosive growth of residential housing to absorb the sudden influx of thousands of people. Substandard dwellings crowded the hillsides along the ravines and extended in files beside the highways at the end of the city. By the 1970s the local government was attempting to remedy this situation by constructing several nationally financed *urbanizaciones* (low-cost housing projects) that were provided with at least a minimum of public utilities.

Brunnschweiler noted that while there were a number of industries in the city (i.e., the brewery, the cotton gin, the meat freezing plant, and several rice mills), these factories provided work for only a small minority of the city's

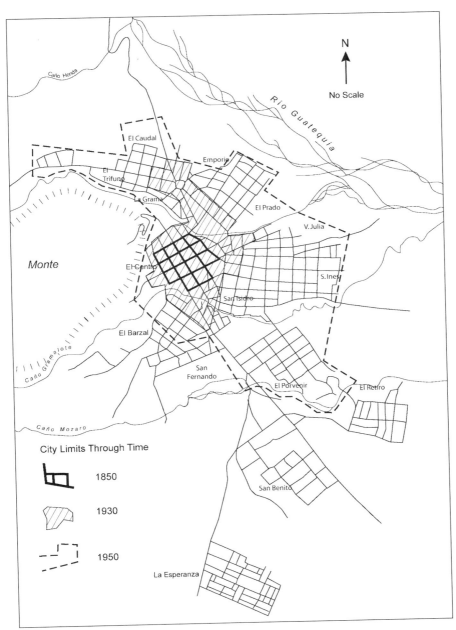

Map 9.1.   Plan of Villavicencio, 1965

population. Most of the industries continued in workshops, where owners with a few helpers applied their special skills to fashion the traditional handicrafts of the horse and cattle country of Meta. Underscoring Villavicencio's enhanced position as a commercial center and conduit for goods from the highlands to all the towns throughout the Llanos, Brunnschweiler concluded that the city urgently needed to develop labor-intensive industries to absorb the large number of unemployed inhabitants.[22]

ELECTRIFICATION AND OTHER URBAN INFRASTRUCTURE

With Villavicencio's rapid growth, the need to improve its basic infrastructure was imperative—especially the expansion of electricity, the improvement of the aqueduct to supply drinking water, and the expansion of sewers. Some residents had enjoyed electric service since 1918 when a hydraulic plant built in Susumuco by Francisco Arango began to operate. Water from the Corrales Quebrada activated the generators, and cables carried the current to a transformer plant located on the northeast side of the old Plaza Bolívar (today the Parque Infantil) from where the current was distributed to subscribers. Electric service was offered from 6:30 AM to 6:30 PM, but power varied from seventy volts during the rainy season to ten volts during the summer due to lack of water to run the generators.

In 1964 Electrificadora of Cundinamarca began to supply 110-volt electricity to Villavicencio and the other seventeen Meta municipios. The service varied from four to eighteen hours a day according to the economic activities of the population. In 1981, a second plant in Villavicencio, the Empresa de Energía Eléctrica, was connected with plants in Bogotá, giving it a power of sixty thousand kilowatts. The electrification of the municipios outside Villavicencio was partially financed by a loan of $COL23 million from the Inter-American Development Bank. Despite this expansion, many citizens even in Villavicencio still did not have electricity, and public lighting remained deficient in all the municipios.[23]

In 1960 only five of Meta's eighteen municipios had aqueducts that could supply drinking water to the residents. Throughout the early twentieth century, Villavicencio had relied on water brought from the La Honda Quebrada, the caños Gramalote and Mizaro, and the Guatiquía River, but without a water treatment plant and an effective distribution network, this system was insufficient to meet demands. Many of the residents' health problems, including diarrhea, malaria, influenza, and whooping cough, were exacerbated by contaminated drinking water. City leaders recognized that continued industrial growth of the capital depended on a better water supply, and by 1973 they had received a presidential subsidy of seven million Colombian pesos to provide Villavicencio with a modern aqueduct that would meet the needs of the residents. At the same time, studies were being carried out to improve sewers in the capital as well as the other municipios.[24]

EDUCATION

When Meta was a national intendancy, Catholic missionaries—specifically the Montfortians, the Hermanos de las Escuelas Cristianas and the Hermanas de Sabiduría—exercised exclusive control over education throughout the territory as well as the Comisaría Especial of Vichada. After it was elevated to a department in 1960, the Catholic schools remained, but government officials became responsible for the diffusion of public education throughout the eighteen municipios. In accordance with Decree 2364 issued in 1956 during the regime of Rojas Pinilla, departments were to create schools, appoint and pay teachers, and supply textbooks and other school materials. They were also enjoined to guarantee educational opportunities for all children of school age and to reserve 24 percent of all collected taxes for educational expenditures.[25] Despite these changes, Catholic priests continued to play an important role even in the public schools, serving as collaborators between the school authorities and municipal officials. They visited the schools two or three times a week to supervise religious teaching and to talk to the children about good behavior and morals.

As previously stated, the Frente Nacional agreement of 1957 stipulated that 10 percent of the national budget had to be spent on education. In the first ten years of joint party rule an array of educational policies and reforms were enacted that were often inconsistent and seldom implemented. In the opinion of Robert F. Arnove, who was an educational advisor to the Ford Foundation during the 1960s:

> The lack of coherence in educational policies during this period is a reflection of the fact that education was essentially a secondary concern of the political leadership of the National Front. Basically there was no unity of purpose, no systematic effort to prioritize education, no sustained commitment to allocate adequate resources to develop the competencies of most Colombians. Two-thirds of the Colombian population received only minimal education while the elite and middle classes used the education system to maintain their social status and gain entry to the most attractive jobs in the economy and decision-making roles in the public bureaucracies.[26]

In Meta, according to the census of 1964, 43.6 percent of the population had obtained a primary education, 3.6 percent had completed secondary studies, and 0.3 percent had achieved a professional degree. The census also determined that 49 percent of the inhabitants were illiterate, a proportion not much above the national average. A review of the statistics between 1961 and 1970 reveals that while church-run institutions remained strong, there was a boom in public education throughout the department. In 1961 there were 1,147 students in private primary schools and 12,092 in public schools. By 1970 there were 2,311 students in private schools and 32,896 in public schools. With regard to teachers, in 1961 there were 425 working in private primary schools and 55 in public schools for a total of 480. By 1970 there were 170 teachers in private schools and 905 in public schools. In other words the number of teachers had more than doubled from 480 to 1,075.

Concerning secondary education, in 1961 there were three private schools with 190 students and seven official schools with 746 students. By 1970 there were seventeen private schools enrolling 2,211 students and nine public schools with 3,457 students. In 1961 there were 24 teachers in private secondary schools and 73 in public schools; in 1970 that figure had expanded to 166 teachers in private schools and 150 in public secondary schools. Of the Meta budget for 1971, 48 percent, or $COL27,429,245, was assigned to education, but given the needs, these funds were still insufficient.[27]

According to Raquel Angel de Flórez, in Villavicencio in 1964 public primary education was offered in four large buildings known as *concentraciones escolares*. Male secondary institutions included the Colegio de la Salle, the Instituto Francisco José de Caldas, and the Escuela Industrial de Artes y Oficios. For young women there were the Colegio de la Sabiduría, the Colegio Feminino de Bachillerato y Comercio, and the Escuela Normal. Four additional private schools for young children included the Domingo Savio, Divino Niño, Liceo Infantil, and a kindergarten.[28]

Despite this expansion of educational opportunities, even in Villavicencio the quality of instruction was not high. The department often failed to supply schools with textbooks or other materials and frequently reneged on paying the salaries of the teachers, most of whom were ill trained. Members of the middle and upper classes tended to send their children to the private religious schools, while the poor were relegated to the public schools. As there was still no university in Meta, those students who completed secondary education sought to enroll in universities in Bogotá or abroad, especially in France.[29]

The poor quality of public education was even more evident in the newly erected municipios. In Granada, for example, there were two urban school buildings in 1964—one for boys and one for girls. Both were without electricity or adequate sanitation. There were no textbooks, and the teachers, all of whom had received some normal school preparation, taught their subjects by rote memorization. Although the department was supposed to pay their salaries, the money often arrived late, and the teachers considered their wages extremely low given the high cost of living in Meta. Their pupils ranged in age from seven to fifteen years. No school lunches were supplied. All of the children suffered from malnutrition, and many from other diseases. Only a small percentage of them ever completed the five-year curriculum. Because of church opposition to co-education, in the rural areas, three-year alternative primary schools were the norm in which the boys attended one day and the girls another.[30]

In 1964 the first six Salesian missionaries arrived in Granada to begin their work in the Prefectura Apóstolica del Ariari. A year later they were joined by the three Hijas de Maria Auxiliadora who immediataely organized the Escuela Normal Feminina María Auxiliadora to train teachers. The prefectura encompassed an area of some thirty-five thousand square kilometers with seven principal settlements, and between 1964 and 1973 the population increased from 30,000 to 180,000, creating serious social problems. In 1972 the Salesians divided this territory into five pastoral regions: Granada, Bajo Ariari, Vega del Ariari, Alto Ariari, and La Macarena. By 1974 Father Angel Martín González reported that the Salesians were operating six secondary schools including the Escuela Agropecuaria La Holanda, the Hogar Campesino de Cumaguaro, and four other Centros in addition to the Escuela Normal, and he stated that there were more than three hundred elementary teachers working in the prefectura.[31] Despite this growth, the schools lacked teaching materials and resources, and their numbers were constantly fluctuating as the colonos frequently moved to other regions.[32] In summing up the situation in 1973 Meta's secretary of education reported that while there had been an enormous growth in primary and secondary education in recent years, "The department is deficient in classrooms and teachers in the primary and secondary sector, being the most deficient in the primary and especially in the rural areas."[33]

COLONIZATION

The one hundred thousand campesinos who poured into the new Department of Meta but did not remain in Villavicencio had been uprooted by the violence in Cundinamarca, Tolima, Huila, and Boyacá. They came hoping to create farms on previously unclaimed and free public land. Because the supplies they needed and the crops they produced had a direct effect on the growing commerce of Villavicencio as well as the renewal of violence in the region, it seems appropriate to review some of their experiences between 1958 and 1974.

One of the first acts of the Frente Nacional government under Lleras Camargo was to pass Laws 20 and 26 of 1959, which created the Plan Nacional de Rehabilitación y Socorro. The Plan Nacional assigned to the Caja Agraria the duty of supervising colonization programs throughout the country including settlement of the Ariari River Valley. Accordingly, the Caja Agraria announced that land parcels would be available for selected colonists in two sections of the Ariari region—both still dominated by ex-guerrilla leaders. The first was the upper Ariari controlled by Dumar Aljure; the second was the Güejar Valley dominated by Bernardo Giraldo.

Unfortunately, despite the good intentions of the government, no previous studies had been carried out about the region, and the colonists arrived without receiving sufficient technical assistance from the Caja Agraria. Because they anticipated reestablishing the same type of farms they had had in the highlands, they were completely unprepared for the geographic and climatic challenges presented by the tropical Llanos of Meta. The campesinos that were already settled under the protection of Aljure were unwilling to cede territory to the newcomers. As a result most of the three hundred twenty "official" colonists settled in the Güejar Valley, where the relatively new municipio of Granada emerged as the principal town of the area. The ineptness of the officials assigned to aid the colonists soon led to the latter's disenchantment, and of the 320 families, some 60 percent decided to sell the parcels they had been assigned and move on to other places, despite the fact that they still owed to the Caja the credit they had received. For this reason many parcels fell into the hands of new owners who bought them at low prices.[34]

Relations between the people in the upper Ariari and those around Güejar remained uneasy, because Aljure remained loyal to the official Liberal Party while Bernardo Giraldo supported the Movimiento Revolucionario Liberal (MRL), a guerrilla organization. Disputes arose between the two factions, leading to incidents of violence and the development of *gamonales* (persons who exercise preponderant influence in a town). Some of the colonos who sold their parcels moved still farther south to the Guaviare Valley that bordered the Sierra de La Macarena, a unique region that congress had designated as a national park in 1948.[35]

Regardless of the region chosen to cultivate, the settlers faced formidable obstacles. The land in the river valleys was fertile and previously unclaimed (offering a greater chance of title security), but it had to be cleared of forests by slash-and-burn methods because the lack of mechanical tools forced the campesinos to rely on machetes and fire. They planted yuca, plátanos, corn, frijoles, and dry rice by hand. Weeding and control of encroaching woody plants was a constant necessity. To provide shelter, they built simple houses out of local materials that included roughly hewn and peeled tree stems and bahareque that they used to reinforce the walls. Lack of manpower hampered all these activities, as did the isolation of the regions that were virtually inaccessible during the rainy season.[36]

The poor performance of the Caja Agraria in promoting the resettlement of colonos prompted Frente Nacional leaders in Bogotá to pass the

Agrarian Reform Law of 1961. This law set up an agrarian reform agency—Instituto Colombiano de Reforma Agraria (INCORA)—and authorized the outright expropriation of privately owned estates for redistribution to those without land. Such expropriation, however, was to be a last resort. "The major emphasis would be on resettling peasants on lands reclaimed for agriculture through irrigation works and the like, or on the existing public domain."[37]

While scholars who have studied INCORA regard its efforts as more attuned to promoting the interests of capitalist expansion and concentrated land ownership than to helping landless peasants gain title to their land, there is no doubt that in Meta, it did achieve some success.[38] In the late 1950s colonists in the Upper Ariari Valley had had to rely on the sporadic action of the Caja de Crédito Agrario, which did little to relieve their hardships. By contrast, after 1964, INCORA began a program known as "Meta No. 1" to protect colonos who duly registered their properties. INCORA also provided trained personnel to assist the occupants of some 150 parcels, ranging in size from 50 to 200 hectares, in building up their farms by providing supervised credit for a carefully planned crop and livestock program, as well as for basic necessities. The Meta No. 1 initiative was centered in the newly established municipio of Vista Hermosa on the Río Güejar.[39]

Since previous to 1960 Meta was dominated by cattle ranches, it is surprising that during the early years of the Frente Nacional, conflict between the ganaderos and the new agricultural farmers was minimal. The explanation appears to lie in the fact that the farmers were settling on land previously forested that was not suitable for cattle, while the ranchers controlled vast stretches of low-cost but almost sterile savanna that provided the large operating units needed for profitable stock raising. Nevertheless, there was a substantial amount of potentially productive land that had been previously claimed but not cultivated.

In 1960 every fifth farm in Meta was held without official legal title. There were more than 10,000 *fincas* (crop farms) as against some 3,000 cattle ranches (haciendas or hatos.) By 1970 the ratio of crop farms to ranches was estimated to have increased to 5:1. The 10,722 crop farms, representing 73 percent of all agricultural enterprises, occupied 468,500 hectares of the more than 3 million hectares considered productive in Meta, while 2,907 cattle ranches comprised 80 percent (2.5 million hectares) of the state's productive land. Brunnschweiler estimated that 400,000 of the 486,500 hectares were occupied but not effectively farmed, suggesting that a substantial amount of potentially productive land was claimed but not cultivated. He concluded, "Considering the impetuous nature of the colonization process in its early phases, penetrating public land without official authority and privately owned land without respect for its legal owner, it is not surprising that the tenancy situation in Meta is a troublesome issue."[40]

Despite all the problems, Meta showed a dramatic increase in crops produced not only for local consumption but also for export to Cundinamarca. In 1972 production figures were as follows: cotton, 10,500 tons; paddy rice, 100,000 tons; dry rice, 30,000 tons; corn, 53,500 tons; soy, 480 tons; yuca, 500,000 cargas; plátano, 11 million bunches; African palm, 5,590 tons of oil; and sugar, 12,500 cargas of panela.[41] There were also two worrying developments. First, more and more peasants were moving into the protected area of La Macarena, and second, by the 1970s the growing of marijuana had become common, especially on both sides of the Güejar River where airplanes were landing to take the harvest to the exterior.[42]

RANCHING

In 1966 DANE estimated that there were 562,000 head of cattle in Meta or 3.7 percent of Colombia's livestock. Although only 2,907, or 18.4 percent, of the 15,835 farms in Meta in that year were classified as exclusively stock-raising operations, their combined acreage amounted to 80 percent of all land farmed in the department. In other words, 228 ranchers, or 1.4 percent of the farmers, whose properties exceeded 2,500 hectares, owned 63 percent of Meta's productive land. The largest ranches were located exclusively in the middle and outer Llanos where the carrying capacity of the natural savanna was extremely low and totally unsuited to agriculture. In DANE's national agricultural census of 1965, only 1 out of every 10 hectares in Meta was classified as improved pasture, and almost all of this land lay in the piedmont region that served as a fattening range for three- to four-year-old cows and steers brought in from the outlying ranches.[43]

Brunnschweiler noted that ranching continued to be carried out in the traditional manner with few innovations. "Except for rotating herds on the various sectors of a ranch, the only measure of pasture "management" is laying fire to the desiccated grasses at the end of the dry season."[44] The poor quality of the cattle produced brought a low price at the slaughterhouse, placing the ranchers in a disadvantageous position. The people who made a true profit from the cattle were middlemen who bought the underweight animals at low cost, fattened them on pastures around Villavicencio, and sold them in the Bogotá stockyards at 300 percent of the original sale price.[45] Despite the lack of modern management techniques, the number of cattle within the department quadrupled between 1960 and 1971, increasing from 313,000 to 1.2 million.[46]

All cattle raised for beef in Meta, excepting those slaughtered for local consumption, were sent to the metropolitan district of Bogotá, a market of well over two million people. In 1973 Villavicencio provided 54 percent of the beef consumed in Bogotá, the rest coming from the Magdalena Valley.

At the end of the Violencia, the sacas, or herding of cattle from Casanare and Arauca, were renewed. With the exception of an estimated ten thousand head sent annually from Casanare ranches to Sogamoso, Boyacá, and perhaps one thousand cows per year flown out from Arauca to the fattening pastures around Cúcuta, most of the cattle from these other Llanos regions were eventually herded along the Villavicencio- Bogotá market corridor through the northern and eastern control stations. Ranchers shipped cattle on barges down the rivers while vaqueros drove the mature animals to the Meta Cercano on old established cattle trails. These drives took more than a month when they departed from Casanare and Vichada, and the weight losses occurring during these migrations were such that the first half of the finishing period was really one of recuperation rather than fattening. It often required as much as a year to bring the animals up to a satisfactory market weight.[47]

When the cattle were ready, they were loaded into trucks that ascended the Villavicencio-Bogotá highway. Because there was a marked seasonal fluctuation in deliveries, acute meat shortages accompanied by simultaneous price rises occurred in Bogotá during the slack periods. During the rainy season when the fattening pastures were most productive, some thirty to forty cattle trucks, each loaded with eight to twelve animals, set off from Villavicencio for Bogotá on an average day. In 1973, 22,162 cattle were slaughtered in Villavicencio to supply local needs, but the departmental planning office warned that the city still did not have an adequate hygienic slaughterhouse.

PETROLEUM

The search for exploitable oil deposits in Meta began in the 1940s when Tropical Oil Company and Shell International explored potential sites and drilled some exploratory wells in the areas of San Martín, Chafurray, Vorágine, and Chaviva. While some of these drillings revealed the presence of hydrocarbons, the results were not encouraging enough to continue operations. According to Tomás Ojeda Ojeda, in 1950, after funding an eight-day fiesta for the people of Villavicencio, "Mr. Rockefeller announced that the Llanos did not have oil," and suspended operations in Meta.[48]

In 1951 Laureano Gómez founded the Colombian Petroleum Enterprise (ECOPETROL), which worked with Tropical Oil to exploit the DeMares region around Barranca Bermeja, Santander. During the Rojas Pinilla years, ECOPETROL developed a policy of working in association with multinational corporations (MNC) whereby the MNCs explored at their own risk and cost. The arrangement specified that if a MNC found economically feasible amounts of petroleum, both it and the government would invest

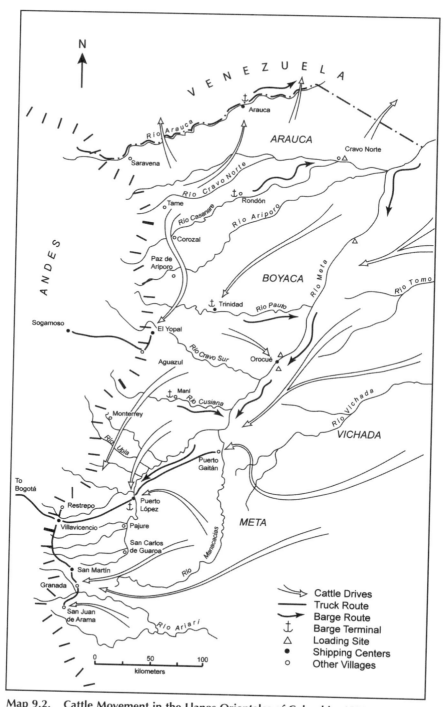

Map 9.2. Cattle Movement in the Llanos Orientales of Colombia, 1972

equally in production activities, with the government receiving royalties, taxes, and 50 percent of the petroleum.[49]

Between 1950 and the 1960s, Intercol, a subsidiary of Exxon, continued exploratory drilling that produced useful knowledge about the geology of the plains. Although no strike was made at the time, the results could not have been entirely discouraging, because there was a veritable rush for drilling concessions in Meta by the end of the 1960s. C. H. Neff, in at article published by *The American Association of Petroleum Geologists Bulletin*, called the renewed interest in the Llanos the most outstanding development in the Colombian oil industry in 1968.[50] In 1969 congress passed Law 20, which authorized the government to declare as a national reserve any zone potentially rich in oil and to deliver it to ECOPETROL without subjecting it to ordinary contractual rule, so that ECOPETROL might explore, exploit, and administer it directly or in association with other companies of public or private capital, national or foreign. By 1973 the national government had awarded four companies—Continental, International Petroleum Colombian, British Petroleum, and Superior Oil—concessions to explore approximately three hundred ninety thousand hectares of Meta land.[51] These exploratory activities were a temporary boost to Meta's economy because, if a major find might be discovered, there was hope that the department's share in the revenues from petroleum production would establish the financial base it needed to improve public institutions and services.

THE REBIRTH OF GUERRILLA ACTIVITY

When Lleras Camargo took office in 1958, guerrillas were still active in parts of Colombia, but the violence had begun to lose its original political justification. Prior to the consolidation of the Cuban Revolution as a Marxist-Leninist phenomenon, the fighting had largely degenerated into self-seeking robbery and murder. As Jorge Osterling points out, the old communist agrarian groups of the early 1950s, such as the Colombian Revolutionary Armed (FARC), continued to be active, but they were now joined by recently created guerrilla groups who, inspired by Cuba's successes, established a number of relatively self-contained, Marxist-controlled areas.[52] These so-called independent republics were located in Marquetalia, Tolima, Río Chiquito in northern Cauca, and El Pato and Guayabero on the border of Huila and Caquetá, where communists worked with the peasants, organizing them politically and militarily and providing them with social services and facilities.

The Colombian army tolerated these enclaves during the Lleras Camargo administration, but when Guillermo Leon Valencia became president in 1962, their presence appeared to pose a challenge to the government's authority. Accordingly, Valencia ordered the army to attack the republics. "After failures in 1962, the army in 1964 employed roughly a third of its force in taking control of the most important enclave, Marquetalia," and it destroyed the other "republics" in 1965.[53] In 1966 the survivors of the Marquetalia republic transformed themselves into the FARC with an estimated 350 to 500 men who operated primarily in Tolima but who also began to move into Meta. Led by Manuel Marulanda, alias "Sure-Shot," the FARC was committed to social revolution but was less politically sophisticated than the Army of National Liberation (ELN), a second guerrilla group inspired by Castro and active in rural Antioquia, Bolívar, and Santander in 1964–1965.

The government's inability to regulate and aid the flow of colonists into Meta offered an ideal opportunity for the infiltration of the FARC, which could give assistance to those peasants fighting off takeovers by large landowners. Until his death on April 5, 1968, Aljure had provided this kind of protection to colonists in the over sixty thousand hectares of the upper Ariari Valley where he had established himself as "the regional political chief with virtual autonomy from the central government, protecting himself with the maintenance of an armed force given to occasional banditry."[54] Aljure's allegiance to the Liberal Party gained him the support of Meta's most prominent Liberal politician, Durán Dussán, and despite Aljure's illegal activities and past criminal acts, Colombian authorities considered him untouchable.

In 1957 Aljure moved his operations to Rincón de Bolívar where his domain grew to include the municipios of Fuente de Oro, San Martín, and Granada. Within this area he built up a prosperous cattle operation. He imposed taxes on the peasant cultivators and cattlemen and, in return, provided them with protection from himself and from incursions by the national government. He helped to elect certain municipal council members, and it was widely believed that he could deliver eight thousand votes, or over one third, of Meta's Liberal electorate.[55]

For many years Aljure marshaled votes for slates of candidates headed or sponsored by Senator Durán Dussán; however, his downfall came when, in the 1968 congressional elections, he reportedly backed the slate of Durán Dussán's opponent, former Minister of Education Daniel Arango Jaramillo. After losing the election, Durán Dussán broadcast a highly emotional speech from Villavicencio in which he implied that a Conservative governor would be named for Meta to punish the disloyal local leaders. In addition, members of the VIII Brigade of the Colombian Army located in Villavicencio were increasingly uneasy with Aljure's open flaunting of the law and freedom of action in his self-proclaimed domain. The army's presence in the area encouraged quite a few peasants to give testimony against the guerrilla chief. A month later, Colombian Army units of the 21st Vargas Battalion stationed in Granada attacked Aljure, killing him, his wife, and thirteen members of his band.

In the view of Richard Maullin, who has written the most extensive account about Aljure's activities, the Liberal guerrilla played a well-developed role in the Meta Department as a political, economic, and social figure. Maullin sees Aljure as representative of the local chief who is adroit at constructing a personal system of power, but although Aljure was said to be motivated by an "almost religious allegiance to Liberalism, his career did not reflect great ideological commitment. In the revolutionary spectrum he must be ranked higher than an ordinary bandit for hire but well below the true believer."[56]

What is clear is that Aljure's elimination paved the way for the infiltration of FARC operatives into the Ariari region who could offer peasants assistance in setting up self-defense groups to resist the seizure of their lands by cattlemen and local farmers. The FARC extended services to people that were not supplied by the government. As in the Aljure era, "The communities influenced and defended by the guerrillas tended toward autonomous forms of political and economic organization, but this tendency did not prevent them from participating in traditional political contests as well."[57] Because the government's policies tended to stimulate the interests of the large landowners instead of helping the colonists through subsidized credit, commercialization, land titles, and roads, the new structure of the FARC could be imposed as an organization system among the colonists and the peasants under its influence, setting up a situation where renewed violence would become inevitable.[58]

VILLAVICENCIO: GATEWAY TO THE LLANOS?

In her excellent study of the history of Villavicencio, Nancy Espinel Riveros has emphasized that at least until the 1960s, the town was far more a reflection of the regional cultures of the highlands that that of the plains."[59] As migrants from the west flowed into Villavicencio during the Frente Nacional era, one might imagine that the city's identification with the eastern plains would become more tenuous; however, the resumption of cattle drives from Arauca and Casanare as well as the eastern part of the department brought a new wave of influence of the unique Llanero culture that had been molded in the plains over a period of three centuries.[60]

Between 1958 and 1973 the town leaders began initiatives that would establish Villavicencio's credentials as a true Llanero city. For example, in 1962 at the suggestion of the Llanero composer, Miguel Angel Martín, Governor Carlos Hugo Estrada agreed that Villavicencio should sponsor the first Festival de la Canción Colombiana with the express purpose of "stimulating and promoting our Llanero folklore and all the national compositions."[61] The success of this event encouraged the addition during the following year of holding a contest to elect a departmental beauty queen and the inauguration of the first Torneo International del Joropo, the most typical dance of the plains. With participants coming from all sections of the plains, including Venezuela, the Torneo had the effect of identifying Villavicencio with Llanero culture and popularizing Llanero dances and songs throughout all of Colombia.

In 1966, with the support of another Llanero composer, Héctor Paúl, Villavicencio began holding a Festival de la Canción Colombiana in November so that it would correspond with the celebration of the "Cuadrillas de San Martín," a folklore event of religious and secular significance that dated back to 1735. This festival that recreates the history of the expulsion of the Moslems from Spain and the Spanish conquest of America through music, dances, and horsemen, is the most authentic celebration of Llanero culture. Over the years it has become an enormously popular tourist attraction.

Another way to solidify Villavicencio's identity with Llanero culture was to establish centers for its study and promotion. Beginning in 1966 a series of decrees brought about the founding in 1971 of the Casa de la Cultura that includes a school of music, art, and dance, a folklore museum, and the departmental library. Despite limited economic resources, in 1972 the music school offered instruction in guitar, cuatro, piano, tiple, bandola, and harp to approximately 250 students. The departmental library held regular lectures, recitals, and music concerts. In addition, in 1962 Miguel Angel Martín began an Academia de Música. The secretariat of education promoted the writings by Llanero novelists and poets and supported the departmental band that offered concerts throughout Meta. In 1972 the department also created an Academia de Historia to promote the study of the Llanos region.[62] Taken together, these various events and cultural entities help to reinforce Villavicencio's claim to be an authentic Llanero city notwithstanding its obviously mixed ancestry.

NOTES

1. Bushnell, *Colombia*, 223. For other studies of the National Front, see Dix, *Colombia: Political Dimensions of Change*; Francisco Leal Buitrago, *Estado y política en Colombia* (Bogotá: Siglo Veintiuno, 1984), and Jonathan Hartlyn, *Politics of Coalition Rule in Colombia* (New York: Cambridge University Press, 1988).

2. Alberto Lleras Camargo, "Paz en los Llanos Orientales" in *El Primer Gobierno del Frente Nacional*, 4 vols. (Bogotá: Imprenta Nacional, 1959–1960), 2: 10–11.

3. Departamento del Meta, *Monografía, folclor, cultura y turismo* (Villavicencio: Oficina de Planeación, 1972) (Hereafter cited as *Monografía*), 13–17; Leonel Pérez Bareño, *Planes de Desarrollo en la Orinoquia y la Amazonia*, 2nd ed. (Bogotá: Editorial Presencia, 1986), 7.

4. Lleras Camargo cited by Paredes Cruz, *Departamento del Meta*, 49–52.

5. Florez, *Conozcamos*, 1: 97–103. The additional governors were Daniel Arango Jaramillo (1964), Jorge H. Acevedo (1965), Ricardo Roa Latorre (1966), Policarpo Castillo Dávila (1968), Gabriel López González (1970), and Julio H. Guevara Castro (1973). For a complete list of governors of Meta up to 1998 see Anexo 12 in Espinel Riveros, *Villavicencio*.

6. Paredes Cruz, *Departamento del Meta*, 128.

7. "Arquidiócesis de Villavicencio" www.geocities.com/diocesis_villavicencio/ (accessed July 7, 2005); Garavito Jiménez, *La Iglesia*, 73; 36–39.

8. Martín Gonzalez, *La Prefectura Apostólica*, 141–43.

9. *Primer Congreso de Territorios Nacionales*, May 1966, Inaugural Sesión, Discursos, p. 3 in *Informe del Director del DTN*, MMG, 1966.

10. *El Tiempo*, June 14, 1974.

11. Brunnschweiler, *The Llanos Frontier*, 56.

12. *El Tiempo*, March 6, 1974.

13. *El Tiempo*, June 18, 1974.

14. *El Tiempo*, June 21, 1974.

15. *El Tiempo*, June 27, 1974.

16. *El Tiempo*, June 30, 1974.

17. *El Tiempo*, July 8, 1974; July 4, 1974.

18. Hernando Vargas Rubiano, "Reflexiones sobre el Transporte en la Orinoquia," in *Llanos de Colombia* (Bogotá: Litografía Arco, 1986), 157; "López responderá a críticos," *El Tiempo*, February l, 1976.

19. *Monografía*, 22–23; Humberto Diez, "Dramática situación del Llano," *El Tiempo*, June 27, 1974.

20. *Monografía*, 18–19; Brunnschweiler, *The Llanos Frontier*, 20–21.

21. Brunnschweiler, *The Llanos Frontier*, 27.

22. Brunnschweiler, *The Llanos Frontier*, 28.

23. Ojeda Ojeda, *Villavicencio*, 323–24; *Monografía*, 25. When the author visited Granada in July 1964, electricity was available in that municipio only between 6:00 to 11:00 PM. Nevertheless, most of the residents had at least a radio and often a refrigerator.

24. Ojeda Ojeda, *Villavicencio*, 307–8; *Monografía*, 26.

25. Colombia, *Una política educativa para Colombia*, 4 vols. (Bogotá: Imprenta Nacional, 1963), 1: 44.

26. Robert F. Arnove, "Education Policies of the National Front," in *Politics of Compromise*, ed. Albert Berry, et al., 407.

27. *Monografía*, 19–21.

28. Florez, *Conozcamos*, 2:44.

29. Ojeda Ojeda, *Villavicencio*, 104–6.

30. These observations are based on a visit by the author to the Granada schools in July 1964. They form part of an unpublished report titled, "A Study of Primary Education in Rural Colombia" (Madison: University of Wisconsin, 1964.)

31. Martín González, *La Prefectura Apostólica del Ariari*, 125–26.

32. Martín González, *La Prefectura Apostólica del Ariari*, 159.

33. *Monografía*, 21.

34. Londoño D., "Aproximación," 396–97.

35. Londoño D., "Aproximación," 396–97.

36. Brunnschweiler, *The Llanos Frontier*, 31–33.

37. Bushnell, *Colombia*, 232.

38. See for example, A. Eugene Havens, et al., "Agrarian Reform and the National Front: A Class Analysis," in *Politics of Compromise,* ed. Albert Berry, et al., 375.

39. Brunnschweiler, *The Llanos Frontier*, 33.

40. Brunnschweiler, *The Llanos Frontier*, 41.

41. *Monografía*, 38–39.

42. Londoño D., "Aproximación," 400.

43. Brunnschweiler, *The Llanos Frontier*, 44–45.

44. Brunnschweiler, *The Llanos Frontier*, 48.

45. Brunnschweiler, *The Llanos Frontier*, 49.

46. *Monografía*, 42.

47. Brunnschweiler, *The Llanos Frontier*, 49.

48. Ojeda Ojeda, *Villavicencio*, 240.

49. Kline, *Colombia*, 113.

50. Neff, "Review of 1968 Petroleum Developments in South America, Central America, and Caribbean Area, *The American Association of Petroleum Geologists Bulletin*, 53:1578-1648 cited by Brunnschweiler, *The Llanos Frontier*, 53.

51. *Monografía*, 17.

52. Osterling, *Democracy in Colombia*, 99.

53. Osterling, *Democracy in Colombia*, 99; J. Mark Ruhl, "The Military" in *Politics of Compromise*, ed. Albert Berry, et al., 195–96.

54. Richard L. Maullin, "The Fall of Dumar Aljure, a Colombian Guerrilla and Bandit," (Memorandum RM-5750-ISA, Santa Monica, CA: Rand Corporation, November 1969), 7.

55. Maullin, "The Fall of Dumar Aljure," 13.

56. Maullin, "The Fall of Dumar Aljure," 32.

57. Alfredo Molano, "Violence and Land Colonization," in *Violence in Colombia: The Contemporary Crisis in Historical Perspective*, ed. Charles Bergquist, et al., (Wilmington, D.E.: Scholarly Resources, 1992), 209.

58. Molano, "Violence and Land Colonization," 209.

59. Espinel Riveros, *Villavicencio*, 201.

60. Espinel Riveros, *Villavicencio*, 201.

61. *Monografía*, 81.

62. *Monografía*, 112.

10

Villavicencio, 1974–Present:
The Search for Civic Identity

The demise of the Frente Nacional as Colombia's political system brought a renewal of competitive politics at the national level with the elections of Liberal Julio César Turbay Ayala in 1978, Conservative Belisario Betancur in 1982, Conservative Virgilio Barco in 1986, Liberal César Augusto Gaviria in 1990, Liberal Ernesto Samper in 1994, Conservative Andrés Pastrana in 1998, and Liberal Alvaro Uribe Vélez in 2002. While this period saw the adoption of the new, reform-minded Constitution of 1991, there was also an increase in rebel fighting augmented by conflicts caused by the massive growth of illegal drug trading in marijuana and cocaine.

During these thirty-two years the population of Villavicencio once again doubled in size, even while the city and the surrounding region were hit by repeated outbreaks of violence brought on by drug trafficking and guerrilla warfare. The challenge of dealing with the dual influx of hundreds of immigrants arriving from the highlands and those displaced from the surrounding Llanos required new initiatives on the part of city officials. After examining various aspects of Villavicencio's expansion between 1974 and 2005 within the context of the development of the Department of Meta as a whole, this chapter will conclude with an exploration of the city's continuing struggle to define its identity. While there is no doubt that Villavicencio remains the dominant city in the plains as well as the "Gateway to the Llanos," the nature of its uniqueness among other Colombian mid-sized urban centers has become a question for debate.

THE POPULATION GROWTH OF VILLAVICENCIO AND META

According to the census of 1973, Villavicencio had 91,559 inhabitants while 151,905 people lived in the rest of the department. Of the other seventeen municipios, the largest was Granada with 20,443 inhabitants, followed by Acacías with 17,927, and San Juan de Arama with 13,449.[1] Twelve years later the adjusted census for 1985 revealed that Meta's population had more than doubled to reach 474,046 with 191,001 of the people living in Villavicencio. The number of municipios had increased from fourteen to eighteen. Granada remained the largest with 32,848 inhabitants, followed by Acacías with 29,201, Vista Hermosa with 24,586, and San Martín with 23,301.[2] Slightly less than half of the people living in urban areas had emigrated from other regions to the department, although the percentage of those born in Meta increased slightly from 57.9 percent in 1973 to 58.7 percent in 1985.[3]

By 2003, the population of Meta, based on the census of 1993 (the next census was due in 2005), was estimated at 618,427.[4] Although the number of municipios had increased to twenty-three, over one half of Meta inhabitants continued to live in Villavicencio with that urban center containing 285,425 people and the rural area an additional 45,992 for a total of 331,417 people.[5] This figure places Villavicencio in the category of intermediate Colombian cities. In terms of size, it is approximately equal to Valledupar (César), Ibague (Tolima), and Santa Marta (Magdalena).[6] Currently the city is divided into 234 barrios arranged in eight *comunas*, sixty *veredas*, and seven *corregimientos*.[7]

TRANSPORTATION

Much of this population growth can be attributed to improvement of the Bogotá-Villavicencio highway that remains the vital lifeline connecting the Llanos to the highlands. Fifty-seven percent of the trade and 60 percent of the passengers traveling between the two regions make use of the road. An average of three thousand five hundred cars travel along the highway every day in spite of the fact that landslides, violence, and other calamities frequently combine to delay or even block transit entirely.[8] In the 1990s the highway was the conduit for twenty thousand head of cattle sent monthly from the Llanos to the capital along with two hundred seventy thousand tons of white rice and forty thousand tons of palm oil and, still today, when service on the road is interrupted, all activity in Villavicencio and the Llanos is paralyzed.

After periodically making minor repairs to reduce the hazardous conditions of the highway, on December 29, 1996, the Ministry of Transport designated it an *obra nacional* (a national project) and called for its widening,

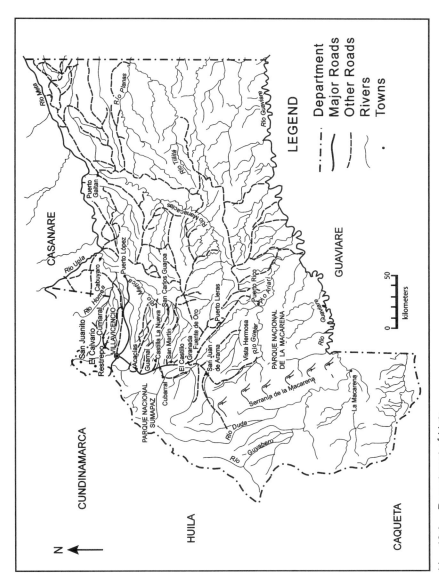

Map 10.1.   Department of Meta

redesign, and repaving. It was believed that the proposed improvements would reduce the time necessary to travel between the two cities from four hours to ninety minutes, but the geographic obstacles confronting this goal remain enormous. For example, in 2004 the ministry signed a contract with the Ingetec Engineering Company to improve a 33-kilometer section between Kilometers 55 and 87. For just this portion of the road, Ingetec agreed to construct twenty-five bridges with a total length of 2.3 kilometers, to stabilize the roadbed, build a new pavement structure, and reinforce existing pavements.[9] Ingetec completed this work satisfactorily, but its efforts affected only about one third of the road, leaving much to be done to ensure transit safety.

The declaration that the Bogotá-Villavicencio highway would become part of the national road network known as Transversal Route 40 bolstered the national government's determination to protect the road from rebel attacks. Beginning at the Pacific Coast port of Buenaventura, Transversal Route 40 is projected to pass through the cities of Ibagué, Bogotá, and Villavicencio and continue on to Puerto Carreño. In addition, plans are in place for the Carretera Marginal de la Selva, an international road, which, following the edge of the Eastern Cordillera for a distance of some one thousand five hundred kilometers through Colombia, would unite the borders of Venezuela and Ecuador. The idea for this second route dates from 1963, and despite its potential importance, up to now little substantial progress has been made. In the opinion of Tomás Ojeda Ojeda, completion of the Carretera Marginal is the key to expanding exports of products from the Colombian Llanos to the outside world.[10]

In recent decades public transport between Bogotá and Villavicencio has become more comfortable. As Ojeda Ojeda points out in 1967, "to get on a bus was no pleasure." He continues:

> The seats at that time were hard and fixed with a system of three passengers on one side and two on the other. Vehicles of more than forty passengers could also serve as transport for such cargo as chickens, plátanos, yuca, beans, cheese, dogs, sausages, etc.[11]

By 1970 transport companies had introduced reclining seats and busses with two seats on each side of the aisle. In 1980 they installed equipment to show videos and curtains for the comfort of the passengers. Soon bathrooms became a common convenience as well. To consolidate the various bus companies in the capital, the city of Bogotá built a central bus terminal. By the mid-1990s eight hundred vehicles were leaving from this main terminal every day to travel between Villavicencio and Bogotá.[12]

Before 1970, within Villavicencio urban transport was limited, with even buses in short supply. By the 1980s, however, the number of personal au-

Photo 10.1.   Villavicencio 2006
Source: www.btinternet.com/~j.rivera/images/villabo.jpg.

tomobiles had increased considerably, and a decade later, buses, taxis, *colectivas*, and motorcycles saturated the town, creating a constant state of congestion. The narrowness of the streets and avenues, absence of traffic lights, lack of control over bus routes, and habitual abuse of traffic rules and speed limits exacerbated this situation. As a result, in 1997 Villavicencio registered the greatest number of deaths by traffic accidents in the country.[13]

If transport along the Bogotá–Villavicencio highway has continued to expand, commerce via the Meta River has diminished despite the often cited advantage of shipping goods from Villavicencio directly to the Atlantic via Puerto López.[14] At the beginning of this era, during the eight months a year when the Meta was navigable, on average five ships a day carrying construction materials, iron, cattle, passengers, and foodstuffs plied their way up and down the river. By the early 1990s, this traffic had declined because of insecurity in the Llanos and Bogotá's decision to concentrate international shipping at Cartagena. In addition, deforestation along the banks of the Meta had created so much sedimentation that even boats with a shallow draft could no longer navigate the river's channels. In 1998 the Ministry of Transport proposed a plan to dredge nine hundred kilometers of the river between Puerto López and Puerto Carreño and to rehabilitate and install ports along its length. The goal was to enable navigation throughout the year, reduce transport costs, and increase trade with Venezuela, which shares two hundred kilometers of the Meta, but to be successful the plan required international cooperation. When Venezuela demanded that Colombia first begin a process of reforestation along the river, the project stalled, but it continues to have supporters. One study suggests that increased river commerce would benefit forty-seven municipios in Orinoquia, and that by 2020 it would generate 14,652 permanent jobs. Apparently Llaneros do not expect river traffic to improve in the near future. As Néstor Restrepo, an official of CorpoMeta (Corporación Regional del Meta), stated:

> If there were the political will to do it, it would give Colombia the opportunity to deliver products efficiently and cheaply along the river . . . But government is *paquidérmico* (elephantine) in the Llanos, and because of this, development of the region goes at a turtle's pace.[15]

For many years, local officials have regarded the creation of an international airport in Villavicencio as the best way to develop the economy of the city and the department. They have repeatedly asked the national government to permit such a facility, suggesting that it would not only expand passenger and cargo capacity but also serve as an alternative to Bogotá's overcrowded El Dorado airport. Nancy Espinel Riveros has argued that installing a customs-free zone in Apiay's Vanguardia Terminal would promote international trade and stimulate tourism. Moreover, it would fulfill an obvious necessity by facilitating regular air communication between the towns of the Llanos. As a corollary to internationalizing the Vanguardia airport, Espinel Riveros suggests that Llanero entrepreneurs should organize a new airline to transport people and cargo to cities throughout Orinoquia and Amazonia as well as other regions of the country. "In this way," she argues, "the myth of the 'alternative airport' would be ended, and dependence on El Dorado would be over, giving way to an international Villavicencio Airport with optimal technical, geographic and strategic conditions."[16]

COLONIZATION

As in previous decades, economic and social pressures in the Colombian highlands, especially violence and land concentration, were the primary forces behind the flow of population into Meta. The bulk of the highland migrants were landless campesinos, fleeing low salaries on *minifundios* or dislodged from their homes by violence. Without any special training or skills, they saw the Llanos as a place of opportunity, a place where they might own land and improve their lives.[17]

In analyzing colonization trends, some scholars divide Meta into three regions. The first is the piedmont area (Llanos Arriba) that includes Villavicencio, most of the other urban centers, and the bulk of the new immigrants.

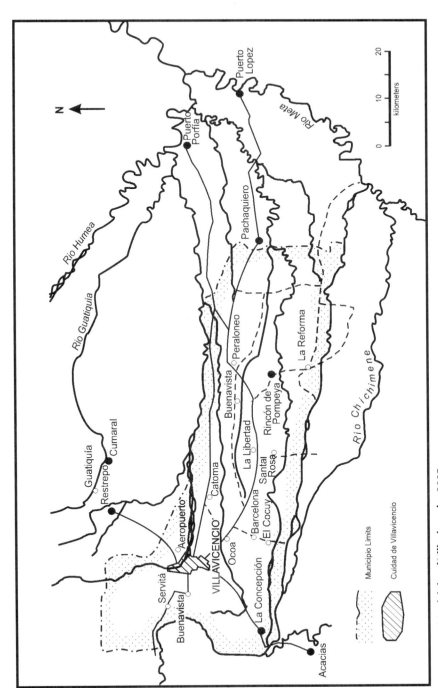

Map 10.2. Municipio of Villavicencio, 2005

The second is the Llanos Abajo that encompasses the savannas and jungles where the population is more dispersed. Finally, there are thirteen Guahibo Indian reservations located in the eastern part of the municipios of Puerto Gaitán, Puerto Lleras, and San Martín. As they have for centuries, these nomadic natives live by hunting, fishing, and farming yuca, sweet potatoes, and tobacco. Their basic food is casaba extracted from yuca. They maintain a collective system of property and elect a *capitán* who directs their activities. In 1980 the government calculated Meta's native population at 3,069, a number that has not changed significantly even though the Guahibos face extinction due to steady and illegal encroachment of cattle ranchers onto their traditional lands.[18]

In her article, "El Ordenamiento Territorial en el Departamento del Meta," Matilde Beltrán Figueredo points out that from a cultural point of view, in addition to the Indian resguardos, there are distinct differences in the lifestyles of the four departmental provinces. The inhabitants of the Provincia de la Cordillera, which includes the municipios of El Calvario and San Juanito, are mainly from Cundinamarca and Boyacá. They identify closely with Andean culture, and the region has often expressed a desire to secede from Meta to join Cundinamarca. The colonists moving to the Provincia del Piedemonte (which includes Villavicencio, Cubarral, Acacías, San Carlos de Guaroa, Castilla La Nueva, Restrepo, and Cumaral) are also from Cundinamarca and Boyacá, but here they have mixed with other migrants returning to these towns from the plains. The people in the piedmont primarily engage in agriculture, commerce, *artesanías*, and mining for oil and salt. Due to the disappearance of most of the hatos, ranching, once important, is now limited to fattening pastures for cattle. Since the colonists tend to reproduce the culture of their places of origin, the Llanero customs that do exist are introduced by people arriving from the savannas. These customs are also promoted by folkloric celebrations and by the stories of those who, year after year, have participated in the roundups that transport cattle from Arauca and Casanare to be fattened at Villavicencio.[19]

By contrast, the Provincia del Ariari, which contains the municipios of Granada, Fuente de Oro, and La Macarena, continues to attract the largest number of immigrants who move there from Tolima, Cundinamarca, Valle, Caldas, Tolima, and Huila, after stopping first in Villavicencio. The region is economically important with the development of irrigated rice, intensive ranching, African palm plantations, and cultivation of cacao, cotton, and sorghum. According to Beltrán Figueredo, the inhabitants of this zone strive to keep their own traditions but are open to including Llanero customs as one of many cultural manifestations. In the years after 1986, given its natural resources and social promise, Ariari province has become one of the principal areas afflicted by violence, guerrillas, drug dealers, and paramilitaries.[20]

The true center of Llanero life is San Martín, which lies in the Provincia de Río Meta, a region that also includes Puerto López, Mapiripan, Cabuyaro, and Barranca de Upía. Thanks to new roads, immigrants coming to this region from Venezuela as well as the Colombian interior are more easily absorbed into the existing Llanero culture. Cattle ranching is the principal economic activity, but crops such as plátano, cacao, maiz, rice, and yuca are grown on the river plain.[21]

VIOLENCE, DRUG WARS, AND DISPLACEMENT

As noted in chapter 9, the Frente Nacional was unable to control the numerous rebel groups that emerged to challenge the alternating rule by Liberal and Conservative presidents. In Meta FARC leaders established a foothold in the plains in 1964 after the Colombian army crushed their so-called independent republic of Marquetalia in Tolima. New colonos were vulnerable to guerrilla pressure, because inadequate government support had left them unable to turn a profit on parcels they had cleared and planted. Often forced to sell their land to large-scale agriculturalists or to ranchers, some of them formed self-defense groups or paramilitary units while others discovered that the FARC's rural-based strategy designed to gain and hold territory would offer them a measure of protection. The continuing efforts of large landholders to evict the colonos combined with the lack of a strong government presence on the Meta frontier permitted the FARC, led by Manuel Marulanda Vélez (alias Tirofijo) to win popular support even though the actual number of committed guerrillas was less than six thousand.[22] As Alfredo Molano explains, "Insofar as the guerrillas were able to create defenses for the colonists, they tended to control the roles of the merchant and the intermediaries and to provide for or attend to the population's most basic needs such as education, health, and justice."[23]

The violence took on a new dimension with the introduction of drug trafficking. In 1975, after the United States cracked down on marijuana grown in Mexico, the center of its production moved to the north coast of Colombia. Thanks "to its direct introduction by U.S. traffickers who distributed seeds and guaranteed to purchase the harvest," between 1977 and 1980 Meta campesinos in Vista Hermosa and Puerto Lleras south of the Ariari also began to grow marijuana.[24] As Renaldo Barbosa Estepa notes, the colonos tended to dissipate the economic bonanza they received in luxurious expenditures, liquor, and prostitution, and the climate was set for the introduction of coca cultivation. Between 1980 and 1986 an understanding emerged between the newly formed Colombian drug cartels, who promoted the cultivation of coca in the Llanos and transferred technology there to process and refine the drug, and the FARC guerrillas, who guaranteed internal order and levied a tax on cultivators and buyers. At this point the guerrillas assumed the posture of protecting the cultivators, but the collapse of a 1984 truce between the FARC and the government of Belisario Bentancur brought down on them the wrath of both the army and paramilitary groups hired by the large landowners to protect their persons and property.[25] The violence was especially intense in the Province of Ariari. During the 1980s a struggle for control of the region degenerated into a confrontation between guerrillas and paramilitaries who declared a war to the death. The paramilitaries targeted for removal any person suspected of sympathizing with the left. During this decade sixty-two people died in more than eight separate massacres, most of which were perpetrated by the paramilitaries.[26]

For the next twenty years leaders in Bogotá struggled either to crush the drug cartels and the various rebel groups that had come to include beside the FARC, the M-19, the Ejército de Liberación Nacional (ELN), and the Ejército de Popular Liberación (EPL), or to reach some kind of truce with them. To cite one extreme tactic, in 1998 as a peace gesture, President Pastrana ceded to FARC uncontested control of a sixteen-thousand-square-mile zone in Caquetá, south of Meta, but his gambit did not achieve the desired goal. Insecurity and terror in the Llanos continued, and hundreds of colonos left the conflicted areas to seek security in Villavicencio.

During the last two decades waves of colonos fleeing the Llanos Abajo have descended on Villavicencio. Similar movements of rural people moving to the cities have occurred throughout Colombia, but the phenomenon is concentrated in eleven departments (Antioquia, Bogotá, Magdalena, Bolívar, Valle del Cauca, Putumayo, Cauca, Sucre, Cesar, Santander, and Meta). Indiscriminate intimidation, armed confrontations, massacres, and specific threats are the principal causes of colono flight. According to one national study, 57 percent of the displacements were caused by paramilitary groups, 12 percent by guerrillas, and 18 percent by more than one of the armed groups.[27]

Although the percentage of displaced individuals in Meta is low compared with the numbers in Antioquia and Bogotá, the ruling elite of Villavicencio was and is unprepared to deal with this phenomenon. The refugees arrive traumatized by terror and the tragedy of the failure of their hopes. Help for such people from the city is minimal, and the National Red Cross and the Centro de Atención Humanitaria Inmediata supply what is forthcoming. The refugees build their homes in marginal areas along the banks of rivers that are subject to flooding, cave-ins, and contamination during the winter months. According to studies carried out by the Secretaría de Planeación Municipal, in 1989 there were 27 *asentamientos* (settlements) in high-risk, unhealthy locations. Ten years later there were 151 such settlements with an estimated forty-six thousand inhabitants.[28] Rather than assisting these people, the municipal authorities have repeatedly tried to evict them. To cite just one example, Amnesty International reported that on February 2, 2001, twelve hundred soldiers invaded the La Nohora asentamiento in an effort to force several hundred internal displaced families to leave the area.[29]

Moreover, even in Villavicencio people are not free from the threat of guerrilla violence. After the collapse of a round of peace talks on February 20, 2002, the FARC detonated bombs in a popular city nightspot on April 7. The explosion left twelve people dead, more than sixty wounded, and damaged homes and businesses in a four-block area. As one commentator warned, increasingly the rebels were turning to civilian targets, attacking power plants, electrical and telecommunications lines, reservoirs, and bridges.[30]

THE CHURCH

On July 4, 2004, Pope John Paul II elevated the Diocese of Villavicencio to the status of archdiocese. Monseñor José Octavio Ruiz Arenas was appointed the first archbishop, and he took possession on August 16, 2004.[31] By this time the archdiocese encompassed an area of 65,470 square kilometers, a population of 512,320 of which 97.2 percent professed the Catholic faith. There were 117 parishes and 120 secular and 20 religious priests. In 1999 the vicariato apostólico de Ariari became the Diocese of Granada and the prefectura apostólica de Mitú, the Diocese of San José del Guaviare. Héctor Julio López Hurtado, a Salesian, was appointed as the first bishop of Granada, and in Guaviare that honor fell to Monseñor Belarmino Correa Yepes, a Jesuit. The five vicariatos apostólicos of Inírida, Leticia, Mitú (formerly Puerto Inírida), Puerto Carreño, and Puerto Gaitán completed the jurisdiction of the archbishop.[32] The Montfortians remained in charge of the mission territories of Puerto Carreño and Puerto Gaitán. In 2005 that order, founded in France by St. Louis Marie Grignion de Montfort in 1705, was preparing to celebrate its 300th anniversary and one hundred years of work in Colombia.[33]

EDUCATION

On July 12, 1973, the Colombian government and the Holy See agreed to a new concordat annulling both the Concordat of 1887 and the Convention on Missions of 1953. In accordance with this agreement, the state issued Law 43 in 1975 nationalizing official primary and secondary education, including schools in the intendancies and comisarías, and in 1976 with Decree 102, it ruled that regional educational funds (FER) would finance both educational levels. Despite this arrangement, the missionary orders signed

Photo 10.2.   Villavicencio Cathedral, 1998
Source: www.llanera.com/galeria/details.php?image_id=98.

three-year renewable contracts with the state to control education in areas primarily populated by Indians. The result was to create two types of schools: official and private. The official schools are run by the government under the direction of the ministerio de educación nacional (MEN), while most of the private schools and those in the prefecturas apostólicas are administered by the missionary orders.

In the 1970s and 1980s the growing population of Villavicencio brought an increase in demand for schools. By 1984 the city had 77 official schools with 27,674 students and 119 rural schools with 5,706 students. There were 898 urban teachers and 235 rural teachers. In addition, many privately financed schools were meeting the needs of the rapidly increasing middle class. In Meta overall, however, only 53 percent of children between six and twelve years of age were attending classes, a low figure even by Colombian standards. Most of the schools had only one or two classrooms and insufficient desks. They lacked restrooms, potable water, gardens, and sports fields. There was a high percentage of school desertion. Children frequently repeated grades, especially in rural areas where they went to work on their parents' farms at an early age or came from poor families who were forced by their precarious economic situation to constantly move about.[34] Sixty-one percent of Meta's secondary students were enrolled in one of the 28 official schools or 20 nonofficial schools in Villavicencio, which was also the site for the department's only university, the Universidad Tecnológica de los Llanos Orientales, founded in 1974.[35]

HEALTH

The tropical climate of the Llanos continues to present serious health problems for white and native inhabitants, although those who live in the piedmont area and especially Villavicencio have much easier access to health centers and hospitals. There have been some successes. Yellow fever has been virtually eradicated, and while malaria affects all age groups, the prevalence of the disease has diminished thanks to departmental controls. A massive vaccination campaign of children against polio, measles, yellow fever, and tetanus has produced good results. On the other hand, tuberculosis remains widespread, especially among people between the ages of 15 and 44. Surprisingly, the primary cause of death reported in Meta in 1985 was diseases of teeth and gums, conditions that stem from the lack of dentists and an unbalanced diet based predominately on consumption of flour and carbohydrates. Other fatal maladies include venereal diseases, diseases of the skin, intestinal parasites, and malaria.

The best health facilities are located in Villavicencio. The city has a regional hospital, four urban health centers, and three rural health centers. Fifty-three percent of the medical personnel living in the department work in Villavicencio, but even there the lack of doctors is notable with only one practitioner for every three thousand three hundred inhabitants. In the rural areas the absence of medical personnel and such basic services as aqueducts and sewers exacerbate unhealthy environmental conditions. The most lethal situations are found in the Guahibo *resguardos* (reservations) that have been constituted by INCORA near San Martín, Puerto Gaitán, Puerto López, and Puerto Lleras. The health of the natives is especially at risk, because they resist white medicine and are prone to alcoholism and drug addiction.[36]

ECONOMY

During the last thirty years sweeping changes have affected the traditional economy of the Llanos in general, and Meta in particular. Villavicencio retains its position as the largest and most important city in the region, but ranching, after showing an increase in the 1980s, began a rapid decline during the following decades. At the same time the mechanization of rice and palm oil transformed those products into the primary exports of the region in 2002. Exports of petroleum have grown so spectacularly that Meta now accounts for 10.9 percent of national production, and of course, the importance of illegal drug-related commerce should not be overlooked. All of these activities tend to bring the greatest returns to entrepreneurs who do not reside in Meta. As Alberto Baquero Nariño explains, the Llano may truly be the future breadbasket of Colombia, but this position has come at the price of an extractive economy by which most of the profits and employment opportunities benefit capitalists outside the region.[37]

CATTLE

In 1974 there were 1.1 million head of cattle in Meta. Of these 173,200 were exported to Venezuela; 8,425 were slaughtered; 40,000 were *reposición* or replaced; and 198,000 were sent to Bogotá.[38] Between 1986 and 1987 violence in Casanare provoked a massive movement of cattle from that province into Meta, swelling the total to 1.6 million. As a result, only 34,763 were shipped to Venezuela; 130,528 were replaced; 45,826 slaughtered; and 285,000 sent to Bogotá. The annual export of cattle in the 1980s averaged 18 percent of the entire herd, an acceptable proportion, but it was already evident that problems lay ahead. Too many female cows were being exported for the preservation of the herds. The hatos that supplied 80 percent of the cattle were located in the savanna where production methods were quite backward, and owner absenteeism was the rule. By the year 2000 cattle hatos in Meta had disappeared leaving only pastures for fattening cattle coming from the outer plains on their way to Bogotá. As Baquero Nariño observes, "The transport of cattle on foot to Bogotá continued to indicate an extractive economy of very little regional value and a minimum generation of employment even in the modern sector."[39]

THE MECHANIZATION OF AGRICULTURE

In contrast to the decrease of cattle, the production of dry and irrigated rice has boomed, promoted by the construction of an ultramodern mill in 1987. In 1949 Meta produced 8,117 tons of dry rice and 3,000 tons of irrigated rice. The production was done primarily by tenant farmers who cultivated plots of between 40 and 100 hectares. Some families rented mills, but more than 40 percent of their harvest was exported without being processed. This situation changed in 1986 when Proexpo, a government agency, gave a grant of COL$120 million to some entrepreneurs to build a modern rice plant in Meta. The resulting mill, known as Induarroz, was a factory with the capacity of processing 12 tons of rice an hour. In 1989 Meta was exporting 55,000 tons of dry rice and 70,000 tons of irrigated rice. By 2001 the department had become the primary Colombian producer of dry rice and ranked second in irrigated rice.[40] The presence of Induarroz encouraged traditional mill owners to streamline their own operations to avoid bankruptcy, but even with these changes, Induarroz processed 60 percent of the rice grown in Meta. Its capacity is so great that it now processes rice from other parts of Colombia, especially Tolima.[41]

Despite modernization, most Meta rice growers continue to adhere to traditional techniques. Only 25 percent own their own land. The other 75 percent are renters. The crop must be rotated, and cultivation requires many low-paid manual laborers. Other rice workers, such as tractor drivers and truckers, live in the *barrios populares* of Villavicencio while the manual laborers live in the asentamientos.

The production of Africa palm oil has undergone a similar expansion. In this case, a multinational corporation, Unipalma, introduced modern techniques and mechanization of the crop. Having acquired nine thousand hectares of land, it imported a labor force from the Pacific coast to cultivate the trees. Other companies, such as Palmar de Oriente and Manuelita, have also established themselves. With eighty thousand hectares under cultivation, Meta has become the number one producer of African palm oil in the country.[42] Other crops of major importance are all primarily grown in the piedmont. They include coffee, citrus fruit, soy, sorghum, yuca, and maíz.

PETROLEUM AND THE LLANOS

The exploration for oil in the Colombian Llanos, first begun in the 1940s, finally struck it rich in Arauca in 1980 when test wells dug by ECOPETROL and Occidental Petroleum in Cravo Norte indicated that there were 500 million barrels of oil reserves in that location. The German company Mannesmann constructed a 186-mile pipeline from Cravo Norte to the Río Zulia oil terminal near the Venezuela border, and Bechtel Engineering built a 305-mile pipeline connecting Río Zulia with the port of Coveñas on Colombia's northern coast. In 1986 the long-awaited "black gold" of the Llanos began pouring through the pipes at the rate of 200,000 barrels a day.[43] By 1991 the Cusiana-Cupiaga oil fields located near Yopal, Casanare, were delivering 200,000 barrels of crude oil daily, a figure expected to rise to half a million barrels by the year 2000.[44]

In 1996 wells at Chichimene, Castilla la Nueva, and Apiay in Meta started to produce oil at the rate of 20,500 barrels a day. All these wells were in a thirty-hectare area known as the Distrito Petróleo, which is in Apiay on the road to Puerto López, thirty minutes from Villavicencio. The Apiay refinery processes the crude oil to extract its principal derivatives: asphalt, cocinol (cooking fuel), CPM, benzine, and gasoline. From the Distrito Petróleo, the petroleum is pumped to the Porvenir station in Casanare, and from there it moves by pipeline to the Bosconía station en César and Barranca Bermeja in Santander to be shipped to the United States and Europe. Apiay also produces daily more than sixteen thousand feet of gas for domestic and industrial consumption in Villavicencio and Bogotá.[45] Despite the fact that guerrillas have repeatedly blown up the pipelines, by 2001 Meta was producing 21 million barrels of oil a year or 11 percent of Colombia's national output. This amount ranked it as the third largest petroleum producing department, exceeded only by Casanare with 45.1 percent of national output and Arauca with 17.7 percent.[46]

In 1996 the Department of Meta received COL$23,093,879,714 in oil royalties and Villavicencio COL$5,745,220,872.[47] While at first glance this huge sum of money may seem to represent the city's long awaited bonanza, Reinaldo Barbosa, in his essay "Frontera Agrícola Orinoquense," cautions that past experience has shown that oil has not necessarily been a blessing to the regions where it has been discovered. In fact, using the example of Caño Limón in Arauca to calculate the economic and social benefits that oil has generated, he concludes that not only has this resource been squandered, but the efforts of department officials to cash in on the revenue has left Arauca in arrears, because they borrowed extravagantly on the expectation of future income only to find themselves saddled with the burden of servicing an enormous debt. Aggravating the situation is the lack of orderly, intelligent, and objective planning that might have avoided the growth of expenses and the deficit in the commercial balance.[48] Writing in 2000, Ojeda Ojeda agreed that just as the extraction of cattle had benefited the capital more than the Llanos, Meta's oil was likewise being exploited because the derivatives were cheaper in Bogotá than in Villavicencio.[49]

DRUGS

While the department does not include income from drug-related activities in its official economy, there is no question that the growing and selling of cocaine is a profitable industry in Meta. The influx of drug money began in the mid-1970s with the cultivation of marijuana. After 1980 the spread of coca growing followed the advance of colonization and undoubtedly served to stabilize developments in the Provincia del Ariari. According to Baquero Nariño, there quickly emerged a drug axis connecting Villavicencio-Granada-San José del Guaviare-Vistahermosa-Villavicencio, and the level of remuneration grew substantially in the years that followed. Many ranches were started with investments made from drug money, and the accumulation of capital had an effect on all the municipios of the region.[50] The extraordinary "dance of the millions" of pesos that filtered through the bank accounts of Villavicencio's different financial institutions is evidence of how its inhabitants were able to modernize ranching and rice milling. Drug money also contributed to the improvement of the infrastructure of hotels and other buildings in the piedmont. According to Baquero Nariño:

> One conclusion stands out: during the ten years of the cocaine economy cities were transformed and improved with greater speed than in the previous fifty years of the economy based on agro-export extraction.[51]

There is of course a dark side to this phenomenon. Drug barons located in other parts of Colombia bought up large amounts of land in Meta, Antioquia, Caquetá, and Guajira. To protect their properties, they encouraged the formation of paramilitary forces, and massacres of civilians caught between the guerrillas and the paramilitaries increased considerably. In addition, the rush to buy land in the Llanos led to a "counter-agrarian reform," as small farmers were coerced into selling their plots to would-be latifundistas.[52] These individuals then faced the choice of moving farther out into the savanna to begin cultivation on unclaimed public lands or to return to Villavicencio to join the growing population of displaced people.

THE GROWTH OF VILLAVICENCIO

Between 1973 and the present, Villavicencio has expanded more rapidly than almost any other city in Colombia. Beginning with the influx of drug money from marijuana and later cocaine, developers from Bogotá and other places began to create new barrios in the city to accommodate the burgeoning population. They constructed buildings in more modern styles. New materials such as *bloque* (cinder blocks), bricks, cement, and *Eternit* roofs replaced zinc and *barriz* (mud), and paint replaced *cal* (whitewash). Kitchens became more functional, bathrooms more hygienic. In the wealthier barrios houses were more comfortable, agreeable, and expensive. Meanwhile, the poor people, who lacked title to land and did not pay taxes, invaded the less desirable parts of Villavicencio, building slums or *turgurios* (slums) similar to those found in highland Colombian cities.

Perhaps even more important, the traditional elite was slowly giving way to a new emerging bourgeoisie that every day acquired more money, power, and influence over the economy and the city government. It is this transformation that most concerns Baquero Nariño, who points out that since 1973, Villavicencio has been the "victim of a lack of an authentic leadership class that understands the urgency of the design of its space in order to avoid the continuation of privilege invoked by pressure groups on specific zones to the detriment of others."[53] As a result, the city has been growing

without any control or order. Parks have been covered over by cement. Historic houses on the great haciendas built at the beginning of the century
have been destroyed, and recreation areas have been abandoned.

Villavicencio is a town located between two rivers: the Guatiquía and the
Ocoa. From the nearby mountains, one can see its disordered growth. The
city is a victim of the cannibalism of its streets, and there are many exam-
ples of a frontal assault by private citizens on public ways. Private contrac-
tors or public entities are constructing the newest barrios on land lacking
adequate drainage. Garbage and *cacarilla* (rice husks) flood the city and its
environs. There is a complete failure to provide adequate sources of puri-
fied water, and to cite only one example of bad management, a new aqueduct inaugurated at the end of 1989 was deficient a year later.[54]

By the 1980s changes in city life were increasingly evident. The traditional small town serenity had been broken. Crowds of people and automobiles clogged Villavicencio's narrow streets. Cafeterías sprang up in all
neighborhoods. As Ojeda Ojeda laments:

> Until 1970 people used to sleep in the park or on the street, and no one would
> rob them of a single peso. After 1980 that security was lost about the same time
> as the appearance of the underground economy and the floating population of
> *raspachines* (thieves).[55]

The city authorities could not control this chaotic, underground economy.
More than two thousand street venders began offering every kind of com-
modity, transforming Villavicencio into a kind of "Persian market." Some
began at dawn offering popular breakfast foods. By 9:00 AM others were selling water, soft drinks, and ice cream. They stood by traffic lights and attempted to hawk their wares to drivers of cars and bus passengers. They pa-
trolled the streets in search of buyers. These venders earned little and
received no social security. Most of them were unemployed or displaced people, single mothers or children who were struggling to support their families.
Even worse, mixed in with this floating population were criminals who stole
motorbikes and then called the owners to demand money for their return.

The police were helpless to stop these practices. At one point the authorities gathered up the venders and removed them from the central plazas of
the city. In response, the venders organized demonstrations to protest the
actions taken against them. Because most of them were displaced people,
they lived in the marginal barrios amid terrible conditions. As Gerardo Enciso, spokesperson for the venders, explained, "We are very needy, and we
want to be in a place where we will not bother anyone. If they dislodge us,
then we will move to another place where we can have a dignified life."[56]

In her 1992 study, Gloria Evelyn Martínez Salas suggested that Villavicencio was like other intermediate Colombian cities, such as Valledupar
(César), Ibague (Tolima), and Santa Marta (Magdalena), in that its acceler-

ated demographic growth was coupled with weak industrial development—a situation that produces marginalization, *sobreurbanización* (superurbanization), and other distortions, such as excessive unemployment and insufficient water supply, electricity, and sewers to satisfy the needs of the expanding population. She noted that in contrast to Bogotá, Medellín, and Barranquilla where 20 percent of the people were employed in manufacturing, in Villavicencio only 6.8 percent of the population were so employed, and most of those individuals worked for small companies rather than large corporations.[57]

Government figures for 2004 support Martínez Salas's hypothesis. In Villavicencio, which contained 42 percent of the total population of the department, 15.4 percent were unemployed, a figure 0.4 points higher than the national average. Of the working age population 56.3 percent had jobs in the city, while 38.1 percent were underemployed, a figure higher than the national average of 31.5 percent. Of those employed, only 9 percent were involved in industry. The commercial sector had the largest number with 32 percent; followed by community and social services, 23 percent; transport, 11 percent; construction, 7 percent; real estate, 7 percent; financial services, 1 percent; and other types, 5 percent.[58]

VILLAVICENCIO'S SEARCH FOR IDENTITY

In 1973 geographer Dieter Brunnschweiler predicted that in spite of the "few hundred thousands" that had crossed the Andes and settled in the Llanos during the twentieth century, they were not "the avant-garde of millions of people who would follow in the path of the frontiersman, settle in the immediate hinterland, consolidate it, and provide a ready market and supply zone for the pioneers." In short, he concluded, "Colombia does not move eastward behind her eastern frontier."[59] As we have seen, the extraordinary political, social, and economic changes that have occurred in Villavicencio and Meta since 1973 appear to prove Brunnschweiler's prediction wrong. Not only has the piedmont region of the Llanos become heavily populated, but the exploitation of petroleum and the development of a massive extractive agribusiness have made Meta a key contributor to the national economy. At the same time, as Martínez Salas has argued, Villavicencio in its urban makeup exhibits the same characteristics as mid-size cities of the highlands. Indeed, as the frontier line has moved away from the piedmont in the twenty-first century, Villavicencio is facing a crisis of identity. As Espinel Riveros warns, improvements in the Bogotá–Villavicencio highway have had the effect of converting Villavicencio into a suburb of the capital. At the same time, the city remains the Gateway to the Llanos. Andean campesinos stream through the city hoping to find free land *más allá* (farther away); at the same time, colonos, discouraged by random violence and seizure of their lands, are returning to the city as *desplazados.*

Espinel Riveros and her Villavicence colleagues, Baquero Nariño and Ojeda Ojeda, seem to agree that the most serious problem facing the city in the twenty-first century is the need to consolidate its identity. Villavicencio has always consisted of heterogeneous cultures. As it adjusts to the impact of closer integration with Bogotá, its ability to retain its unique character depends on its citizens' willingness and ability to recover their history and reaffirm the city's position as the "Portal and Sultana de los Llanos."

The magnitude of this challenge became clear on October 21, 2000, when the town dignitaries celebrated the 150th anniversary of Villavicencio's erection as a Distrito Parroquial and the 160th anniversary of the city's founding. The day's events included a reading of academic papers, the announcement of the creation of the Fundación Centro de Historia de Villavicencio, and the playing for the first time of the city's official hymn.[60] The words are as follows:

I
Hermosa estampa tropical (Beautiful tropical portrait)
son los divinos paisajes de mi tierra (are the divine landscapes of my land,)
con mucho orgullo tu eres majestad, (with much pride, you are sovereign)
y capital de la tierra llanera (and capital of the Llanos land.)

II
Villavicencio luces con honor, (Villavicencio you display with honor)
a tus centauros con lanzas fieras (your centaurs with savage lances)
que son guardianes y velan soberanos (that are guardians and keep watch over)
toda tu extensa tierra ganadera (all your extensive ranch land.)

III
Naciste al mundo en el siglo diecinueve (You came into the world in the nineteenth century)
Fuiste fundada en la década del cuarenta (You were founded in the decade of the '40s)
Cuando tus padres venían de la cordillera (When your parents came from the cordillera)
te bautizaron cual caño Gramalote. (they baptized you caño Gramalote.)

IV
La fuerza brava de tu raza guerrera (The brave strength of your warlike race)
Se ha levantado majestuosa y dominante (has raised you up sovereign and dominant)
Cuando incendiada te erguiste altanera (When burned down you proudly rose up again)
Y hoy eres casa de todo visitante. (And today you are home to every visitor.)
Coro: Villavo la bella (bis)[61] (Chorus: Villavo the beautiful one [bis])

Photo 10.3.   Breaking a Wild Horse
Source: *Llanos de Colombia* (Bogotá: Litografía Arco, 1986), 930.

The words of this hymn celebrate the duality of cultures that have characterized Villavicencio from the day of its founding. The original settlers came from Cundinamarca, Tolima, and Boyacá, bringing with them their *guate* (highland) way of life, while the influx of vaqueros who accompanied their cattle from the Llanos Adentro left in their wake such elements of "Llanero" culture as ranching, music, folklore, and food.

Indeed, to this day the city has a dual economy, for although it is the principal urban center of the Llanos region, the products grown in the Llanos Adentro, Casanare, and Arauca pass through it to supply the demands of the vast Bogotá market. Socially, Villavicencio remains a human crucible in which are mixed the Andean traditions and the customs of the Llanos. If the city is largely Andean and modern in character (in 2005 merchants were looking forward to the construction of its first Centro Comercial Unicentro or mall),[62] its systematic celebration of traditional Llanero culture, which includes sponsoring the annual Torneo Internacional de Joropo (International Joropo contest), El Reinado Nacional del Joropo (national beauty contest to select the Queen of the Joropo), the Festival de la Canción Colombian (Festival of Colombian Song), along with the unending flow through its streets of eager immigrants looking for a new life in the plains combine to reinforce Villavicencio's image as the Gateway to the Llanos and its heritage as a frontier metropolis.

NOTES

1. Colombia, La población en Colombia, 1973, XIV *Censo Nacional de Población yIII de Vivienda, Octubre 24, 1974* (Bogotá:Departamento Administrativo Nacional de Estadística, 1980), 5.

2. Colombia, *La población de Colombia en 1985* (Bogotá: Departamento Administrativo Nacional de Estadística, 1990), 147–48.

3. Martínez Salas, "Crecimiento Urbano, 200–3.

4. *Colombia a su alcance* (Bogotá: Planeta, 1999), 134.

5. Gobernación del Meta, "Villavicencio-ciudad pujante y cosmopolita" from www.gobernaciondelmeta.gov.co/inforNoticia.asp?IdNot=58 (accessed July 7, 2005).

6. Martínez Salas,"Crecimiento Urbano," 199.

7. Gobernación del Meta, "Villavicencio-ciudad pujante y cosmopolita."

8. To cite just one example, on January 22, 2002, at 9:30 AM the FARC set up a roadblock on the highway fifteen minutes outside of Villavicencio. After shooting one driver of a private car, they stopped a bus, forced the twenty-five passengers to get out, and burned the vehicle. The government responded by sending soldiers from the army's VII Brigade to engage the guerrillas. As a result the road was closed for several days, cutting off the Llanos from the highlands. See "Acciones Terroristas FARC y Paramiltarismo," wib.matriz.net/2002colombia/ene02/ene_colomb04_es.html (accessed July 7, 2005).

9. "Bogotá-Villavicencio Highway," www.ingetec.com.co (accessed July 9, 2005).

10. Ojeda Ojeda, *Villavicencio*, 26.

11. Ojeda Ojeda, *Villavicencio*, 31.

12. Ojeda Ojeda, *Villavicencio*, 31.

13. Ojeda Ojeda, *Villavicencio*, 38.

14. Maltilde Beltrán Figueredo, "El Ordenamiento Territorial," in *Por los caminos del llanos*, 2: 74–76.

15. *Llano 7 Días*, July 13, 2005.

16. Espinel Riveros, *Villavicencio*, 206.

17. *Diagnóstico Geográfico Orinoquia Colombiana*, Vol. 1, *Población* (Bogotá: Instituto Geográfico Agustín Codazzi, 1986), 1: 24–26.

18. *Diagnóstico Geográfico*, 1: 69–74.

19. Beltrán Figueredo, "El Ordenamiento Territorial," 77.

20. Beltrán Figueredo, "El Ordenamiento Territorial," 77.

21. Alberto Baquero Nariño, *El caso llanero: Villavicencio* (Villavicencio: Editorial Siglo XX, 1990), 74–80.

22. Renaldo Barbosa Estepa, "Para-Estados y Crisis Institucional en la Orinoquia Colombiana," in *Iglesia, movimientos y partidos: Política y Violencia en la historia de Colombia*, ed. Javier Guerrero Baron (Tunja: Asociación Colombiana de Historiadores, 1997), 149.

23. Molano, "Violence and Land Colonization," 205.

24. Barbosa Estepa, "Para-Estados," 151.

25. Barbosa Estepa, "Para-Estados," 151.

26. Elisender Adan Ovalle, "La Violencia Política y la Acción Guerrillera en los Llanos Orientales en la Década de los años Ochenta" in *Por los Caminos del Llanos*, 3: 314.

27. Red de Solidaridad Social, *Informe sobre Desplazamiento Forzado en Colombia, primer trimester de 2001* (Bogotá, July 3, 2001), 6.

28. Ojeda Ojeda, *Villavicencio*, 67.

29. AMR 23/009/2001, "Fear for safety, internally displaced people at the La Nohora camp, city of Villavicenio, Meta Department," web.amnesty.org (accessed June 14, 2004).

30. "Colombia Copes with Latest Bombing," CBS NEWS.com (accessed April 7, 2002).

31. On June 29, 2005, Pope Benedict XVI bestowed palliums or woolen shawls on thirty-two metropolitan archbishops from around the world to symbolize their bond with the Vatican. Included in that group was José Octavio Ruiz Arenas, Archbishop of Villavicencio. In his speech, the pope appealed to Orthodox Christians saying that a united church could help a world that is "full of skepticism and doubts" to believe. "Pope Benedict XVI bestows the Pallium," it.news.yahoo.como/050629/38/3a9qi.html (accessed July 9, 2005).

32. "Diócesis de Villavicencio-Colombia," www.geocities.com/diocesisvillavicencio/ (accessed January 8, 2005).

33. "Company of Mary (Montfort Missionaries)," www.montfor.org/English/index.htm (accessed July 5, 2005).

34. *Diagnóstico geográfico*, 2: 2–9; Ojeda Ojeda, *Villavicencio*, 104.

35. *Diagnóstico geográfico*, 2: 13.

36. *Diagnóstico geográfico*, 2: 99–102.

37. Baquero Nariño, *El caso llanero*, 135–43.

38. Baquero Nariño, *El caso llanero*, 67.

39. Baquero Nariño, *El caso llanero*, 70. "Reposición" cattle were brought into Meta from other Llanos territories.

40. Colombia, Ministerio de Comercio, Industria y Turismo, "Estructura Productiva y de Comercio Exterior del Departamento del Meta" (Bogotá, April 2004), 7.

41. "Estructura Productiva," 75.

42. "Estructura Productiva," 75.

43. Diana Jean Shemo, "Oil Companies Buy an Army to Tame Colombia's Rebels," *New York Times*, August 22, 1996.

44. "Colombia Hopeful on Huge Oil Find," *New York Times*, December 23, 1991. The Cusiana-Cupiaga oil fields were developed by a consortium that included ECOPETROL, British Petroleum, the Triton Energy Corporation, and Total Compagnie Française del Petroles.

45. Ojeda Ojeda, *Villavicencio*, 143.

46. "Estructura Productiva," 13–14. On October 4, 2002, Juan Forero reported counter-insurgency troopers were to be assigned to protect the 500-mile pipeline from Arauca to Coveñas on the Caribbean coast. In 2001 repeated pipeline bombings by the guerrillas had cost the government nearly $500 million dollars—a blow

in a country where oil accounts for 25 percent of revenues. "The two main rebel groups, which view Occidental [petroleum] as a symbol of American imperialism, have bombed the pipeline 948 times since the 1980s, while extorting oil royalty payments from local government officials." *New York Times*, October 4, 2002.

47. Ojeda Ojeda, *Villavicencio*, 143.

48. Reinaldo Barbosa Estera, "Frontera Agricola Orinoquense: De la precariedad estatal a la crisis de derechos humanos," in *Conflictos regionales: Amazonia y Orinoquia* (Bogotá: Tercer Mundo, 1998)," 164–68.

49. Ojeda Ojeda, *Villavicencio*, 245.

50. Baquero Nariño, *El caso llanero*, 128.

51. Baquero Nariño, *El caso llanero*, 132.

52. Ricardo Rocha García, "Drug Trafficking and Its Impact on Colombia: An Economic Overview," *Canadian Journal of Latin American and Caribbean Studies*, 28: 295.

53. Baquero Nariño, *El caso llanero*, 32.

54. Baquero Nariño, *El caso llanero*, 32.

55. Ojeda Ojeda, *Villavicencio*, 245.

56. Cited by Ojeda Ojeda, *Villavicencio*, 67.

57. Martínez Salas, "Crecimiento Urbano, 2: 200–3.

58. "Estructura Productiva," 18.

59. Brunnschweiler, *The Llanos Frontier*, 62.

60. Nancy Espinel Riveros, comp. *Otra Mirada*, 10–12.

61. "Himno," Gobernación del Meta, http://www.gobernaciondelmeta.gov.co (accessed July 7, 2005).

62. *Llano 7 Días*, July 7, 2005.

11

Villavicencio and the Llanos Frontier

Ever since Frederick Jackson Turner published his paper in 1893 on "The Significance of the Frontier in American History," the study of the role of frontiers in national experience has been a well-defined historical subfield. Until the 1980s, it was not uncommon for scholars from many disciplines to associate the concept of *frontier* with the rapid expansion of U.S. settlement across the North American continent and to suggest that this series of moving frontier zones helped to fashion a distinctly North American culture that emphasized individuals and limitless opportunities.

In the last twenty-five years, however, the emergence of a highly publicized group of historians identified as New Western Historians, has presented a darker vision of the American West. These younger scholars reject Turner's interpretation as too time bound and ethnocentric, and they seek to offer a more realistic interpretation of the nature of the American West. Instead of regarding the frontier as a source of American egalitarianism, they suggest that it promoted class conflict and inequality and, through violence, it reinforced unequal relations of power. Instead of seeing Anglo-Americans moving westward along the edge of Turner's line that separated savagery and civilization, New Western historians concern themselves with multiethnic and multiracial worlds described as zones of transculturation.[1] Despite their efforts to dismiss Turner's model, his thesis has continued to attract scholars who find it useful in modified forms, and the concept of frontier remains a compelling heuristic device, used even by Turner's detractors.[2]

With the notable exception of Argentine and Brazilian historians, Latin American intellectuals have seldom considered their own frontiers central to the formation of their national identities or national institutions.[3] Nevertheless, frontier theories have been applied to Latin American history, primarily by North Americans, and as in the case of the United States, these interpretations have undergone significant changes in the last thirty years. The object of this chapter is to examine the way ideas concerning the impact of the Llanos frontier on the shaping of the Colombian nation have changed during the twentieth century and to examine contemporary theories about the role of Villavicencio as a frontier city.

INTERPRETATIONS OF THE
LLANOS FRONTIER BEFORE 1974

In 1923 Peruvian Victor Andrés Belaúnde was one of the first Latin American *pensadores* to consider the Turner Thesis as it might apply to South America. In an essay entitled "The Frontier in Hispanic America," he argued that the expanding frontier in the Turnerian sense appeared only rarely in Spanish America. In contrast to the modest barrier posed by the Alleghenies to westward movement in the United States, the South American Andes presented such insuperable obstacles for reaching the Amazon valley that the most typical of Hispanic American republics—Colombia, Ecuador, Peru, and Bolivia—could not be classified as "frontier countries," and, therefore, developed differently from the United States. To be more specific, Belaúnde suggested that the absence of accessible free land in these nations was responsible for the lack of dynamism in their cities, which he described as remaining "motionless with stagnant populations."[4]

Writing in 1931, geographer Isaiah Bowman essentially agreed with Belaúnde's analysis. He noted that the first burst of European settlement into South America was "one of the most extraordinary human events this earth has ever witnessed."[5] The Spanish quickly incorporated into their New World empire the Amerindians living in the high Andes and along the coasts, but their impetus was checked when they arrived at the inhospitable jungles of the Amazon basin and the equally unattractive tropical plains broken up by the Orinoco River and its tributaries. Blocked by geographic obstacles, deadly climate, native resistance, and lack of material incentives, they contented themselves with extending nominal rule over thousands of miles of unexplored wilderness.

For three hundred years this frontier line, established by the seventeenth century along the edge of the Eastern Andean Cordillera, expanded eastward only slightly despite improved health conditions and technology that made the tropical lowlands potentially more accessible in the early twentieth century. As a result, Bowman was joined by other geographers writing in the 1930s who agreed that Colombia, Ecuador, Peru, and Bolivia, unlike the United States with its moving frontier, were characterized by permanent frontiers and that the people who lived in these eastern frontier regions might rightfully be called pioneers even though they had lived on farms or in villages occupied by their families for generations.[6]

From colonial times to 1940, the settlement pattern in the Colombian Llanos conformed to this general definition of a permanent frontier. Moreover, pre–World War II scholars were not optimistic about the possibilities for future growth. As Clarence F. Jones stated, with no railroad likely to bridge the cordillera to reduce the isolation of Meta and Casanare, and with the Venezuelan Llanos offering easier access and much greater potential for oil and livestock exploitation, future development of the Colombian plains region was unlikely to occur for many decades.[7] Even after a period of rapid population growth in Meta, as late as 1973 geographer Dieter Brunnschweiler, as previously noted, maintained that the Llanos frontier was not "expanding" at a pace similar to the western frontier of North America, and he concluded that "Colombia does not move eastward behind her eastern frontier."[8]

THE TRANSFORMATION OF META AND VILLAVICENCIO IN THE SECOND HALF OF THE TWENTIETH CENTURY

Notwithstanding Brunnschweiler's pessimism concerning Meta's future, during the second half of the twentieth century the development of the Llanos took a sharp turn. A major theater of La Violencia, the bloody civil war that broke out in 1948 and lasted until 1958, was located in the Llanos, and as 6,000 people abandoned the plains seeking safety in the cities, their loss was more than compensated for by the arrival of 16,000 new emigrants fleeing violence in other parts of Colombia. Enticed by modern health measures that reduced the morbidity of the climate and by the opportunity to colonize public lands, these new settlers came with the hope of beginning a new life for their families.[9] By 1972 Meta, elevated to departmental status in 1959, was the fastest growing region in Colombia with a population of 322,361 people of which 35 percent, or 112,130, resided in Villavicencio.[10]

This phenomenal expansion continued despite the renewed outbreak of guerrilla warfare, the influx of drug cartels, and the operations of paramilitary organizations and the Colombian Army. The discovery of exploitable oil brought in new revenues, as did the expansion of commercial farming of cattle and other products. The Constitution of 1991 recognized the population growth in the other Llanos territories by declaring Casanare, Arauca, and Vichada departments.

By 2005, inhabitants of the Llanos constituted only about 1 percent of Colombia's estimated total population of more than 40 million people , but the region remained one of the most rapidly growing segments of the country, both in terms of economy and demography. The Bogotá-Villavicencio highway had undergone major improvements to cut the travel time between the two cities to less than three hours. The population of Meta alone had reached 618,427 people, with nearly one third of those, or 272,118 people, living in Villavicencio. The department was providing a large portion of the basic foods consumed by the residents of Bogotá. Oil exploitation was proving extremely lucrative.[11] There was serious talk of establishing an international airport outside of Villavicencio to relieve the pressure on Bogotá, and one of the greatest fears of leaders in the city was that within a few more decades, Villavicencio would be reduced to becoming a suburb of Bogotá.[12]

Underscoring this concern is Gloria Evelyn Martín Salas's 1992 study in which she argues that despite its location on the far side of the Eastern Cordillera, Villavicencio shares the same characteristics as other intermediate Colombian cities in the interior such as Valledupar (César), Ibague (Tolima), and Santa Marta (Magdalena). Each of these urban centers exhibit exaggerated demographic growth coupled with weak industrial development. Their unbalanced economy produces marginalization, sobreurbanización and such other distortions as excessive unemployment and insufficient water supply, electricity, or sewers to satisfy the needs of the expanding population. In Villavicencio, for example, only 6.8 percent of the population were employed in manufacturing, in contrast to Bogotá, Medellín, and Barranquilla where 20 percent of the people had factory jobs, and most of that 6.8 percent worked for small companies rather than large corporations.[13] Alberto Baquero Nariño supported Martinez Salas's interpretation by affirming that Villavicencio's development since 1960 has reflected the socioeconomic model that has been applied throughout Colombia "which stimulates the growth of cities to the detriment of the country . . . In this sense, Villavicencio also has become ruralized, and the consequences of unemployment and underemployment have made inevitable the *barrios de invasión* and turgurios."

If Villavicencio exhibits characteristics similar to comparable cities in the interior, then we must conclude that Brunnschweiler was wrong in predicting that "Colombia does not move eastward behind her eastern frontier." In fact, the cutting edge of the frontier has moved out beyond Villavicencio to lie in Ariari and San José de Guaviare. As Father Angel Bianchi, the Salesian priest serving the Diocese of Ariari, commented in 1977, continuous colonization into the eastern plains created in the nascent settlements many characteristics of the North American West. Referring to Ariari, he observed that in the early years there was little appreciation for human life as immigrants moved out to claim public lands. These recent arrivals came from all parts of the interior and were quite diverse with regard to their "degree of culture, their mentality and their customs." It was necessary to overcome enormous difficulties to survive, which is why "Ariari can be called a 'new frontier' country, as in the films of the 'Far West.'" [14]

SOME INTERPRETATIONS OF VILLAVICENCIO AND
META AS A FRONTIER

During the 1990s four Llanero scholars offered frontier interpretations of Villavicencio and Meta that agree on essential points but diverge in their emphasis. In his 1997 book, *Un pueblo de frontera: Villavicencio 1840–1940*, historian Miguel García Bustamante challenged the now familiar theory that the Llanos formed a permanent frontier by pointing out that, not withstanding the geographical difficulty of intercourse between them, the proximity of Villavicencio to Bogotá had, from the seventeenth century, involved a reciprocity characterized by unequal relations between the town and the capital because Villavicencio was dependent politically on Bogotá, and its export economy of cattle and rice was directed almost exclusively to the national capital.[15]

García Bustamante further refined his analysis in 2003 to suggest that the Llanos region per se consisted of two different frontiers. Reflecting Father Bianchi's observations, he argued that the piedmont area (also known as the *Llanos arriba*) was a *frontera provisoria* (temporary frontier) characterized by constant interactions with the highlands and where settlements were dependent on Bogotá with regard to trade, investment, and services. On the other hand, the grasslands east and north of the piedmont or the *Llanos abajo* remained a so-called permanent frontier where development has been much slower.[16]

As the epicenter of a frontera provisoria Villavicencio is a frontier city from the standpoint of the east as well as the west, for just as it receives a constant stream of emigrants from Colombia's highland departments, it continues to be the western terminal for sacas or cattle regularly driven from the northern and far eastern plains of Casanare and Arauca to be sold eventually in Bogotá. In her books Nancy Espinel Riveros has emphasized that, given this dual frontier situation, Villavicencio has been, since its founding, a mixture of two distinct cultures. The earliest inhabitants who arrived there before 1940 emigrated primarily from eastern Cundinamarca or Tolima, bringing with them a guate (highland) way of life, while the influx of vaqueros who accompanied their cattle from the east or Llanos abajo left in their wake, especially after 1940, elements of Llanero culture, such as music, folklore, and food.[17]

This duality of cultures exists to the present day. On the one hand, the majority of Andean people who come to Villavicencio have no intention of remaining. Imbued with a romantic vision of the Llanos as a land of cowboys and freedom, they regard the city as the jumping off place from which to set forth to claim their fortunes. Such people do not intend to establish roots in the town and show little civic concern for its well-being. On the other hand, for discouraged colonos returning from the Llanos abajo, forced off their lands by guerrilla threats, government violence, or economic failure, Villavicencio is a potential gateway to a new life in the highlands.[18]

Because of this mixture of regional cultures brought from several highland departments as well as those that have evolved in Arauca and Casanare, Espinel Riveros writes that the ethos of the city is in a process of hybridization, and she adds, "It is necessary to insist that Villavicencio is not the Llano, and the Llano is not Villavicencio. Even though they participate in the same region and maintain mutual and intense relations, they have different commercial and cultural geographies." In her view Villavicencio has been converted into a human "crucible" in which all these distinctive customs have been mixed:

> As a result the city is open to the stranger and the persecuted of whatever condition. [It is] cosmopolitan in its social composition, multiple and diverse in its creative dynamic, but lacking a defined cultural identity because today it neither personifies the Llano as such, nor reproduces the highland ancestry, nor has it sufficiently assimilated the heterogeneous subcultural contributions of the migrants.[19]

Taking a dependency point of view, Baquero Nariño, an economist at the Universidad Nacional, describes the same phenomenon of a dual frontier, but he substitutes the term *frontera interior* for Bustamante's frontera provisora. Baquero suggests that Villavicencio exhibits the characteristics of a frontera interior because "immigrants pass through the city with little desire to settle in it; residency is impermanent; there is little substantial financial investment in the region, and the inhabitants do not display a sense of civic concern." Although there are some organizations in Villavicencio, such as the Corporación Cívica Sesquicentenario, La Casa de la Cultura, and the Cámara de Comercio, that nurture a collective spirit, Villavicencio lacks a consolidated, directing class that could implement an economic plan for the city and the department. For more than four decades the city has grown without any control or order, a fact that further demonstrates "the lack of an authentic leadership class that understands the urgency of the design of its space in order to avoid the continuation of privilege invoked by pressure groups on specific zones to the detriment of others."[20]

Still worse, from Baquero's point of view, is that although Villavicencio is the center of Llanero economy, since 1950 that economy has been characterized by "savage capitalism" by which he means that it is dominated by "the continued exportation of economic products and the absence of a real agroindustrial economy that might generate wealth for the region."[21] Twenty percent of the cattle that leave Meta for Bogotá arrive from hatos located in the piedmont while 80 percent come from hatos near San Martín and Puerto López. Thus, the bulk of the cattle come from ranches characterized by traditional ranching techniques, absentee landlords, low pay for the workers, and the selection of too many female animals to preserve the inventory. In short, "The transport of cattle on foot for Bogotá continues to indicate an extractive economy of very little regional value and minimal generation of employment."[22]

The situation of rice and African palm production is little better. Domination of these crops by large processing firms, such as Indaruz and Fanagra (a large corporation which produces refined palm oil, margarine, and other industrial derivatives), has driven many smaller operations out of business. These giant companies have their headquarters in cities other than Villavicencio, and the taxes they pay do not return to the region.

In addition, sawmills, carpenter shops, and furniture making that are located in Villavicencio remain technologically backward. Throughout the Llanos, in clear decline are small-time processors of cotton, coffee, and cacao. Land tenancy is skewed with less than 2 percent of the proprietors owning more than 61 percent of the land. According to the Corporación Llanos de Colombia, the economic growth of the Llanos "has been undervalued and products from the Llanos are regarded as inferior."[23] Llanero cattle slaughtered in Bogotá bring a cheaper price despite the excellent quality of the meat. Rice mills and palm oil processors that acquire raw materials from the Llanos commonly pack them with different names to sell them at higher prices.[24]

Baquero does not consider the impact of the Meta petroleum boom in his analysis, but it is clear from the writings of Reinaldo Barbosa Estera that oil exploitation has been similarly skewed to profit multinational corporations rather than the economic growth of the department. Colombia's Orinoco plains have a proven reserve of 500 million barrels of oil, but in those locations where it has been extracted, petroleum revenues have not fulfilled the promise of generating the expected revenue. Using the example of Caño Limón to calculate the economic and social benefits that oil has generated in Arauca, Barbosa concludes that "not only has the resource been squandered, but efforts to capitalize on the investment have placed the department in debt by imposing a deduction on its incomes that will surely remain for a long time." This situation occurred because of the lack of orderly, intelligent, and objective planning. Barbosa further asserts that the ministerio de minas y energía's decision to hand over the pipelines to a multinational company for ninety-nine years "can be seen as a rebirth of colonialism."[25]

Baquero does point out that the underground economy, which is something that affects all of Colombia, also plays a major role in the Llanos. After 1978 the extensive settlement in Meta by colonos, whose expectations of satisfying their minimum needs had been postponed for many years due to absolute government neglect, combined with a cultural predisposition for easy money and the precarious nature of an authentic governing class to provide an ideal environment for the growing and processing of cocaine. On the one hand, the arrival of guerrillas and drug traffickers helped to create a horrific climate characterized by massacres, assassinations, extortion, and kidnapping. On the other, profits from the underground drug economy stabilized the colonization of the Ariari in a relatively short time and considerably improved hotel infrastructure; public amusements such as restaurants, inns, and discotheques; roads; and housing in many sections of the Llanos and Villavicencio.

Baquero concludes that the impact of the Llanos economy on Colombia as a whole is extraordinary. Meta is among the top five departments in national production of six agricultural products (rice, African palm, soy, cacao, sorghum, and papaya), in addition to supplying 60 percent of Bogotá's meat and 11 percent of the nation's petroleum. Nevertheless, even as entrepreneurs are transforming the region, the bulk of the resources are going to Bogotá, and the Llanos are locked into a syndrome of an extractive economy that must be broken. To arrest this process of "growth without development," Baquero suggests that the state needs to create a special development plan for the Llano Adentro. It should consider a new law on agrarian reform and find easier ways to provide credit for campesinos. In addition, the asymmetric interchange between Bogotá and the Llanos must be corrected, and Villavicencio must be given more power to take charge of regional development.

In the future, local leaders need to elaborate policy toward two ends: first to prepare the territory for a wave of colonization that will come with the opening of the Carretera Marginal de la Selva, and second, to foster a solid base of cultural identity rooted in the history of the Llanos to prepare for the influx of people from other regions. Baquero notes that Villavicencio lacks historical houses and museums, and he describes the cultural apathy of its citizens as "the result of savage capitalism that pushes to the side spiritual development."[26] He concludes:

> Villavicencio and the zone that it influences has an enormous possibility of improvement if it decides to implement strategies that motivate and develop community and supports its initiatives in the fields of culture, recreation, participation in service and community activities, sport and physical education. The demonstration of this effort will be able to transform the present notions that human beings and society are merely exclusive instruments for the obtaining of material ends.[27]

THE POWER OF MYTH

García Bustamante, Espinel Riveros, Barbosa Estera, and Baquero all agree that Villavicencio and Meta as a whole are rapidly modernizing but in ways that bode ill for the future unless a new and committed directing class takes control of the various political and economic forces. They also agree that old myths about the Llanos still play a role in Colombian perceptions of the region. For example, Baquero opens his book with the following statements: "The Llano is a mythology from which nobody escapes and as all mythology, it sounds better if it is accompanied by lyricism:

> Thus it is easy to say: "Its rivers, deep and tumultuous or still and light, carry in their waters enchanted wealth, united in imagination as a necklace of foam put around the neck of Mother Earth."[28]

He adds that for the people of the Llanos, Villavicencio is the end of the road. It is a cosmopolitan space in which the patria is nearer, but for Andean travelers reaching the city from the interior, Villavicencio represents mystery, life, hope, and uncertainty. They come inspired by an idea of Llanero music or a romantic vision far from crude reality.[29]

Historically speaking three myths have been perpetuated about the Llanos since the era of independence. The first, fueled by the heroism of Bolívar's Llanero army against the Spanish during the Battles of the Pantano de Vargas, July 25, 1819, and Boyacá, August 7, 1819, is the myth of the romantic, picturesque Llanero described by an American traveler in 1913 as a "half-Spanish, half-Indian, wild, brave, restless, devil-may-care cowboy Cossack of the Colombian steppes and boastful Tartar full of poetic fire."[30] The second more horrifying myth popularized by José Eustacio Rivera in his novel La vorágine published in 1924, depicted the Llanos as a "*devoradora de hombres*" (devourer of men)—a godforsaken land filled with cannibals, wilds beasts, and poisonous snakes.[31]

The third myth, which had roots in the nineteenth century, presented a picture of the Llanos far from being a devoradora de hombres but rather as "the future of Colombia." Promoted by official pronouncements beginning in the second half of the nineteenth century, government authorities frequently referred to the plains as a region of untold wealth and resources that within a few short years would become the heartland of Colombian prosperity. The following statement taken from a congressional report of September 18, 1882, is representative of this rhetoric:

> The vast and rich eastern region of the Republic known by the name of the Llanos of Casanare and San Martín, by its topography, by the fertility of its soil, and by the abundance and wealth of its natural products is called to be in the more or less distant future, the center of a civilization more advanced perhaps than that which the now occupied interior regions will reach.[32]

President Alfonso López Pumarejo enthusiastically adopted this view in 1934, and by making the development of Meta one of the centerpieces of his

Revolución en Marcha, firmly supported the idea that the Llanos represented the "Future of Colombia."

It is this third myth that the officials of Villavicencio and Meta have energetically cultivated during the last thirty years. For example, in July 1988 to celebrate the twenty-seventh anniversary of the creation of the Department of Meta, the secretaría general proudly proclaimed:

> Somos un solo pueblo (We are a single people)
> Un pueblo orgulloso (A proud people)
> Trabajador (Hardworking)
> Valiente (Brave)
> Somos el Meta (We are Meta)
> El futuro (The future)
> Vamos pa'lante (We march forward)
> Vivimos en paz (We live in peace)
> EL FUTURO IS AHORA (THE FUTURE IS NOW).[33]

Given the strength of the violence occurring in the department at the time, one has to question the credibility of this pronouncement, but in recent years, Villavicencio has chosen to identify itself with the best of Llanero culture: the folk music, the dance known as the joropo, and the notion that the city and the department offers immigrants a vista of unlimited opportunities.

With the proliferation of radio, television, and Internet communication surmounting the geographic obstacles that have traditionally cut Villavicencio and the Llanos off from the national heartland and given the news of the petroleum reserves as well as countless assassinations, massacres, and bombings perpetrated by guerrillas, paramilitaries, and the army, one might imagine that Colombian awareness of Villavicencio and the Llanos in general would be at an all-time high. However, in 2004 a random survey of some Colombian scholars elicited some intriguing answers to the question "How do you think contemporary Colombians envision the Llanos frontier today?" For example, a professor based in Medellín replied that in her view, "If *antioqueños* think of the Llanos at all, they see it as an unknown, remote and mysterious region. No one would plan a vacation there. There is an enormous ignorance about the Llanos, as if it were not part of Colombia." But she added, "Opinions may be very different in Bogotá because there people own ranches in the plains; Llaneros come to the city, and one finds restaurants that sell meat that is cooked *a la llanera.*"[34] Another scholar from Bogotá responded, "I believe that the romantic view of cowboys, open plains, and lovely skies still exists. However, I think that the war has done much to make people think about the Llanos as one of Colombia's most dangerous territories, that is, with guerrillas, paramilitaries, and oil."[35] A scholar in Yopal, Casanare, had a different answer. In his view Colombian history has remained the history of the interaction between the highlands and the Caribbean coast with the peripheral territories playing a negligible role. "Moreover," he wrote with undisguised bitterness, "the inhabitants of the highlands see us as children, which explains why they rule us from Bogotá notwithstanding the decentralization established in the Constitution of 1991."[36]

The variety of these opinions inspired the commissioning of a broader survey of Colombian attitudes regarding the Llanos. In January 2005 three Colombian social scientists questioned ninety-eight individuals to ascertain their views concerning the Llanos.[37] The respondents included forty-seven females and fifty-one males. They ranged from under twenty years of age to over sixty years of age. Originally born in twenty different departments, all were living in Bogotá at the time of the survey. Of the ninety-eight respondents, forty-four stated that they had been to the Llanos, and sixty-one confessed that they would like to travel there. With regard to the three stereotypes, concerning the romantic image of freedom fighters, thirty-one replied that they had learned in school that Llaneros had been a key factor in winning the Battle of Boyacá, while nine disagreed. Surprisingly, over half or fifty-seven stated that they did not know anything about the role of the Llaneros in the War of Independence. Concerning the "Llanos as the future of Colombia," eighty-three respondents stated that the Llanos were important because of their beauty while sixty-five stressed their importance due to the existence of oil, agriculture, and cattle.

With reference to the negative image of the Llanos as a *devoradora de hombres* the answers were mixed. Some fifty-three people stated that the tropical environment would not deter them from visiting the Llanos, but forty-three people agreed that the activities of armed groups have made the Llanos one of the most dangerous places in the country. On this last question, the twenty-three dissenters stated that the media had exaggerated the violence occurring in the Llanos and that the region was no more dangerous than any other section of Colombia.

Perhaps, in terms of the issue of national identity, the most important question was the statement that the Llanos Orientales were known in Colombia principally for their distinctive music, culture, and folklore. Sixty-four respondents agreed, noting that Llanero music was not only beautiful and original, but it was also played throughout the country. They expressed a particular fascination with the joropo. As one individual explained, "Where one hears the joropo or a harp, one identifies it with the Llanos."

IS VILLAVICENCIO A FRONTIER METROPOLIS?

Ever since its founding in 1840, Villavicencio, until recently, has regarded itself as a frontier town, par excellence. With its sponsoring of the Festival de la Canción Colombiana, an annual Torneo Internacional de Joropo, and El Reinado Nacional del Joropo, the city continues to identify strongly with Llanero culture, even though the true center of regional life is located in San Martín and the Llanos of Arauca and Casanare. A case has been made that it remains a frontera provisoria or frontera interior because it is the dual launching place for Andean colonists for setting off for the Llanos and for colonos fleeing from the plains seeking to return to the highlands. Nevertheless, as chapters 10 and 11 have made clear, in recent years, Villavicencio has taken on characteristics similar to cities of its size in the highlands, and it is increasingly under the economic and political control of Bogotá. It is obvious that the cutting edge of the frontier has moved beyond it to places such as San José de Guaviare and Granada. In its search for an authentic cultural identity Villavicencio may rightfully celebrate its colorful past, but just as the former towns of the Old West in the United States can no longer pretend to lie along the frontier, Villavicencio has been fully integrated into Colombian society and culture.

Despite this transformation, as long as the Bogotá-Villavicencio highway remains the principal link between the highlands and the plains, Villavicencio can rightfully claim to be the Gateway to the Llanos. After negotiating the hair-raising road that twists its way down the Eastern Andean Cordillera, travelers reach the outcropping known as Buena Vista just above Villavicencio. From here they gain their first view of the immense plains, whose natural beauty holds a bewitching fascination. When the German traveler Ernst Röthlisberger made the trip by horseback in 1882, he dismounted at Buena Vista and saw, spread out before him, "the boundless plains." He wrote in his journal, "How can I describe my astonishment and rapture":

> No greater contrast can be imagined than that between the intricate massiveness of the Cordillera, rising to the region of perpetual snow, and this uniform tropical plain. Great and majestic in its solitude and mystery is the ocean; greater and more impressive are the Llanos. The ocean waves are rigid and dead, an image of dread and of blind Might, but the Llanos have movement of color and endless diversity. They are the image of Life—Life that preaches to man not his puny impotence, but awakens in him Hope, such as aroused the companions of Colombus on hearing the magic cry, "Land! Land!"[38]

Fifty-two years later in 1934 the Liberal journalist Luis Eduardo Nieto Caballero explained that his first impression of the Llanos was like a mystical seduction:

> The attraction of the Llanos is irresistible. . . . The Llanero is perhaps the only Colombian who rarely complains. Badly dressed, badly fed, with rustic shelter, absolutely alone, like a point in the immensity, it is clear that he is satisfied.

. . . I felt the mysterious call of the Llanos, and I understand, exalt and envy the life of the Llanero.[39]

Given the lamentable condition of the majority of people living in Villavicencio or Meta today at the beginning of the twenty-first century, probably no one would agree with Nieto Caballero in envying life in the plains, but the geographic grandeur of the Llanos continues to enthrall unsuspecting travelers who see them for the first time. As the Gateway and "Sultana" of this unique region, Villavicencio, whether frontier town or modern metropolis, will always hold a unique place among Colombian cities.

NOTES

1. David J. Weber and Jane M. Rausch, eds. *Where Cultures Meet: Frontiers in Latin American History* (Wilmington, D. E.: Scholarly Resources, 1994), xxxii.

2. See, for example, Andrew R. L. Cayton and Peter S. Onuf, *The Midwest and the National: Rethinking the History of an American Region* (Bloomington: Indiana University Press, 1990).

3. The classic Argentine work is Domingo Faustino Sarmiento, *Life in the Argentine Republic in the Days of the Tyrants; or Civilization and Barbarism*, trans. Mrs. Horace Mann (New York: Knopf, 1961). For a more recent Argentine interpretation see Hebe Clementi, *La frontera en América*, 4 vols. (Buenos Aires: Editorial Leviatan, 1986–1988). For an early Brazilian study see Clodomir Vianna Moog, *Bandeirantes and Pioneers*, trans. L. L. Garrett (New York: G. Braziller, 1964).

4. Victor Andrés Belaúnde, "The Frontier in Hispanic America," *Rice Institute Pamphlets* No. 10 (October 1923), 208.

5. Isaiah Bowman, *The Pioneer Fringe*, Special Publication, No. 12 (New York: American Geographical Society, 1931), 296.

6. Bowman, *The Pioneer Fringe*, 299; Raymond E. Crist, "Fixed Physical Boundaries and Dynamic Cultural Frontiers: A Contrast," *American Journal of Economics and Sociology* 12, no. 2 (April 1953), 230; Notable among Latin American scholars who have considered the role of frontiers are Silvio Zavala, "The Frontiers of Hispanic America," *The Frontier in Perspective*, ed. W. D. Wyman and C. B. Kroeber (Madison: University of Wisconsin Press, 1957), 35–58; José Honório Rodrigues, "Webb's Great Frontier and the Interpretation of Modern History," in *The New World Looks at Its History*, ed. A. Lewis and T. McGann (Austin: University of Texas Press, 1963), 155–64; and the aforecited Vianna Moog, *Bandeirantes and Pioneers*. The British historian Alistair Hennessy also examines this thesis in *The Frontier in Latin American History* (Albuquerque: University of New Mexico Press, 1978).

7. Clarence F. Jones, *South America* (New York: Holt, 1940), 607. Other geographers sharing this view included Bowman, *The Pioneer Fringe*, 296, and Raye Platt, "Opportunities for Agricultural Colonization in the Eastern Border Valleys of the Andes," in *Pioneer Settlement*, Special Publication, No. 14 (New York: American Geographical Society, 1932), 84.

8. Brunnschweiler, *The Llanos Frontier*, 62.

9. Ojeda Ojeda, *Villavicencio,* 187, 205.
10. *Monografía,* 13–17.
11. *Colombia a su alcance,* 134.
12. Espinel Riveros, *Villavicencio,* 208.
13. Martínez Salas, "Crecimiento Urbano," 199.
14. Martín González, *La prefecture apostólica del Ariari,* 231.
15. García Bustamante, *Un pueblo de frontera,* 11.
16. García Bustamante, *Persistencia y cambio,* 40–41.
17. Espinel Riveros, *Villavicencio,* 201–2.
18. Espinel Riveros, *Villavicencio,* 201–2.
19. Espinel Riveros, *Villavicencio,* 201–2.
20. Baquero Nariño, *El caso llanero,* 32–34.
21. Baquero Nariño, *El caso llanero,* 18.
22. Baquero Nariño, *El caso llanero,* 69.
23. Baquero Nariño, *El caso llanero,* 105.
24. Baquero Nariño, *El caso llanero,* 106.
25. Barbosa Estera, "Frontera Agrícola Orinoquense," 164–68.
26. Baquero Nariño, *El caso llanero,* 152.
27. Baquero Nariño, *El caso llanero,* 152.
28. Baquero Nariño, *El caso llanero,* 21.
29. Baquero Nariño, *El caso llanero,* 36–38.
30. Phanor James Eder, *Colombia* (London: T. Fisher Unwin, 1913), 235.
31. "Los colonizadores del llano," 145.
32. *Anales del Senado,* vol. 21, September 29, 1892, 167.
33. *Trocha* #153 (July 1988), 31.
34. E-mail to author, November 2, 2004.
35. E-mail to author, November 17, 2004.
36. E-mail to author, November 19, 2004.
37. The investigators were Leticia Arteaga, Stan Malinowitz, and Natali Perozzo.
38. Röthlisberger, *El Dorado,* 228–29.
39. Luis Eduardo Nieto Caballero, *Vuelo al Orinoco* (Bogotá: Librería Colombiana, Camacho Roldán, 1935), 124–25.

Bibliography

ABBREVIATIONS USED IN NOTES AND BIBLIOGRAPHY

AC	Archivo del Congreso, Bogotá
AHN	Archivo Histórico Nacional, Bogotá
BHA	Boletín de Historia y Antigüedades
CE	Comisario Especial
Cod. Nac.	Codificación nacional de todas las leyes de Colombia desde el año de 1821
DANE	Departamento Administrativo Nacional de Estadística
DIC	Departamento de Intendencias y Comisarías
DTN	Departament de Territorios Nacionales
GB	Gobierno de Bogotá
MG	Ministerio de Gobierno
MMF	Memorias del Ministerio de Fomento
MMG	Memorias del Ministerio de Gobierno
NHC	Nueva Historia de Colombia

ARCHIVAL MATERIALS

Archivo Histórico Nacional, Bogotá
Archivo Histórico Nacional, Bogotá. *José Caicedo, Province de los Llanos: Padrón formado en el año de 1778.* Morcote, October 14, 1778.
Archivo del Congreso: Cámara
Baldios (1879–1898)
Gobernación de Bogotá (1832–1857)
Ministerio de Gobierno (1879–1898)

PUBLISHED DOCUMENTS

Government Documents

Colombia. *Codificación de todas las leyes de Colombia desde el año de 1821.* 32 vols. Bogotá: Imprenta Nacional, 1924.

——. DANE: *La Población de Colombia en 1973: XIV Censo Nacional de Población y III de Vivienda,Bogotá, 1978.*

——. DANE: *La Población de Colombia en 1985: XV Censo Nacional de población y IV de vivienda,* Bogotá: 1990.

——. Memorias del Congress. *Discursos a la Inaugural Session del Primer Congreso de Territorios Nacionales,* 1966.

——. Ministerio de Comercia, Industria y Turismo. "Estructura Productiva y de Comercio Exterior del Meta." Bogotá, April 2004.

——. Ministerio de Fomento. *Memorias.* 1881.

——. Ministerio de Gobierno. *Memorias.* 1881.

——. Ministerio de Hacienda y Fomento. *Memorias.* 1869–1870.

——. Ministerio de Industrias. 1931.

——. Ministerio de Obras Públicas. 1936.

——. *Informes,* Prefect of San Martín. 1873–1882.

——. *Un año de gobierno 1950–1951.* 2 vols. 1951.

——. *Una política educativa para Colombia.* 4 vols. 1963.

Departamento de Boyacá. *Ordenanzas expedidas por la asamblea departamental de Boyacá en sus sessiones de 1892.* Tunja, 1892.

Departamento del Meta. *Monografía, folclor, cultura y turismo.* Villavicencio: Imprenta Departamental, 1972.

Galindo, Anibal. *Anuario estadístico de Colombia, 1876.* Bogotá: Imprenta Nacional, 1878.

Gobernación del Meta. Villavicencio-"Ciudad Pujante y Cosmpolita." www.gobernaciondelmeta.gov.co.

Lleras Camargo, Alberto. *El Primer Gobierno del Frente Nacional.* 4 vols. Bogotá: Imprenta Nacional, 1962.

Rojas Pinilla, Gustavo, ed. *Rojas Pinilla ante el Senado.* Bogotá: Editorial Excelsior, 1959.

——. *Mensajes y Discursos.* Bogotá: Empresa Nacional de Publicaciones, 1955.

Church Documents

Arquidiócesis de Villavicencio. www.geocities.com/diocesis_villavicencio/.

Bodas de plata misionales de la Compañía de María en Colombia: 1904–1929. Villavicencio: Imprenta San José, 1929.

Company of Mary (Montfort Missionaries). www.montfor.org

Conferencias Espicopales de Colombia, 1908–1953. 2 vols. Bogotá: Editorial El Catolicismo, 1956.

Dieres Monplaisir, Maurice, and Gabriel Capdeville. *Las misiones católicas en Colombia: informes de los años 1919, 1920, 1921, 1922, 1923.* Bogotá, Imprenta Nacional, 1921–1923.

Diócesis de Villavicencio, Colombia. www.geocities.com/diocesis-villavicencio/.

Ganuza, Marcelino. *Monografía de las misiones vivas de agustinos recoletos (candelarios) en Colombia*. 3 vols. Bogotá: Imprenta de San Bernardo, 1921.

Martín González, Angel. *La Prefectura Apostólica del Ariari (Colombia): Estudio Histórico*. Madrid: Central Catequisita Salesiana, 1977.

Mesanza, Andrés. *Apuntes y documentos sobre la orden dominicana de Colombia (de 1680 a 1930): apuntes o narración*. Caracas: Editorial Sur America, 1936.

Ortega Torres, José Joaquín. *La obra salesiana en Colombia: Los primeros cincuenta años: 1890–1940*. Bogotá: Escuelas Gráficas Salesianas, 1941.

Pérez Gómez, José. *Apuntes históricos de las misiones agustinianas en Colombia*. Bogotá: Casa Editorial de la Cruzada, 1924.

Vela, José de Calasanz. "Visita de las poblaciones del Meta," *Anales religiosos* (Bogotá) 1 (1884), 351–53.

Zamora, Alonso de. *Historia de la Provincia de San Antonio de Nuevo Reino de Granada*. Caracas: Editorial Sur America, 1930.

Official Periodicals

Anales del Senado, 1883–1930.
Diario Oficial, 1868– .
El Constitucional de Cundinamarca, 1832–1852.
Gaceta de Cundinamarca, 1886–1898.
Gaceta de la Nueva Granada, April, 1838–1846.
Gaceta Oficial, 1850.

Newspapers and Periodicals

Bogotá:
El Diario Nacional, 1916–1919.
El Espectador, 1917–1923.
El Liberal, 1948–1949.
El Siglo, 1949–1950.
El Tiempo, 1902–1932, 1934–1939, 1946–1950, 1969, 1974, 1976, 1991.
Semana, 1946–1953.
New York City:
"Colombia Hopeful on Huge Oil Find." *New York Times*, December 23, 1991.
New York Times, October 4, 2002.
Shemo, Diana Jean. "Oil Companies Buy an Army to Tame Colombia's Rebels." *New York Times*, August 22, 1996.
Villavicencio:
Eco de Oriente 1916–1939.
El Ferrocarril del Meta, 1917.
Llano 7 Días, 2005.
Trocha, 1989–1994.
Trocha #153 (July 1988), 31.

Theses and Dissertations

Baquero, Omar. "Departamento del Meta: Historia de su integración a la nación, 1536–1936." Thesis, Universidad Nacional–Bogotá, 1986.

Loy, Jane M. "A Study of Primary Education in Rural Colombia." Unpublished paper. Madison: University of Wisconsin, 1964.

Ramsey, Russell. "The Modern Violence in Colombia, 1946–1965." Ph.D. diss., Gainesville: University of Florida, 1970.

Books and Articles

Abel, Christopher. *Política, iglesia y partidos en Colombia, 1868–1953*. Bogotá: FAES-Universidad Nacional de Colombia, 1987.

Acevedo Latorre, Eduardo. *Geografía pintoresca de Colombia*. Bogotá: Litografía Arco, 1968.

Aguado, Pedro de. *Recopilación historial*. 4 vols. Bogotá: Empresa Nacional de Publicaciones, 1956.

Arbeláez, Tulio. *Espisodios de la Guerra de 1899–1903*. Manizales: Tip. Caldas, 1904.

Arcila Robledo, Gregorio, O. F. M. *Las misiones franciscanas en Colombia*. Bogotá: Imprenta Nacional, 1910.

Arnove, Robert F. "Education Policies of the National Front." In Berry, et al., *Politics of Compromise*, 381–411.

Baquero Nariño, Alberto. *El caso llanero: Villavicencio*. Villavicencio: Editorial Siglo XX, 1990.

Baquero Riveros, Omar. *Villavicencio ayer y hoy*. n.p. n.p., 1900.

Barbosa Estera, Reinaldo. "Frontera agrícola Orinoquense: de la precariedad estatal a la crisis de derechos humanos." In *Conflictos Regionales: Amazonia y Orinoquia*, 155–95. Bogotá: Tercer Mundo, 1998.

———. "Llanero conflicto y sabana: historias presentes." In *Los Llanos: Una historia sin fronteras*, 343–84. Bogotá: Academia de Historia del Meta, 1988.

———. "Para-Estados y Crisis Institucional en la Orinoquia colombiana." In *Iglesia, movimentos y partidos: Política y violencia en la historia de Colombia*, edited by Javier Guerrero Baron, 135–77. Tunja: Asociación Colombiana de Historiadores, 1997.

Bates, Nancy Bell. *East of the Andes and West of Nowhere*. New York: Charles Scribner's Sons, 1947.

Belaúnde, Victor Andrés. "The Frontier in Hispanic America." *Rice Institute Pamphlets* No. 10. (October 1923): 202–13.

Beltrán Figueredo, Matilde. "El Ordenamiento Territorial en el Departamento del Meta." In *Por los Caminos del Llano*, 2: 71–83.

Bergquist, Charles W. *Coffee and Conflict in Colombia, 1886–1910*. Durham: Duke University Press, 1978.

Berry, R. Albert, et al. *Politics of Compromise: Coalition Government in Colombia*. New Brunswick, N. J.: Transaction Books, 1980.

Bethell, Leslie, ed. *The Cambridge History of Latin America*. 10 vols. Cambridge: Cambridge University Press, 1984–1995.

Blydenstein, John. "Tropical Savanna Vegetation of the Llanos of Colombia." *Ecology* 48, no. 1 (Winter 1967): 1–14.

Bonnet, José. *Comercio oriental por el Río Meta*. Bogotá, 1884.

Bowman, Isaiah. *The Pioneer Fringe*. Special Publication, No. 12. New York: American Geographical Society, 1931.

Brisson, Jorge. *Casanare*. Bogotá: Imprenta Nacional, 1896.

Brunnschweiler, Dieter. *The Llanos Frontier of Colombia: Environment and Changing Land Use in Meta*. East Lansing: Michigan State University, 1972.

Buckland, Francis Trevelyan. *Curiosities of Natural History*. New York, 1859.

Burgos M., Carlos. *Crónicas y anécdotas regionales: Villavicencio años 1900*. (1999).

Bushnell, David. "Elecciones presidenciales colombianas, 1825–1856." In Urrutia and Arrubla, *Compendio de estadísticas históricas de Colombia*, 219–314.

———. *The Making of Modern Colombia: A Nation in Spite of Itself*. Berkeley: University of California Press, 1993.

Cabrera Becerra, Gabriel. *La iglesia en la frontera: misiones católicas en el Vaupés, 1850-1950*. Bogotá: Universidad Nacional de Colombia-Sede Leticia, 2002.

Camacho Leyva, Ernesto. *La policía en los territories nacionales*. Bogotá: Editorial ABC, 1947.

Camacho Roldán, Salvador. *Escritos varios*. 3 vols. Bogotá: Editorial Incunables, 1983.

Casas Aguilar, Justo. *La violencia en los Llanos Orientales*. Bogotá: ECOE Ediciones, 1986.

Cayton, Andrew R. L., and Peter S. Onuf. *The Midwest and the Nation: Rethinking the History of an American Region*. Bloomington: Indiana University Press, 1990.

Clementi, Hebe. *La frontera en América*. 4 vols. Buenos Aires: Editorial Leviatan, 1986–1988.

Codazzi, Agustín. *Geografía física y política de las provincias de la Nueva Granada*. Archivo de la Economía Nacional. vols. 21–24. Bogotá: Banco de la República, 1959.

Colmenares, Germán. *Las haciendas de los jesuítas*. Bogotá: Universidad Nacional de Colombia, 1969.

Colombia Hoy, 9th ed. Bogotá: Siglo Veintiuno, 1985.

Colombia a su alcance. Bogotá: Planeta, 1999.

Crist, Raymond E. "Fixed Physical Boundaries and Dynamic Cultural Frontiers: a Contrast." *American Journal of Economics and Sociology* 12, no. 2 (April 1953): 221–30.

Crist, Raymond E., and Ernesto Guhl. "Pioneer Settlement in Eastern Colombia." In *Annual Report of the Smithsonian Institution*, 391–413. Washington, D.C.: Smithsonian, 1956.

Crist, Raymond E., and Charles M. Nissly. *East from the Andes*. Gainesville: University of Florida Press, 1973.

Cuervo Márquez, Carlos. *El Llano*, Archivo de la Economía Nacional vol. 7. Bogotá: Banco de la República, 1955.

Curtin, Philip D. *Death by Migration: Europe's Encounter with the Tropical World in the Nineteenth Century*. New York: Cambridge University Press, 1989.

Deas, Malcolm. "Colombia, Ecuador and Venezuela, c. 1880–1930." In Bethell, *The Cambridge History of Latin America*, 5: 645

de Greiff, Luis. *Semblanzas y comentarios*. Bogotá: A B C, 1942.

de la Pedraja Tomán, René. *Los llanos: colonización y economía*. Bogotá: CEDE Documento 072, June 1984.

Delpar, Helen. *Red against Blue: The Liberal Party in Colombian Politics, 1863–1899.* Tuscaloosa: University of Alabama Press, 1981.

———, ed. *Encyclopedia of Latin America.* New York: McGraw-Hill, 1974.

———. "Thousand Days, War of the (1899–1902)." In Delpar, *Encyclopedia of Latin America,* 582.

*Diagnóstico Geográfico Orinoquia Colombiana.*Vol.1 Población; Vol. 2, Servicios sociale, educación y salud. Bogotá: Instituto Geográfico Agustín Codazzi, 1986.

Díaz Díaz, Oswaldo. *La reconquista española.* vols. 11, 12. In *Historia extensa de Colombia.* Bogotá: Ediciones Lerner, 1964–1967.

Dieres Monplasir, Mauricio. *Lo que nos contó el abuelito: El centenario de Villavicencio, 1842–1942.* Villavicencio: Imprenta San José, 1942.

Diot, Joelle."Baldíos, 1931–1971: Legislación y adjudicaciones," *Boletín Mensual de Estadística* (DANE) no. 296 (March 1976): 92–127.

Dix, Robert. *Colombia: Political Dimensions of Change.* New Haven: Yale University Press, 1967.

Eder, Phanor James. *Colombia.* London: T. Fisher Unwin, 1913.

Espinel Riveros, Nancy. *Villavicencio, Dos siglos de historia comunera: 1740–1940,* 2nd ed. Villavicencio: Editorial Juan XXIII, 1997.

———. *Otra mirada a la historia de Villavicencio.* Villavicencio: Fundación Centro de Historia de Villavicencio, 2000.

Flórez, Raquel Angel de. *Conozcamos al Departamento del Meta.* 3 vols. Bogotá: Fonda Rotatorio Judicial Penitenciaria Central, 1962–1963.

Fluharty, Vernon. *Dance of the Millions: Military Rule and Social Revolution in Colombia, 1930–1956.* Pittsburgh: University of Pittsburgh Press, 1957.

Fosdick, Raymond B. *The Story of the Rockefeller Foundation.* New York: Harper Brothers, 1952.

Franco Isaza, Eduardo. *Las guerrillas del llano.* Bogotá: Librería Mundial, 1959.

Garavito Jiménez, Gregorio. *Historia de la iglesia en los llanos.* Villavicencio: Imprenta Departamental del Meta, 1994.

García Bustamante, Miguel. *Un pueblo de frontera: Villavicencio 1840–1940.* Bogotá: Universidad de los Llanos, 1997.

———. *Persistencia y cambio en la frontera oriental de Colombia: El piedemonte del Meta, 1840–1950.* Medellín: Fondo Editorial Universidad Eafit, 2003.

Gast Galvis, Augusto. *Historia de la fiebre amarilla en Colombia.* Bogotá: Ministerio de Salud, 1982.

Gibson, William M. *The Constitutions of Colombia.* Durham, N. C.: Duke University Press, 1948.

Gómez, Fernando."Los censos en Colombia antes de 1905." In Urrutia and Arrubla, *Compendio de estadísticas históricas de Colombia,* 9–30.

Guerra Azuola, Ramón, "Apuntamientos de Viaje." *BHA* (January 1907) 4: 43, 415–30.

Gustavo, R. P., ed. *Rojas Pinilla ante el Senado.* Bogotá: Editorial Excelsior, 1959.

Gutiérrez, Rufino. *Monografías.* 2 vols. Bogotá: Imprenta Nacional, 1920–1921.

Guzmán Campos, Germán, Orlando Fals Borda, and Eduardo Umana Luna. *La Violencia en Colombia,* 2nd ed. 2 vols. Bogotá: Tercer Mundo, 1962–1964.

Hartlyn, Jonathan. *The Politics of Coalition Rule in Colombia.* New York: Cambridge University Press, 1988.

Havens, A. Eugene, et al. "Agrarian Reform and the National Front: A Class Analysis." In Berry, *Politics of Compromise*, 341–80.

Henao, Jesus María and Gerardo Arrubla. *Historia de Colombia*, 5th ed. Bogotá: Librería Colombiana, Camacho Roldán, 1929.

Henderson, James D. *Modernization in Colombia: The Laureano Gómez Years, 1889–1965.* Gainesville: University Press of Florida, 2001.

Hennessy, Alistair. *The Frontier in Latin American History.* Albuquerque: University of New Mexico Press, 1978.

Hettner, Alfred. *Viajes por los andes colombianos* (1882–1884). Translated by Heinrich Henk. Bogotá: Banco de la República Archivo de la Economía Nacional, 1976.

Introducción a la Colombia Amerindia. Bogotá: Instituto Colombiano de Antropología, 1987.

Jimeno Santoyo, Myriam. "Los procesos de colonización: Siglo XX." In Tirado Mejía, *Nueva historia de Colombia*, 5: 371–96.

Jones, Clarence F. *South America.* New York: Holt, 1940.

Kline, Harvey F. *Colombia: Portrait of Unity and Diversity.* Boulder, CO: Westview Press, 1983.

Leal Buitrago, Franciso. *Estado y política en Colombia.* Bogotá: Siglo Veintiuno, 1984.

LeGrand, Catherine. *Frontier Expansion and Peasant Protest in Colombia, 1830–1936.* Albuquerque: University of New Mexico Press, 1986.

Londoño D., Oscar Gonzalo. "Aproximación a la historia regional del Ariari (1950–1970)." In *Los Llanos: Una historia sin fronteras*, 385–402. Villavicencio: Academia de Historia del Meta, 1988.

"Los colonizadores del Llano." *Revista Pan.* (Bogotá, 1937): 15: 145–150 ff.

Martin, F. O. "Exploration in Colombia." *Geographical Review* 19 (1929): 621–33.

Martínez Salas, Gloria Evelyn, "Crecimiento Urbano Accelerado y Marginalidad Reciente de la Ciudad de Villavicencio." In *Por los Caminos del Llano*, 2: 197–221.

Maullin, Richard L. "The Fall of Dumar Aljure, A Colombian Guerrilla and Bandit." Memorandum RM-5750-ISA. Santa Monica, CA: Rand Corporation, November 1969.

Mecham, J. Lloyd. *Church and State in Latin America.* Rev. ed. Chapel Hill: University of North Carolina Press, 1966.

Mesa, Darío. "La vida política después de Panamá," in Manual de Historia de Colombia. 3 vols. (Bogotá: Instituto Colombiano de Cultura, 1978–1980), 3: 83–176.

Michelsen U., Carlos. *Suplemento. Estudio sobre las quinas esploitadas en el Territorio de San Martín*, July 19, 1971.

Michelsen U., Carlos, and A. Saenz. *Informe de los exploradores del Territorio de San Martín. Exposición Nacional 20 de julio 1871.* Bogotá, 1871

Montenegro Colón, Feliciano. *Geografía general.* 4 vols. Caracas: Imprenta de Damiron y Dupouy, 1834.

Moog, Clodomir Vianna. *Bandeirantes and Pioneers.* Translated by L. L. Barrett. New York: G. Braziller, 1964.

Molano, Alfredo. "Violence and Land Colonization." In *Violence in Colombia: The Contemporary Crisis in Historical Perspective*, edited by Charles Bergquist, et al., 195–216. Wilmington, D. E.: Scholarly Resources, 1992.

Nieto Caballero, Luis Eduardo. *Vuelo al Orinoco.* Bogotá: Librería Colombiana, Camacho Roldán, 1935.

Ocampo, José Antonio. *Colombia y la economía mundial, 1830–1910.* Bogotá: Siglo Veintiuno, 1984.

Ocampo López, Javier. *Historia básica de Colombia.* Bogotá: Playa & Janes, 1987.

Ojeda Ojeda, Tomás.*Villavicencio entre la documentalidad y la oralidad.* Villavicencio: Oscar Giraldo Durán Ediciones, 2000.

Oquist, Paul. *Violence, Conflict and Politics in Colombia.* New York: Academic Press, 1980.

Orlando Melo, Jorge."La República Conservadora." In *Colombia: Hoy,* 52–101. Ortega Díaz, Alfredo. *Historia de los ferrocarriles Colombianos.* 3 vols. Bogotá: Imprenta Nacional, 1932.

Ortega Ricarte, Enrique. *Villavicencio (1842–1942): Monografía.* Bogotá: Prensa de la Biblioteca Nacional, 1943.

Ospina, Joaquín. *Diccionario biográfico y bibliográfico de Colombia.* 3 vols. Bogotá: Editorial Aguila, 1939.

Ossa Varela, Peregrino. *Geografía de la intendencia nacional del Meta.* Bogotá: Ministerio de Agricultura y Comercio, 1937.

———. "La Ganadería en los Llanos Orientales." *Revista Nacional de Agricultura* 23, nos. 303–4 (September-October 1929): 96–103.

Osterling, Jorge P. *Democracy in Colombia: Clientelist Politics and Guerrilla Warfare.* New Brunswick, N. J.: Transaction, 1989.

Otero d'Costa, Enrique. "La revolución de Casanare en 1809." *BHA* 17 (1928): 530–46.

Ovalle, Elisender Adan. "La Violencia Política y la Acción Guerrillera en los Llanos Orientales en la Década de la Años Ochenta." In *Por los Caminos del Llanos,* 3: 311–17.

Pabón Monroy, Oscar."Restrepo." *Trocha* (Villavicencio), no. 168 (December 1989), 18–19.

Pacheco, Juan Manuel. *Historia eclesiástica: La consolidación de la iglesia—siglo XVII.* Vol. 21, tomo 13, parte 2. In *Historia Extensa de Colombia.* Bogotá: Ediciones Lerner, 1975.

Palacios, Marco. *Coffee in Colombia 1850–1970): An Economic, Social and Political History.* Cambridge, U. K.: Cambridge University Press, 1980.

Pardo, Nicolás. *Correría de Bogotá al territorio de San Martín.* Bogotá: Imprenta de Gaitan 1875.

Paredez Cruz, Joaquín. *Departamento del Meta.* Villavicencio: Cooperativa Nacional de Artes Gráficas, 1961.

Paris Lozano, Gonzalo. *Guerrilleros del Tolima,* 2nd ed. Bogotá: El Ancora Editores, 1984.

Park, James. *Rafael Núñez and the Politics of Colombian Regionalism, 1863–1886.* Baton Rouge: Louisiana State University Press, 1985.

Pérez, Felipe. *Geografía general, física y política de los Estados Unidos de Colombia.* Bogotá: n.p., 1883.

Pérez Bareño, Leonel. *Planes de Desarrollo en el Orinoquia y la Amazonia,* 2nd ed. Bogotá: Editorial Presencia, 1986.

Platt, Raye."Opportunities for Agricultural Colonization in the Eastern Border Valleys of the Andes." In *Pioneer Settlement,* Special Publication, No. 14, 80–107. New York: American Geographical Society, 1932.

Plazas Olarte, Humberto. *Los territories nacionales con una introducción al estudio de su geografía y de su historia.* Bogotá: Editorial Pax, 1944.

Por los Caminos del Llano: A Través de su Historia. 4 vols. Arauca: Academia de Historia de Arauca, 1992.

Ramos, Albelardo. "Puente de Fierro sobre el Rio Negro." *Anales de Ingeniería* (Bogotá) 1, no. 9 (April 1, 1888): 257–60.

Ramsey, Russell W. *Guerrilleros y Soldados*, 2nd ed. Bogotá: Tercer Mundo, 2000.

Rausch, Jane M. *Colombia: Territorial Rule and the Llanos Frontier.* Gainesville: University Press of Florida, 1999.

———. *The Llanos Frontier in Colombian History, 1830–1930.* Albuquerque: University of New Mexico, 1993.

———. *A Tropical Plains Frontier.* Albuquerque: University of New Mexico Press, 1984.

Red de Solidaridad Social. *Informe sobre Desplazamiento Forzado en Colombia, primer trimester de 2001.* Bogotá, July 3, 2001.

Restrepo, Emiliano. *Una excursion al territorio de San Martín.* 1868. Biblioteca de la Presidencia vol. 45. Reprint, Bogotá: Editorial Kelly, 1957.

Rice, Hamilton. "Further Explorations in the Northwest Amazon Basin." *Geographical Journal* 44, no. 2 (August 1914), 137–68.

Rocha García, Ricardo. "Drug Trafficking and its Impact on Colombia: An Economic Overview," *Canadian Journal of Latin American and Caribbean Studies* 28: 55–56, 277–304.

Rodrigues, José Honório. "Webb's Great Frontier and the Interpretation of Modern History." In *The New World Looks at its History* edited by A. Lewis and T. McGann, 155–64. Austin: University of Texas Press, 1963.

Rojas de Moreno, María Eugenia. *Rojas Pinilla, mi padre.* Santa Fe de Bogotá: Panamerican Formas e Impresos, 2000.

Romoli, Kathleen. *Colombia: Gateway to South America.* Garden City, N. Y.: Doubleday, Doran, 1941.

Röthlisberger, Ernst. *El Dorado.* Bogotá: Banco de la República, Archivo de la Economía Nacional, 1963.

Ruhl, J. Mark. "The Military." in Berry et al., *Politics of Compromise,* 181–206.

Safford, Frank. *The Ideal of the Practical: Colombia's Struggle to from a Technical Elite.* Austin: University of Texas Press, 1976.

Sarmiento, Domingo Faustino. *Life in the Argentine Republic in the Days of the Tyrants; or Civilization and Barbarism.* Translated by Mrs. Horace Mann. 1868. Reprint, New York: Knopf, 1961.

Serrano Camargo, Rafael. *El General Uribe.* Bogotá: Tercer Mundo, 1978.

Tavera B., Juan de Dios. *Eco de Oriente.* Bogotá: Imprenta Popular, 1879.

Tirado Mejía, Alvaro, ed. *Nueva historia de Colombia.* 8 vols. Bogotá: Planeta, 1989.

Triana, Miguel. *Al Meta.* Bogotá: Casa Editorial de "El Liberal," 1913.

Urrutia, Miguel, and Mario Arrubla, *Compendio de estadísticas históricas de Colombia.* Bogotá: Dirección de Divulgación Cultural, Universidad Nacional de Colombia 1970.

Uribe, Antonio José. *Anales diplomáticos y consulares de Colombia.* 6. vols. Bogotá, Imprenta Nacional, 1920.

Uribe Celis, Carlos. *Los años veinte en Colombia: ideología y cultura.* Bogotá: Ediciones Aurora, 1984.

Uribe Uribe, Rafael. *Documentos políticos y militares.* 4 vols. Medellín: Beneficencia de Antioquia, 1982.

Vargas Rubiano, Hernando. "Refleciones sobre el Transporte en la Orinoquia." In *Los Llanos de Colombia,* 155–62. Bogota: Litografía Arco, 1986.

Vela, José de Calasanz. *Desde Villavicencio hasta San Fernando de Atabapo.* Ed. In *América Española* (Cartagena), edited by Andrés Mesanza, 2 (1935): 222–40, 353–77; 3(1936): 150–78, 210–39, 304–24.

———. *Dos viajes por la Orinoquia colombiana 1889–1986.* Bogotá: Fondo Cultura Cafetero, 1988.

Velandía, Roberto. *Encyclopedia histórica de Cundinamarca.* 5 vols. Bogotá: Cooperativa Nacional de Artes Gráficas, 1979.

Villar Borda, Carlos J. *Rojas Pinilla: El Presidente Libertador: Biografía.* Bogotá: Editorial Iqueima, 1953.

Villegas, Jorge, and José Yunis, eds. *Sucesos colombianos, 1900–1924.* Medellín: Universidad de Antioquia, 1976.

Weber, David J., and Jane M. Rausch, eds. *Where Cultures Meet: Frontiers in Latin American History.* Wilmington, D. E.: Scholarly Resources, 1994.

Zapata Olivella, Manuel. *El hombre colombiano.* Bogotá: Canal Ramírez-Antares, 1974.

Zavala, Silvio. "The Frontiers of Hispanic America." In W. D. Wyman and C. B. Kroeber, eds. *The Frontier in Perspective,* edited by W. D. Wyman and C. B. Kroeber, 35–58. Madison: University of Wisconsin Press, 1957.

Zuleta Angel, Eduardo. *El presidente López Pumarejo.* Medellín: Ediciones Albon, 1966.

WEBSITES

"Acciones Terroristas FARC y Paramiltarismo." wib.matriz.net/2002colombia/ene02/ene_colomb04_es.html.

AMR 23/009/2001. "Fear for Safety, internally displaced people at the La Nohora camp, city of Villavicenio, Meta Department," web.amnesty.org.

"Arquidiócesis de Villavicenico." www.geocities.com/diocesis_villavicencio/.

"Bogotá-Villavicencio Highway." www.ingetec.com.co.

"Colombia Copes with Latest Bombing." www.CBS NEWS.com.

"Company of Mary (Montfort Missionaries)." www.montfor.org/English/index.htm.

"Diócesis de Villavicenio-Colombia." www.geocities.com/diocesisvillavicencio/.

Gobernación del Meta. "Villavicencio-ciudad pujante y cosmopolita." www.gobernaciondelmeta.gov.co/inforNoticia.asp?IdNot=58.

Gobernación del Meta. "Himno." www.gobernaciondelmeta.gov.co.

Ocampo López, Javier. "Antonio de Villavicencio y Verástegui." In *Gran Enciclopedia de Colombia.* www.lablass.org/blassvirtual/letra-b/biogcircu/villanto.htm.

"Pope Benedict XVI betstowes the Pallium." it.news.yahoo.como/050629/38/3a9qi.html.

Index

Abadía Méndez, Fidel, 97, 103
Acacías Penal and Agricultural Colony, 92
Acero, Antonio, 33–34
Achagua people, 2, 4, 33
Act No. 2 (1959), 151
Act of Medina (1902), 69
Agrarian Reform Law (1961), 163
agriculture, 8, 110; coffee, 57; mechanization, 186–87; rice, 94, 131
Aguirre, Esteban, 1, 13
Aljure, Dumar, 140, 143, 161, 168–69
American Association of Petroleum Geologists Bulletin (journal), 167
Anales Religiosos (periodical), 35
André, Edouard, 37, 45n49
Angel, José Jesús, 88, 94, 96, 97
Aparicio Escobar and Associates, 31
Apostolic Vicariate of the Llanos of San Martín, 79
Apuntamientos de viajes (Guerra Azuola), 15
Arango, Francisco, 83, 95, 96
Ariari River, 4
Arnaud, Juan Bautista, 49, 81; as colonizer, 91; as trained engineer, 99
Article 5, 30

Article 24, 29
Article 25, 53
Article 78: codification of system of territories, 23
Augustinians, 4–5

bandits, 39, 50–51
Baquero, Omar, 61, 73; on the War of the Thousand Days, 69
Baquero Nariño, Alberto, 192; on cattle economy, 186; on cocaine economy, 188; on Villavicencio's lack of leaders, 189; on Villavicencio's negative economic aspects, 202–4; on Villavicencio's retarded development, 200
Barbosa Estera, Reinaldo, 105, 188, 203, 204
Bates, Nancy Bell, 110, 112–13
Battle of Boyacá (1819), 6–7, 207
Battle of Bucaramanga (1899), 65
Battle of El Guavio (1902), 69
Battle of El Oratorio (1860), 17
Battle of El Playón (1899), 67
Battle of Las Peñas (1900), 67
Battle of Peralonso (1899), 66
Bavaria Consortium (brewery), 110, 145

Bejarano, Carlos, 129, 131
Beltrán, Habacuc, 50, 56
Beltrán Figueredo, Matilde, 180
Blydenstein, John, 10
Bogotá-Villavicencio Road, 44n5, 55, 78, 145; early construction, 26–28; efforts to modernize, 97; first attempts, 15–17; improvements, 153, 174–77; landslides, 153–55; opened (1936), 103–4
Bolívar, Simón, 7
Bonnet, José, 55, 57, 59, 115n23
"bonos territoriales," 30
Briata, Ernesto, 54, 71, 73
Brunnschweiler, Dieter: on Meta's cattle production, 164–65; on Meta's frontier, 191; on Meta's land problems, 162–63; on roads, 152–53; on Villavicencio's growth, 156
Bushnell, David, 143, 150

Calvario, El, 81
Campela, Juan, 66, 70
Capdeville, Gabriel, 81, 83
Cáqueza (town), 15
Caro, Miguel Antonio, 51, 53, 56
Casanare: agriculture in, 8; colonization, 33; designated a national intendancy, 48; impact of Wars of Independence, 6; population, 5, 8, 69; towns of, 4–5
Casanare River, 2
Catholic Church, 183, 195n31; declared state religion, 47; and education, 87–88, 159, 161; and "La Violencia," 118; missions, 5, 9–10, 53–54, 73, 146. *See also* Villavicencio: Catholic Church in
cattle, 130; Federación Nacional de Ganaderos, 142; theft, 144. *See also* Meta; Villavicencio
CELASP, 84
Chalarca, Efraín, 85
chulavitas (security forces), 118
cinchona tree bark, 32, 91
Codazzi, Agustín, 10, 17, 21n34

Código Fiscal (1873), 30
Colombia: administration of new territories, 8, 24; established (1863), 23; investment in the territories, 25; land reform, 91, 93–94; military coup (1953), 135–36; presidents, 24–25; territorial policies, 47–48
Colombian Petroleum Enterprise (ECOPETROL), 165
colonization, 140, 200; of Colombian Llanos by Spanish, 3–4; land policies, 29–32, 93–94, 105–6; in Meta, 161–64, 178–81; penal colonies, 92–93, 106; spontaneous, 13–14; town settlement, 5–6, 91–92
Comisaría Especial del Vichada (1913), 70, 78
Communist party, 118, 140; as guerrillas, 167
Community of Apiay, 94; land dispute and Law 51, 105
Compañía de Colombia, 31, 40; dissolved, 59
Compañía del Sumapaz, 32
Compañía de San Martín, 32
Compañía Herrera y Uribe, 59; out of business, 68
Compañía Lorenzana y Montoya, 59
"Concentración Nacional" (National Unity), 101
Concordat of 1887, 47, 55
Conservative party, 12–13, 17, 23, 47; conflict with Liberals, 50, 84–87; and "La Violencia," 117–124; moderates support Olaya, 101; and National Front, 119; in power (1909–1930), 77; against Rojas, 140
"Conservative Republic," or "Era of National Harmony" (1909–1930), 77
Constitution of 1886, 43, 53; provisions, 47
Constitution of 1991, 199
Convención Sobre Misiones (1953), 146

Convers, Sergio, 37, 48, 58, 59; and coffee plantation (1865), 18; and land dispute in Apiay, 94; war problems, 71
Corporación Llanos de Colombia, 203
Cuervo, Rufino, 9

Daza, Camilo, 96, 103
Declaration of Benidorm (1956), 149
Decree 102 (1976), 183
Decree 112 (1955), 142
Decree 238 (1909), 78
Decree 392 (1893), 48
Decree 392 (1897), 48
Decree 1130 and 1131, 92
Decree 2364 (1956), 159
Decree of July 6, 1868, 38
de Flórez, Raguel Angel, 89, 160
Departamento Administrativo Nacional de Estadística (DANE), 151, 156, 164
Diario Nacional, El, 84
Dières Monplaisir, Mauricio, 21n42, 81, 84–85, 87, 88, 90; accused of obstruction, 86–87; anecdotes of, 115n36; on attractions of Villavicencio, 112–13; completed doctorate, 98n12; on completion of Bogotá-Villavicencio road, 104; death of, 115n36; as filmmaker, 97; interview with, 98, 99n20; as newspaper editor, 82; report on schools, 108; support of public health measures, 107; supporter of railroad building, 96
diseases, 9, 114n17; controversy over causes of, 20–21n34; in Llanos, 11, 185; in Meta, 106–8. *See also* Villavicencio
Dominicans, 5, 53, 74; exiles to Llanos of San Martin, 33
drug trafficking, 181–82, 188–89, 203–4
Duarte, Francisco, 52
Duarte Blum, Alfredo, 136, 138
Durán Dusán, Hernán, 124, 151, 168
Durán Quintero, Argelio, 154–55

Echeverría Brothers, 96
Eco de Oriente, 82, 86; on disease prevention, 90, 107; offices stormed, 122; on Villavicencio, 112
economic development, 56–60, 65, 94–96, 199–200; in Llanos, 202–4; in Meta, 108–11, 185–86. *See also* Villavicencio: economy
elections, 43, 72, 77; of presidents, 101, 124–25, 173. *See also* Meta; Villavicencio
Electrificadora of Cundinamarca, 158
Empresa de Energía Eléctrica, 158
Enfermedades dominantes en los llanos de la región oriental de Colombia (Acero), 90
Espectador, El, 87, 128
Espinel Riveros, Nancy, 21n42, 145, 169, 192, 204, 218; on Apiay dispute, 106; on dual frontier, 201–2
excursión a los llanos de San Martin, Una (Restrepo, E.), 18

Fajardo, Nicolas, 38, 41
FARC (Colombian Revolutionary Armed Forces), 167–69, 181–82, 194n8
Federación Nacional de Cafeteros, 142
Federación Nacional de Ganaderos. *See* cattle
Federation Era (1863–1888), 18
Ferrocarril del Meta (periodical), 96
Festival de la Canción Colombiana, 170
"First Law of the Llanos," 128
Foreno, Eliseo, 38, 42
Franciscans, 5, 9, 53
Frente Nacional. *See* National Front (1957–1974)
"Frontera Agrícola Orinoquense" (Barbosa), 188
Frontier Expansion and Peasant Protest in Columbia (LeGrand), 18
"Frontier in Hispanic America, The" (Belaúnde), 198
Fundamental Law of 1831, 8

Gaitán, Jorge Eliécer, 113, 120; reaction to assassination, 122–23
García Bustamante, Miguel, 201, 204
Giraldo, Bernardo, 140, 162
Gómez, Eduardo, 66–67
Gómez, Laureano, 118, 132n4, 144; begins oil company, 165; elected president, 124; and National Front, 149; overthrow of, 135
González Reyes, Enrique, 130, 150
González Valencia, Ramón, 68; president (1910), 77
González Vargas, Juan Nepomuceno, 27
Gramalote, 1, 13, 21n36
Granada, 162; education in, 160–61, 171n30
Gran Colombia, 8
Guahibos (Chiricoas) people, 2, 4, 6, 33, 180; Health of, 185
Guatiquía River, 1, 13; settlement, 91
Guaviare River, 1
Guayabero River, 60
Guerra Azuola, Ramón, 15–17, 22n47
guerrillas, 7, 162, 181–82, 188; amnesty, 118, 135–36, 147n7; attack pipelines, 195–96n46; attempted negotiations, 127; cease-fire, 137–38; demands of, 140; leaders, 125, 126; letter to López, 127; rebirth of (1960s), 167–69; and the "Second Law of the Llanos," 128, 137; tax on cattle controversy, 130; during the War of the Thousand Days, 65–68. *See also* Velásquez, Eliseo
Guiot, José María, 83, 85, 88; authorizes mission in Guatiquía, 91; as bishop of San Martín, 73, 79
Gutiérrez, Rufino, 35, 41, 42, 51
Gutiérrez, Santos, 24–26, 29, 103
Guzmán Campos, Germán, 125, 144

Hacienda El Buque, 31, 37, 95; beginnings, 18; and coffee, 57–58; and war, 70–71
Hacienda El Salitre, 18

Hacienda La Vanguardia, 18
Hacienda Ocoa, 18, 31, 37
Hacienda of Apiay, 5, 21n42; legal battle over, 5, 20n12
Hermanas de la Caridad, 53
Hernández, Tobías, 49, 51–52; report of 1904, 71
Herrera, Benjamín, 66, 69
Hettner, Alfred, 29
Hijas de Sabiduría (Daughters of Wisdom), 73, 79, 81, 83, 146; schools, 88, 91

La iglesia en la frontera: misiones católicas en el Vaupés (Cabrera Becerra), 87
immigration, 28–29, 44n21, 106, 178–80. *See also* colonization
Independent party, 47
Induarroz (rice factory), 186
Ingetec Engineering Company, 176
Instituto Colombiano de Reforma Agraria (INCORA), 163
Inter-American Development Bank, 158

Jesuits, 5
Jiramena, 13
Junta de Beneficencia Pública del Meta, 107
Junta de Propaganda Fide (conversions), 5

land, 59–60, 105–6; controversy over, 44–45n29
Law 11 (1874), 33
Law 18 (1890), 49
Law 20 and 26 (1959), 161
Law 28 (1948), 109
Law 39 (1868), 24, 29, 38, 39, 41
Law 40 (1868), 33
Law 43 (1975), 183
Law 45 (1870), 33
Law 47 (1926), 93
Law 48 (1882), 30
Law 51 (1943), 105
Law 60 (1918), 92

Law 61 (1874), 30–32
Law 61 (1882), 56
Law 66 (1874), 33
Law 71 (1917), 93
Law 105 (1922), 92
Law 118 (1959), 151
Law 200 (1936), 105
Law of June 22, 1850, 14
Law of May 10, 1846, 14
LeGrand, Catherine, 18, 93
Leo XIII (pope), 47, 53, 54
Ley 20 (1969), 167
Liberal, El, 30
Liberal party, 60, 140, 162, 168; as
    "*cachiporros*," 122; call for
    revolution, 51; in disarray, 77; and
    "La Violencia," 117–28; moderates
    support Olaya, 101; and National
    Front, 119, 149; political conflicts,
    84–87; reforms, 12; revolt of 1859,
    17; against Rojas, 143
"Liberal Republic" (1920–1946), 101
Liberal Revolt of 1859, 17, 51–52
Libertador (ship), 56, 115n23
Llanero, El (newspaper), 146
Llaneros, 6, 13; description of (1913),
    79
Llanos frontier, 1, 19; of Arauca, 2; of
    Casanare, 2; geography of, 1, 2;
    interpretations of, 198–99; and
    mythology, 204–7; rubber, 59–60;
    of San Martín, 2; settlement patterns
    of, 199
Llanos of San Martín, 24, 181;
    development, 25–26; drugs in, 181;
    ecology and climate, 10–11;
    economy, 9; guerrilla control over,
    128; land acquisition, 29–32;
    population of, 9; spontaneous
    colonization in, 13; towns in, 5–6;
    Venezuelan immigrants, 28–29;
    Wars of Independence, impact
    upon, 6–7
Llanos Orientales: policies of Rojas
    Pinilla, 136–38
Lleras Camargo, Alberto, 101, 104,
    144; on importance of Meta,

150–51; and National Front, 149;
    speech on creation of Department of
    Meta, 151
*Lo que nos contó el abuelito: El Centenario
    de Villavicencio* (Dières Monplaisir),
    112
Londoño, Manuel Antonio, 38–39
López Pumarejo, Alfonso, 98, 104,
    127–28, 142, 205; on future of
    Meta, 103, 114n3; policies as
    president, 101
Luna Ospina, Jorge, 86; enforcing Law
    71, 93

Macarena, La (plateau), 2
Magdalena River, 69
Manrique, Boshell, 107
Mariana, La (plantation), 60
Marists, 84
Marroquín, José Manuel, 52, 65, 66;
    reorganizing the intendancies, 70;
    signed a Convention on Missions,
    73
Martínez Salas, Gloria Evelyn, 190–91,
    200
Maullin, Richard, 169
Medina, 13; coffee and economic
    development of, 57–58; to
    Cundinamarca (1910), 78;
    Dominicans in, 5; population of, 69
Medina, Elisea, 49–50
Meta: administration, 144–45;
    agriculture, 163–64, 186–87;
    Catholic Church in, 183; cattle
    raising, 115n25, 164–65, 186;
    colonization, 91–94, 104–6, 140,
    161–65, 178–81; Conservative-
    Liberal struggles in, 120; into a
    department, 150–52; description of
    intendants, 78; drug trafficking,
    188–89, 204; economy, 108–11,
    185–86, 204; education in, 159–61;
    elections, 120–21; electricity, 158;
    frontier interpretations, 201–4;
    governors, 151–52, 171n5;
    immigration, 131; Intendant
    turnover (1946–1947), 120–21; as

Jefe Civil y Militar, 144; "La Violencia," 119–21; land reform in, 93; Law 200, affect on, 105; missionaries in, 88; penal colony in, 92; petroleum, 165–67, 187–88; population, 104, 151, 174, 199–200; public health, 185; reestablished as intendancy, 78; schools in, 87–88; transportation in, 152–56, 174–78

"Meta No. 1," 163

Meta River, 2, 5, 15, 96, 177; navigation of, 62–63n39; steam navigation of, 55

Michelsen U., Carlos, 32, 37

missionaries, 4–5, 73, 79–83, 91. *See also* Catholic Church

Mistralia, La, 60

Montfort Fathers (Company of María), 78, 79–83, 183; in Llanos of San Martín, 73; Meta, influence in, 87; settlement building, 91–92; Villavicencio, power in, 79–83, 146, 152

Montfort Hospital, 107

Moreno, Juan Nepomuceno, 7

Moreno, Lisandro A., 60

Mosquera, Tomás C., 17, 18, 33, 74; and anticlericalism, 23

Movimiento Revolucionario Liberal (MRL), 162

National Assembly (1909), 77

National Department of Hygiene, 106

National Front (1957–1974), 119; on colonization, 161–62; and education, 159; origins, 149

National Liberal Directorate, 124–25

National Secretariat of Social Assistance (SENDAS), 136, 141–42

New Granada, 1, 7; presidents of, 12; as republic (1831), 12; struggle for independence, 6–7; transformed to Colombia, 23

Novoa, Aristides, 52, 84–87

Núñez, Rafael, 43, 53, 55, 60; election of 1886, 47

oil. *See* petroleum

Ojeda Ojeda, Tomás, 120, 131, 192; on cattle, 95; on crime in Villavicencio, 190; on oil, 165, 188; on refugees to Villavicencio, 141; on roads, 176

"Olaya Herrera" (night school), 108

Oquist, Paul, 125, 138

"Ordenamiento Territorial en el Departamento del Meta, El" (Beltrán Figueredo), 180

Organic Decree of Public Primary Instruction (1870), 41

Orinoco River, 1, 2; steam navigation of, 55

Orocué (port), 57; to Casanare (1912), 78

Ospina, Pedro Nel, 92, 120

Ospina Camacho, Mariano, 66–67, 70

Ospina Pérez, Mariano, 118, 120, 123, 127; coup, 124

Pact of Sitges (1957), 149

Panama secession (1903), 66

Paul VI (pope), 146

"Paz, Justicia, Libertad y Orden" (Peace, Justice, Liberty and Order), 139–42

penal colonies. *See* colonization; Meta

petroleum, 165–67, 187–88, 195n44, 203

Piapocos people, 33

Plan Nacional de Rehabilitación y Socorro, 161

political prisoners, 74

politics, 49–52, 84–87, 101, 121; Liberal-Conservative struggle, 117–19; military coup (1953), 135; National Front (1957–1974), 149

Pore, 6

presidente López, El, (Zuleta Angel), 103

Provincia de los Llanos, 4, 7

public health, 89–91, 185; in Meta, 106–8. *See also* Villavicencio: health care

Público, El, 30

Un pueblo de frontera: Villavicencio 1840–1940, (García Bustamante), 201

Puerto López (town): massacre, 127; reaction to Gaitán's assassination, 122–24
Pulido, Cesáreo, 68–70
Punchard, McTaggard, Louther, and Company, 55

Quebradablanca, 153–55
quinine, 32–33
Quinquenio: dictatorship of Reyes, 65; dismantled, 77
Quintana, Commandant, 121

Rabagliati, Evasio, 53
racism, 29
Radical Liberal party, 23, 25, 28, 47; land policies, 29; losing power, 43
Recoletos, 5, 53; exiles to Casanare, 33
"Regeneration" (1886–1899), 47
Reina, Oliverio, 85–86
Rengifo, Ricardo Julio, 120–21
Republican Union party, 77
Restrepo, 74, 92
Restrepo, Carlos E., 77, 92
Restrepo, Emiliano, 48, 58, 74; on Apiay controversy, 31; career, 18; on cattle raising, 95; newspaper articles on land purchases, 30; on quinine workers, 32; on rubber trees, 59; Villavicencio described, 36–37
Restrepo Herrera, Bernardo, 49, 54
Revista Nacional de Agricultura, 94
"Revolución en Marcha" (Revolution on March), 101
Reyes, Narciso, 18, 37, 58
Reyes, Rafael, 51, 52; abolished "Intendencia Oriental," 70; as dictator (1904–1909), 65, 72; election as president, 72; exile (1909), 77; exiles critics, 74
Rice, Hamilton, 81, 89
Río Negro bridge, 27
Río Negro River, 1, 13, 16
Rionegro Constitution of 1863, 23
Rockefeller Sanitary Commission, 90, 106–8

Rojas de Moreno, María Eugenia, 136, 138, 141, 142
Rojas Pinilla, Gustavo, 117, 127, 149, 150; coup attempt, 118; exile, 144; on guerrillas, 137–38; impact of dictatorship, 136–37; Llanos policies, 137–38, 142; military coup, 135–36; refugee policy, 144
Roldán, Antonio, 52–53
Roldán, Camacho, 25, 27, 28
Rosas, Avelino, 67, 71, 75n6
Röthlisberger, Ernst, 28, 35, 208
rubber, 58–60
Rueda Sierra and Company, 96
Rueda Vargas, Bernardo, 104, 106; increased education budget, 108
Ruiz Arenas, José Octavio, 183, 195n31
Ruiz Mora, Gustavo, 91, 106

Sabana de Apiay, 31
Salcedo, Guadalupe, 125, 127, 137
Salesians, 67, 73, 148, 152; and leper hospitals, 53; in San Martín, 54; schools, 161; war impact on, 71. *See also* Villavicencio: Catholic Church in
Sáliva people, 2, 6
salt mining, 13, 37, 40–41, 71, 108
San Juan de Arama (city), 4
San Juan de los Llanos (1555), 4
San Juanito (town), 91–92
San Martín, 43; as apostolic vicariate, 54; budget of 1874, 39; coffee, 57–58; colonization, 33; division into corregimientos (1869), 24–25; land grants, 31; Liberal party in, 50; as national intendancy, 48; political unrest in, 50; population, 25, 69; quinine in, 32; during the Quinquenio (1904–1909), 71–74; Regeneration Era, summary of impact, 60–61; reorganized (1850), 14; special territory (1846), 14; taxes in, 39; and War of the Thousand Days, 65–71
San Martín (town), 4, 5, 13
Sanclemente, Manuel A., 52, 65

Santacoloma, Rubén, 90; and land reform, 93; road booster, 97
Santander, Francisco de Paula, 7, 12
Santos, Eduardo, 101, 120
Santos Martinez, Manuel, 74, 76n31
Semana, 129, 131, 141, 145
Siglo, El, 137
Silva, Alfredo, 124; prison and exile, 133n26
Silva, Elisio, 54, 60
Silva, Federico, 18, 37
Sociedad Anónima de Aviación Llanero, 97
Sociedad de Agricultores de Colombia, 95
Soto, Foción, 52, 69
Spain, 6–7
Stiebel, Rothschild, and Son, 15

Tiempo, El, 113, 119, 121; on "La Violencia" impact, 138–39; offices destroyed, 128; political attacks against Dieres Monplaisir, 84–87; on roads, 154
Torneo International del Joropo, 170
Transversal Route 40, 176
Treaty of Neerlandia (1902), 69
Treaty of Wisconsin (1902), 69
Triana, Miguel, 78, 89
Tunebos people, 2, 6
Turner, Frederick Jackson, "The Significance of the Frontier in American History," 197–98
Turriago, Luis Carlos, 140, 146–47

Upín River, 41
Urdaneta Arbelaez, Roberto, 127, 132n4, 135; fights guerrillas, 118, 126
Uribe, Carlos, 59, 96
Uribe Uribe, Rafael, 66, 68–69

Valencia, Guillermo, 153, 167
Vanegas, Rafael, 29, 38–39
Vargas Santos, Gabriel, 51, 69
Vela, José de Calasanz, 33–36, 48–49; burial stone, 62n9

Velásquez, Eliseo, 124; guerrilla leader, 123; killed, 128
Vichada River, 2
Villavicencio, 1; administration for Meta Intendancy, 78; air travel, 97–98, 155, 178; bandits, 39; banking, 82, 110; beer brewing, 110–11, 145; boom town, 112–13; bridges, 105; capital of Intendancy of Meta, 78; capital of San Martín territory (1869), 24–25; Catholic Church in, 14, 33–36, 49, 54, 61, 71, 79–83, 146, 152, 183; cattle raising, 58, 95, 108–10, 131; centennial, 112; city expansion, 156, 189–91; date of founding controversy, 21n42; descriptions of, 36–37, 42, 112–13, 156, 190; diseases in, 14, 89–91, 106–8; districts of, 42–43, 46n68; divided into two *partidos* (1848), 14; early settlers of, 1860s, 17–19; earthquake (1917), 83; economy, 42, 57, 96, 119, 145, 156–58, 202; education, 108, 183–85; elections, 38–39, 52, 87, 121; electricity, 83, 158, 171n23; employment, 191; fires in, 37, 48–49, 129; folklore in, 170; founding of, 14, 19n1, 19n12, 21n37; frontier interpretations, 201–4, 207–9; Gaitán's assassination, reaction, 122–24; gateway to the Llanos, 61, 65, 113, 169–70, 194, 208; geography, 1–3; guerrilla violence, 68, 183; health care, 89–91, 106–8, 185; hospital in, 81, 83; identity crisis, 191–94; immigration to, 17–19, 131, 139–40, 145; impact of violence, 128–29, 138–39; jefe civil y militar (1954–1957), 144; land grants, 59, 93–94; lawlessness, 13; liquor company, 145; location, 1; meat freezing plant, 133n43; as metropolis, 78; military in, 50, 86, 123–24, 168; motion pictures, 83, 145–46; and mythology, 204–7;

named, 14; naming controversy, 21n42; official hymn, 192; out-migration, 131; police and politics, 121; political power, 129; political unrest in, 50, 84–87; population, 14, 37, 42, 69, 83, 91, 104, 131, 151, 156, 174, 199–200; prefects of, 38; progress (1949–1953), 129; public administration in, 38, 74, 129–30; during the Quinquenio (1904–1909), 71–74; railroads, 55, 96; refugees, 182–83; riots, 85–86, 122; roads, 40 (*see also* Bogotá-Villavicencio Road); Rockefeller Sanitary Commission, 90; Rojas era, 139; rubber, 60; schools in, 82, 88; sewer construction, 107; slaughterhouse, 109; taxes, 39, 145; trading companies in, 57;

transportation in, 174–78; Vicariato Apostólica del Meta, seat, 146; "La Violencia" in, 119–24, 126, 138–39; and War of the Thousand Days, 66–71; water system, 83, 158; water ways, 55

"La Violencia," 114; key phases, 117–19; resettling refugees, 126; resurgence, 143, 148n33

"Voice of Liberty, Free Radio of Colombia," 125

vorágine, La, (Eustacio Rivera), 205

War of the Thousand Days (1899–1902), 60; overview, 65–66

Wars of Independence (1809–1819), 6–7

Zuleta Angel, Eduardo, 103, 151

About the Author

Jane M. Rausch specializes in Colombian history and the study of comparative frontier regions. She earned a B.A. at DePauw University (1962) and an M.A. (1964) and Ph.D. (1969) at the University of Wisconsin in Madison. She joined the history department at the University of Massachusetts, Amherst in 1969, where she has taught Latin American history up to the present. In 1984 she was promoted to full professor. Professor Rausch is the author or editor of eight books. Three of them, published both in English and Spanish, deal with the history of the Llanos or eastern plains of Colombia as a tropical frontier spanning the years from 1530 to 1946. In addition she has published over two dozen articles, which have appeared in the *Hispanic American Historical Review* (HAHR), *Latin American Research Review*, *Boletín Americanista* (Barcelona), *The Americas, Boletín Cultural y Bibliográfico* (Bogotá), *Américas, Historia y Sociedad* (Medellín), and *Lateinamerika Studien* (Universität Erlangen-Nürnberg). In 1987 she was a Fulbright lecturer in Colombia. She has been a contributing editor for the *Handbook of Latin American Studies* since 1985, focusing on Colombian and Ecuadoran history in the nineteenth and twentieth centuries. She regularly reviews books for the *HAHR, Boletín Cultural y Bibliográfico, Inter-American Review of Bibliography,* and *The Latin Americanist.* She is currently at work on a study of the writings of Rafael Reyes, president of Colombia from 1904 to 1909.